Volume 28, Number 1

differences

Bad Object

BAD OBJECTS

ESSAYS

POPULAR

AND

UNPOPULAR

NAOMI SCHOR

Cover art by Mira Schor

*E*ditors' note. Two decades ago, Naomi Schor, founding coeditor of *differences*, published a collection of essays titled *Bad Objects*. Admittedly contrarian, Schor confessed to being drawn to what "the carefully policed precincts of the academy" deemed taboo or critically unworthy. And underpinning all her bad objects (universalism, essentialism, feminism, and so on) was her mourning for the literary, a sense that her work, and feminist theory more generally, had broken off from the textual readings in which they were grounded. She asked, "Will a new feminist literary criticism arise that will take literariness seriously while maintaining its vital ideological edge?" (xiv).

The "bad object" in this issue of *differences* is "literariness." Indeed, the very word, which in Schor's problematic entailed language, the signifier, may well be illegible to many of today's readers. So successful was the thematized reception of the "linguistic turn" that critical studies have happily made several new turns since its demise. Language is once more a medium, more or less transparent depending on one's disciplinary perch. More or less illegible as well today, then, Catherine Belsey's 1999

Volume 28, Number 1   DOI 10.1215/10407391-3821652

essay "English Studies in the Postmodern Condition: Towards a Place for the Signifier," which tells us that language is precisely *not* a medium and that "meaning is neither referential nor psychological: on the contrary, it is an effect of language" (135).

This is not a thematic issue; we did not ask contributors to *address* the question of language, or the new formalism, or debates about reading, nor to engage literary texts—though all those things were welcome. Our wager was that the essays, collected as a "Bad Object," would be at once an invigorating and unsettling reading experience and would thus "speak for themselves."

Works Cited

Belsey, Catherine. "English Studies in the Postmodern Condition: Towards a Place for the Signifier." *Post-Theory: New Directions in Criticism.* Ed. Martin McQuillen, Graeme Macdonald, Robin Purves, and Stephen Thomson. Edinburgh: Edinburgh UP, 1999. 123–38.

Schor, Naomi. *Bad Objects: Essays Popular and Unpopular.* Durham: Duke UP, 1995.

Comes a Letter in the Mail:
Ellipses of Reading

*T*he invitation to write for this issue inspired by Naomi Schor and her fierce defense of what she called "bad objects" held me at bay for a long time.[1] Even though she would not read it, I felt I should try to respond with something Naomi might receive with approval or even pleasure. For part of her so sadly shortened life, we shared a lot, mostly at a distance, through writing and reading but also by situation as women of the same generation of u.s. feminist literary scholars working in university French departments (a very small world). As a result, the dynamics she analyzed in *Bad Objects* in 1995 were very familiar to me then. It is a book of melancholy, which I cannot not share especially now, when more than twenty years have passed, for only a few of which Naomi was alive to continue chronicling the disappearance of her bad objects.

Whether or not melancholy played a part (no doubt it did), these thoughts led me to unearth, from the hard drive, texts that had lain dormant there for the greater part of those twenty-plus years. They are shards of an aborted project that never really got very far. It was on the subject (so to speak) of reading, which is probably why the association with Naomi took

Volume 28, Number 1   DOI 10.1215/10407391-3821664

me back to them. *Au fond*, the good bad object she wants to preserve is first and last of all reading, reading that takes time and attention. Her defense of narrative, for example, defends reading in the figure of what Peter Brooks had called "reading for the plot." This comes near the end of the book when, after posing that "current work on gender has contributed little to our understanding of narrative" and that the performativity that has displaced narrativity in queer and gender theory treats literary fiction as just another discourse and "in the process fiction loses its distinctive formal properties and is reduced to a series of scenes," Naomi concludes her paragraph with the image of a "chop shop" of literary fiction: "At a time when the grand narratives have been pronounced dead, it is in fact the narratives of fiction which have vanished in the chop shop, where people go to furnish themselves with spare narrative parts" (*Bad* 160).

Let this image be an excuse for bringing together here this assortment of spare parts.

I would say just a little more about the abandoned project. Over several years, I sank test holes around the subject of reading, that is, I dug into research on its identified pathology, dyslexia, and I also probed the recent field that had spun off from history of the book, which called itself history of reading. For a while all this activity was sustained by a rather delirious vision of intervening into these discourses from the side of what deconstruction has understood about reading, unreadability, writing, the unsaturability of context, the divisibility of the letter, and so forth. I call the vision or idea "delirious" for a couple of reasons: First, because it had a "mad" thesis, to wit, that reading disorder was a general condition because no one ever really *knows* how to read. This preposterous-sounding proposition was aimed at the reductive object that science recognizes as reading, which it defines and measures as information extraction. Second, because *delirious* evokes the French word *délire*, from which Hélène Cixous forges the homonym and synonym, *dé-lire*: to un-read, dis- or dys-read. *Lire/délire*: reading is mis- or dis-reading, madness.

Before abandoning this delirium, I was led to try to reread famous scenes in a familiar literature of reading and learning to read. These I thought to counterpose against various assumptions I saw shaping the scientific study of reading. One of the most prevalent and determining of these (determining, for example, where the largest portion of research funding in these disciplines goes) was the assumption that the interiority of reading could be mapped, explained, imaged; therewith, its pathologies could be diagnosed and maybe corrected. As if, then, the other reading, the other's reading were no longer irreducibly strange, having become a matter for knowledge equipped with the technology of fMRI. To this I wanted to respond by reading from Augustine's *Confessions* a passage about the other reading or at least seeming to read. (This is spare part number one.)

■

In the passage, Augustine describes how he reacted when he first observed someone, it was St. Ambrose, engaged in the practice of silent reading. It occurs toward the beginning of book 6 and records one of the rare experiences prior to his conversion that Augustine seems to relate more because of its curiosity than for its role in that retrospective narrative. And yet, although he does not make it explicit, there is a connection to the event of his own conversion when, some years later, Augustine hears the voice "as of a child" chanting the phrase "Take up and read," whereupon he opens the epistle of Paul to the Romans lying on a table and reads the verses that await him there. And he reads them, he notes, "in silence" (167), recording perhaps with these two words his conversion to the practice that, when he first observed it, had struck him enough to warrant the following description:

> *But when [Ambrose] was reading, his eye glided over the pages, and his heart searched out the sense, but his voice and tongue were at rest. Ofttimes when we had come (for no man was forbidden to enter, nor was it his wont that any who came should be announced to him), we saw him thus reading to himself, and never otherwise; and having long sat silent (for who durst intrude on one so intent), we were fain to depart, conjecturing that in the small interval which he obtained, free from the din of others' business, for the recruiting of his mind, he was loth to be taken off; and perchance he dreaded lest if the author he read should deliver any thing obscurely, some attentive or perplexed hearer should desire him to expound it, or to discuss some of the harder questions; so that his time being thus spent, he could not turn over so many volumes as he desired; although the preserving of his voice (which a very little speaking would weaken) might be the truer reason for his reading to himself. But with what intent soever he did it, certainly in such a man it was good [*quolibet tamen animo id ageret, bono utique ille vir agebat]. (Augustine 98–99)*

Augustine recalls that he and his companions hesitated as to how to explain Ambrose's behavior. Without resolving which of the possible reasons he might have had for reading in silence rather than aloud as was customary even when alone, Augustine nevertheless concludes that in such a man as the saintly Ambrose, it was for a good purpose and with good intentions. It is, however, as if assurance were needed here to dispel a contrary thought, perhaps even the first one to occur to this witness when he initially came upon the strange behavior: might not that silenced tongue be keeping to itself some secret guilt, an evil and not a good purpose? This conclusion ends up lending a note of excuse to the possible reasons Augustine offers to explain Ambrose's reading habits, as if he had to forestall the idea of the fault there was in keeping to oneself what was meant to be proffered openly and viva voce.

What makes this text so extraordinary is not just its historical value as a document, one that suggests how such an important transformation in reading practices might have been experienced by those who underwent it, those who like Augustine began one day to silence their own voices as they read.[2] At the same time as it records the advent of this novel experience, the text also uncovers and brings clearly into focus a condition of the reading experience that is not first of all or above all historical. For Augustine's account reveals nothing less than the ground or rather the gulf of unfathomable, irreducible alterity across which and on the condition of which reading can take place. In effect, we see, we read Augustine, who believes that he is seeing reading happen because Ambrose's "eye glided over the pages," even though he cannot see to the heart of the other's reading, to what precisely he locates here in Ambrose's heart, which "searched out the sense." Thus he neither sees nor hears the other's reading taking place; he can only believe that it takes place nowhere that he can hear or see, cut off, therefore, from his own understanding. So long as reading manifests itself in the openly spoken voice, then its conditioning ground of alterity can appear to disappear into that powerful figure of sameness Jacques Derrida has called *s'entendre-parler*, hearing/understanding-oneself-speak.[3] Augustine's experience is one in which that precise figure is thrown out of alignment with the figure of reading and with a reading figure who silences the voice without thereby suspending the reading that is *apparently* taking place. For Augustine sees or at least believes he can see that Ambrose *is* reading, there before him, openly and yet not so openly—reading also in secret because "to himself." What has been made manifest, therefore, is reading as phenomenon of alterity, that is, as the appearance and disappearance of some otherness, alterity no sooner showing itself as phenomenon then it disappears into the belief in the reliability of appearances. It is as if Augustine's startled and startling account had recorded a moment when alterity obtruded itself into his world as phenomenalized by the voice and hearing-oneself-speak, and to do so it had to appear as *the other reading, the other's reading.* In that moment, the reading that appears to be taking place appears also suspended from its condition, which is unfathomably secret and irreducible alterity.

■

Some years later I came to connect Augustine's phenomenology of the-other-reading with a scene his great emulator, Jean-Jacques Rousseau, staged in book 2 of his *Émile, or On Education.* (This is spare part number two. My translation of the passage is overly literal and thus rather clunky.)[4]

> *I see a man: blooming, gay, vigorous, in good health; his presence inspires joy, his gaze announces contentment, well-being; he carries with him the image of happiness. Comes a letter in the mail; the happy man looks at it; it is to his address; he opens it, he reads. Instantly his appearance changes; he turns pale; he falls into a faint. Returning to his senses, he weeps, he rushes about, he moans, he tears his hair out, he fills the air with his cries, he seems to be having an attack of dreadful convulsions. Mad man, what harm has this paper then done you? Which of your limbs has it removed? What crime did it make you commit? Finally, what did it change in yourself to put you into the state in which I see you? (307–8)*

The passage occurs in a section of *Émile* where Rousseau is arguing that the true source of all our misery is *la prévoyance*, foresight, looking ahead, neglecting the present "of which one is sure" for a future "that so rarely comes" (307). The present is not just a temporal category, however, for the same *prévoyance* also displaces man in space to the point that "[e]veryone spreads himself, so to speak, over the whole earth and is sensitive over this whole great surface. Is it surprising," he then asks, "that our ills proliferate in all the points where we can be wounded?" (307). To illustrate this operation of suffering at a distance from where one is presently, Rousseau, as we've just read, calls up the figure of a healthy, contented man who receives a letter one day; upon reading it, he falls down in a fit of moaning and despair. The letter itself, a piece of paper with traces of writing, has done nothing to harm him and yet he is now utterly miserable.

To say that the passage is about reading (or writing) may seem to be forcing things. Surely the effects of temporal and spatial dislocation, of transgression of the enclosure that is anyone's present existence, are only incidentally produced by reading. In other words, it is not reading or writing *as such* that are being identified as the source of misery. This point is made, moreover, quite clearly by Rousseau himself. The page of writing or the paper the man reads is explicitly declared innocent of any violence or crime. And yet we can also recognize all the links in this passage to Rousseau's overarching accusation against writing, reading, or, let us say in general, *the letter*, the accusation that led Derrida, some time ago, to reserve an important place for Rousseau's thought in the history of the West's metaphysics of presence.[5] In Derrida's account, Rousseau would have taken over this history, inherited it more or less straight from Plato, but with the difference of a certain inward turn, a turning toward the idea of sameness, as in Plato, but now the idea is placed within; it is the idea of the self-sameness within the self, that the self simply is (the same as itself).

But we are drawing things too broadly and going too quickly. Let us slow down and actually try to read this passage, presuming that we can and that it is readable.

Rousseau begins by posing that he sees a man, a happy man: "I see a man: blooming, gay, vigorous, in good health; his presence inspires joy, his gaze announces contentment, well-being; he carries with him the image of happiness." It is to this man whom Rousseau pretends or imagines he sees—"I see a man"—to this happy self of a man that the letter arrives as a catastrophe. He will not have seen it coming, he had no *prévoyance* of this event that will reduce him to trembling, even to "dreadful convulsions." Remember the argument and the implied lesson here: it is precisely because he did not see it coming, because he had forgotten or never learned to be *prévoyant*, that he was happy. If *prévoyance* is the source of all misery, then a man who would be happy must have no foresight. His contentment, his joy is in the present, his present, his present presence. He is happy there where he is, present to himself.

But of course he is not present to himself alone; he is present with others and in the presence of others, standing before them: "I see a man [. . .] his presence inspires joy, his gaze announces contentment, well-being; he carries with him the image of happiness." This man is not alone; he appears to and before others, if only in someone's imagination, Rousseau's for instance. But as here imagined, he is really happy, or at least one must say that so he appears. He figures present happiness, but not present only to itself. It is in a world with others, others who may see him and say something like, "[H]e is the very image of happiness." Rousseau puts it somewhat differently: "[H]e carries with him the image of happiness." This "with him" marks the image as not the same as him. The image is set a little bit aside, separated, something to be carried or borne. This separation between self and image, the gap that opens up in that space where one is seen, heard, or imagined with others, the gap in presence and the present, the gap of difference between this present and that, this place and that, this time and that, this opening into and from the world with others is there from the instant Rousseau imagines to write, "I see a man." So in this sense, the happy man had to have already begun to exist not simply where he was, and in his own body, but already also where he was not, in others and with others. That's what it means to be in the world *with* others, with others as one is with the image of happiness one carries as one's own. But there you go, that's the problem, which Rousseau will end up calling a "strange problem" (308). The image of one's own happiness has never been simply one's own to bear and keep safe, if possible and for as long as possible. The passage we are trying to read will turn around this strange problem of not-being where one is as soon as one is more than one, and that is as soon as anyone can imagine, say, and write: I see a man.

But in the parable—for it, indeed, has the structure of parable, fable, or allegory—this misfortune of being in more places than one and at more times than one's own present, this misfortune apparently arrives only when "[c]omes a letter in the mail." Rousseau's elliptical and inverted phrasing permits one, I believe, to read this coming of the letter as a kind of exemplary allegory of the general event being figured here: the arrival of the "letter" or the trace of absence that knocks happy self-presence for a loop so that, as we read on, it ends up existing where it is not, no longer present to itself where it is. Rousseau is very precise, I would say, in the way he stages this event of the letter. The inversion in the phrase "[c]omes a letter in the mail [(v)ient une lettre de la poste]" delays the arrival from arriving anywhere yet. Arrival at address happens only in the next moment, but it happens as or in an ellipsis: "[T]he happy man looks at it; it is to his address."

The happy man looks at it. He looks at it, it says; it does not say he reads it. He looks at it; "it is to his address." Rousseau inserts an ellipsis here between looking and reading, a kind of *prereading* that has to take place in order to "read" one's own address. We'll come back to this suggestion of prereading.

Notice that Rousseau does not let us read whatever message the letter contains. Perhaps because he would not want to arouse our pity for this poor man by revealing any details of the terrible thing that has been announced to him, that happens to him at some remote distance from himself but happens and arrives at his address. Rousseau needs his reader to remain lucid so that she can see what he is about to show her. Because, of course, the point is that *nothing* has happened to the man, to him himself, in the present, in his body or the soul of his conscience. The letter, itself, its paper and its traces, its material thing, is innocent. We might not be able to see this innocent thing so well if we had been told the terrible news the man just received. Rousseau's is a description of the phenomenon of misery; we are to continue to see the man solely from the outside, as appearance, and for the moment we must not try to identify or identify with his interior state. Yet, by appearing to keep us from seeing into the man's affective interior, Rousseau's rhetorical finesse has also, and by the same token, conjured up the figure of something to be seen, an image in space: but it is the figure of interiority, which precisely *as* interiority is nothing to be seen. Rousseau's rhetorical technique here is such that we are almost induced to forget the invisibility of what is being conjured up as "in yourself."

Almost, but not quite. We've already remarked the phrasing that distinguishes between looking (at the address) and reading (the letter as message to his address). This difference between looking/seeing and reading is one of the central pivots around which turns the conjured figure of interiority, a fact that might go unremarked if we weren't reading Rousseau's text in a certain way. We have to read it not just for what it says or describes but also for what it does. To keep us from seeing that a text, a letter, can also do something, although not necessarily something harmful, this is the condition on which this passage produces its figure of interiority that cannot be harmed by a letter, that cannot be harmed in itself, by the letter itself. But while we may suspect that, on some level, Rousseau's text seeks to keep one from seeing something about its own production, it cannot prevent anyone from reading whatever it is trying not to show. No, it cannot prevent this, but neither can it prevent the figure of its own unreadability from precipitating out when the other figure it has conjured up, the figure of interiority, deconstructs, that is, when it undoes the figuration and displaces all the oppositions that held it in place. It does this on the condition of reading. Unreadability may be the figure or the symptom of our deconstructed interiority, but it still needs to be read.

Thus, for example, one must try to read the mode of the final question asked of the poor, miserable man: "Finally, what did it change in yourself to put you into the state in which I see you?" Given that the passage has blocked any view of the message just read, this question hovers between the mode of a rhetorical question—it says in effect that the paper changed nothing "in yourself [dans toi-même]"—and the mode of a true inquiry. In the latter case, it asks, What is no longer the same in your interior landscape, in your affective world? What new grief has befallen you? The greatest equivocation here, however, is in the figure of interiority that the series of questions builds up to and that this final question—"Finally"—renders explicit or names. Of the possible harms that the letter didn't commit, it did not sever a limb (*membre*, which could include the sexual member), that is, it did you no bodily harm, and it did not cause you to commit a crime. This second remark disculpates the letter not for physical harm but for some internal damage, damage to one's conscience or to what Rousseau might have assimilated to one's basic *amour de soi*, love of self. In any case, it is a matter of self-relation, and thus of what Derrida has called *auto-affection*, of which hearing-oneself-speak is an example. By suggesting this particular figure of interiority, distinct not just from the "exterior" body whose members can be severed but also perhaps from other representations of "interiority," Rousseau contrives, once again, to keep out of sight another view of this internal space, an affective interiority that is a shared space, an affective world *within*. It is this internal world, with its multiplicity of affective ties, that Rousseau hides until he can point to it and ask how it has changed. As if to imply that this "in yourself" were bounded solely between one's body and one's relation to self, yourself, as if "in yourself" meant yourself only within yourself, without others.

■

Rousseau's passage continues and so did my attempt to read it, to read it reading reading. But this will suffice. I want to leave room for at least one more spare part, which was originally written for the Nineteenth-Century French Studies conference in 2010. Because Naomi was first of all a *dix-neuviémiste*, because her books on Émile Zola and George Sand, her studies of Madame de Staël, Honoré de Balzac, Stendhal, and Gustave Flaubert—the pantheon of nineteenth-century French narrative fiction—remain mandatory reading for whoever approaches these writers from our shores today, especially if they are asking questions of sexual difference, well then, the musings I ventured on that occasion on some reading issues in Flaubert might well have been addressed to Naomi's ghost at the conference. As it happens, I was enjoined with others to respond to the then-recent manifesto in an issue of the journal *Representations* titled *The Way We Read Now.* Cosigned by Stephen Best and Sharon Marcus, this manifesto bore its own title: "Surface Reading." I venture to believe that as the author of *Reading in Detail* (1987), Naomi would have had much to say in my place about this so-called surface reading, whereby its inventors (of the phrase, if not the thing) sought to displace what they called "symptomatic" reading as modeled by the interpretive practices of the likes of Sigmund Freud, Fredric Jameson, Louis Althusser, Umberto Eco, Paul Ricoeur, and so on (the implication being that there had been a general contagion of "symptomatic reading" of which it was time to cure ourselves).

I deposit here, then, as on a compost heap, the text I wrote in these circumstances. It was called "Reading 'Surfaces.'"

∎

"You are attacking details, and it's the whole you should be taking on. The brutality is in the depths and not on the surface" (Flaubert, *Correspondance* 2: 650). This is Gustave Flaubert in December 1856 writing to Léon Laurent-Pichat, one of the editors of *La Revue de Paris*, which was about to deliver its next installment of *Madame Bovary* minus the notorious "coach episode." What Flaubert calls "details" and "surface," as distinct from the "whole" and the "depths" referred thus to the wickedly hilarious sequence that, in the unbowdlerized novel, follows the very pregnant one-sentence paragraph: "And the heavy machine got underway [Et la lourde machine se mit en route]" (*Oeuvres 1*: 514). (On its surface, this would be an unexceptional assertion, were it not for the adjective "heavy [*lourde*]" weighing it down, pulling at that surface and signaling toward the allegorical machine that language just is—always saying more or less, more *and* less than it can appear to say, "appearance" being perhaps precisely the wrong way to think about surfaces when they are made up of written traces.) So Flaubert's remark to Laurent-Pichat about "depths" and "surface" is occasioned by what may well be the most notorious scene in all of French letters to confound that very distinction, at least to the extent that it is taken to be a matter of *seeing* what is on a surface as distinct from what is hidden, concealed, veiled, unrevealed, and so forth. Flaubert, obviously (but how so "obviously"?), counted on readers to read the sequence not for what can be seen there but for what cannot be seen, unlike the poor driver of the coach who—but it's hard to believe anyone could be so *bête*—"didn't understand what furious mania for locomotion compelled these individuals not to want to stop ever" and unlike the bourgeois in the streets of Rouen "whose astonished eyes opened wide in the face of this thing that was so extraordinary in the provinces, a coach with blinds drawn, and that kept appearing over and over" (*Oeuvres 1*: 515) (a remark that recalls both the second title of the novel, *Provincial Customs* [*Moeurs de Province*], and the "irresistible argument" that Léon had used to get Emma into the coach: "'Ah! Léon! . . . Really . . . I don't know . . . if I should,' she simpered. Then, with a serious tone: 'It's very improper, you know?' 'How so?' the clerk replied. 'It's done in Paris!' And this remark, like an irresistible argument, made up her mind" [513]).

Just to take one last measure of the stupor or *hébétement* into which this "heavy machine" throws whoever confuses visibility with readability or whoever invokes a self-evident distinction of manifest surface from hidden depths, one could cite the plodding insights of Maître Ernest Pinard, who was the prosecutor at the trial that began about a month later of *Madame Bovary*'s author and publisher. Pinard knew about the deletion of the coach episode from the serial publication, but he was still made indignant by what remained of it, which he duly cited into the court transcript as quite enough evidence to suggest *la suite* in all of its hidden obviousness. The comments he went on to make, however, show just how far he had lost his bearings among all these treacherous appearances and disappearances: "We know now, gentlemen, that the fall does not take place in the coach. With a scruple that does him honor, the editor of the *Revue de Paris* deleted the passage of the fall in the coach. But if the *Revue de Paris* lowers the blinds of the coach, it allows us to penetrate into the bedroom where the meetings are held" (Flaubert, *Oeuvres 1*: 626). And, alas, we penetrate this intimate interior, laments the prosecutor, "without the considerations of art. With [Flaubert], no gauze, no veils, it is nature in all its nudity, in all its coarseness!" (627). Notice how what is so biblically referred to here as "the fall" is both thought not to take place when and where it nevertheless is also thought to take place behind the blinds of censorship lowered on the already lowered blinds of the coach. One has to feel a little sorry for poor Pinard, tangled up in all these veils of "nature in all its nudity."

All of this seems embarrassingly obvious, even if one would be hard put to say exactly where it is showing up, on what surface other than the depthless surface of readability. If I've ventured even a very little way onto this too obvious terrain, it is as a result of reading "Surface Reading: An Introduction." I admit that I've given in too easily to the too obvious, but would allege the excuse of that essay's insistent invocation, I quote *ad seriatim*, of the "immediately apprehensible" (Best and Marcus 4), "what is evident, perceptible, apprehensible" (9), "what insists on being looked *at* rather than what we must train ourselves to see *through*" (9), "'pure, untranslatable, sensuous immediacy'" (10), "presented meaning" (11), "what is present" (11), "face value" (12), "what lies in plain sight" (18)—and here the essay's authors do not fail to allude to the much-sought-after purloined letter in Poe's tale (which you may recall prompted a much earlier debate, unmentioned by Best and Marcus, that in important ways was also about the dizzying pitfalls of a certain kind of symptomatic reading, *mais passons*)[6]—all of this so that we may "see a text more clearly" (18).

What has to fall away in this incessant predication of reading by evidence, apprehension, presence, perception, looking, sight, or vision is the experience of reading as a nothing-to-see, as what no more engages with visible surfaces per se than with invisible depths. These are but figurative stopgaps for what has no other dimension than the movement of a gap, from gap to gap, across intervallic differences, for instance, the difference between surface and depth, the one gapping into the other as the possibility of meaning either the one or the other, but always therefore both the one and the other. When it comes to reading, surface or depth is the same difference.

This could take us back to Flaubert's complaint: "The brutality is in the depths and not on the surface." None could know better than Flaubert that he calls upon here an illusion of verticality or depth put in place by his own doggedly or let us say, rather, froggedly horizontal practice. In December 1853, he writes to Louise Colet:

> *Continuity constitutes style, just as constancy makes for virtue. To swim against the currents, to be a good swimmer, your body must be stretched out along a same line, from the back of your head to your heel. You draw yourself in like a frog and you spread yourself across the whole surface, rhythmically, with all your limbs, head low and gritting your teeth. The idea must do the same thing across words and not paddle while striking out right and left.* (Correspondance 2: 481)

The previous year, writing to the same, he employs a similar image of movement across a surface of water:

> *And yet I have a conception of one, of a style: a style that would be beautiful, that someone will do one day, in ten years or ten*

*centuries, and that would be rhythmical like verse, precise like the language of the sciences, and have waves, the throbbing of the cello, plumes of flame; a style that would enter into your ideas like the blow of a stiletto, and where your thoughts would finally float on smooth surfaces, the way you do on a boat with a good wind behind you. (*Correspondance *2: 79)*

What is also repeated on the surface of these passages is the conjunction of style with idea, two terms that are not deployed according to any distinction of form from content, or surface from depth, but rather as a continuity across or within a difference. There is idea and there is style, but the idea of style—dreamed of, conceived of—is of "a style that would enter into your ideas like the blow of a stiletto."[7]

Because I have begun to suggest a pattern across Flaubert's watery surfaces, I can't resist quoting another passage from the correspondence, where he compares himself to an alpine lake: "I am like those Alpine lakes that become agitated under valley breezes (what blows up from below along the ground); but the great winds from the summits pass over them without wrinkling their surface and just serve to blow away the fog" (*Correspondance* 2: 491).

If, as Buffon's aphorism would have it and as Flaubert was wont to recall, "style is the man," then the man-style Gustave Flaubert bids, perhaps, to be received according to some novel idea of "writ in water" that would undo the Keatsian conceit. Casting his thoughts ahead, in 1876, to the writing of "Hérodias," he claims to see "(clearly, as *I see* the Seine) the surface of the Dead Sea shimmering in the sun" (*Correspondance* 5: 143).

The question I am turning around, then, concerns a literary "surface" that cannot be opposed to some depth, but neither does it appeal to visibility, appearance, or perception, and that has as its only dimension or effect a possibility of writing/reading. Or rather, that just is that possibility. Not, then, a surface at all, which is but a metaphor for an unfigurable interface that is no less temporal than spatial. Instead of a name or a noun, however, be it surface or any other, perhaps it is only the verbal register that can hold off the familiar—tired and tiresome—metaphors.

■

Maurice Blanchot opens a chapter of *Thomas the Obscure*, which many consider his most important fictional work, with a scene of Thomas reading as seen from within, *as it were* (this "as it were" is, of course, the mark of fiction). When the scene begins, one is reminded of Augustine's description of coming upon St. Ambrose reading in his room: "Thomas remained reading in his room. He was seated, his hands joined above his forehead, his thumbs leaning against the root of his hairline, so absorbed that he did not move when the door was opened. Those who entered, seeing his book always open to the same pages, thought that he was pretending to read." But at this point Blanchot's language passes beyond appearance or pretense and affirms simply: "He was reading." If it seemed that he was not, if unlike the saintly St. Ambrose his eyes did not glide "over the pages" but remained fixed on "the same pages," that is because, the text goes on, "[h]e was reading with an unsurpassable minuteness and attention [(i)l lisait avec une minutie et attention insurpassables]." At this point, the text fashions an image—a simile or an analogy—that is but the first of many in this long description that breaks off only at the end of the paragraph two pages later. It is, you could say, a striking image, this first stab at saying what *it was like* when Thomas read in this way: "In relation to each sign, he was in the situation in which the male finds itself when the female praying mantis is going to devour him. Each of them looked at the other." This uncanny relation is then unfolded in a detail of "unsurpassable minuteness" as Thomas comes to realize "all the strangeness [*étrangeté*] there was in being observed by a word as by a living being." And these livings beings, these words, these praying mantises already "were grabbing hold of him and beginning to read him. He was caught up, kneaded by intelligible hands, bitten by a tooth full of sap; he entered with his living body into the anonymous forms of the words, giving them their substance, forming their relations, offering to the word being its/his being [offrant au mot être son être]." While reading, he is read, the words drawing their substance from his living body, to the point that he "recognized himself with disgust in the form of the text he was reading." This disgust with reading's solipsism, when he recognizes himself not just *in* but *as* the text in his hands, does not, however, have the last word. There is an after-image, so to speak, a ghostly image left by this passage itself whose descriptions and images have unfolded *as if* from within Thomas's experience. For even after he breaks off reading, "he kept the thought that in his person [. . .] there abided obscure sayings [*paroles*], disincarnated souls, and angels of words that were exploring him profoundly" (Blanchot 27–29).

But who, him? Who is reading? And who is reading whom? Or what? Thomas is a fictional character, the name given by Blanchot to this invisible site of reading as interior experience of the other. But can this site be figured or configured without the fiction of some "as if"? That is doubtless one of the questions this passage presses on us as one tries to read it. The fiction puts reading *en abyme,* and as a consequence Thomas's experience is the reader's, but also it is *as if* Blanchot's text were the one Thomas stared at. This reversibility or repetition of the reader in the read and the read in the reading figures, moreover, in the passage when (as we read), as Thomas was reading, or believed he was reading ("believing he was a profound reader"), the words already "were grabbing hold of him and beginning to read him." What does it mean for words *to read*, active transitive, instead of *being read*, passive? What is called reading if the words to be read are already living beings that (who?) read, which is to say also, bite, knead, grab?

But that, of course, is a fiction.

PEGGY KAMUF writes on literary theory and contemporary French thought. She has translated numerous texts by Jacques Derrida and several works by Hélène Cixous. Director of the Derrida Seminars Translation Project, she also coedits the series publishing Derrida's teaching seminars in English. She is Marion Frances Chevalier Professor of French and Comparative Literature at the University of Southern California.

Notes

1   I am thinking in particular of the chapter in *Bad Objects* "The Righting of French Studies: Homosociality and the Killing of 'La pensée 68,'" a title that announces clearly enough the counterattack mounted there against the male coterie of academics who led the backlash against "French theory" and especially feminism in U.S. university French departments.

2   According to historians of reading, silent reading was known among the ancient Greeks even if, as Jesper Svenbro writes, it "was probably practised by only a limited number of readers and was unfamiliar to a good many Greeks, especially to illiterates who knew about writing only 'from the outside'" (51).

3   See, for example, Derrida, *Voice and Phenomenon*, ch. 6, "The Voice That Keeps Silent."

4   All translations from the French that follow are my own.

5   See Derrida, *Of Grammatology*, esp. part 2.

6   See Derrida, "Le facteur de la verité," and Lacan, "Seminar on 'The Purloined Letter.'"

7   On this idea of Flaubert's style, see Derrida, "An Idea of Flaubert: 'Plato's Letter.'"

Works Cited

Augustine. *The Confessions of Saint Augustine.* Trans. E. B. Pusey. New York: Modern Library, 1999.

Best, Stephen, and Sharon Marcus. "Surface Reading: An Introduction." *The Way We Read Now.* Spec. issue of *Representations* 108.1 (2009): 1–21.

Blanchot, Maurice. *Thomas l'obscur.* Nouvelle version. Paris: Gallimard, 1950.

Derrida, Jacques. "An Idea of Flaubert: 'Plato's Letter.'" Trans. Peter Starr. *Psyche: Inventions of the Other.* Vol. 1. Ed. Peggy Kamuf and Elizabeth Rottenberg. Stanford: Stanford UP, 2007. 299–317.

—————. "Le facteur de la vérité." *The Post Card: From Socrates to Freud and Beyond.* Trans. Alan Bass. Chicago: U of Chicago P, 1987. 413–96.

—————. *Of Grammatology.* Trans. Gayatri Chakravorty Spivak. Baltimore: Johns Hopkins UP, 1976.

—————. *Voice and Phenomenon: Introduction to the Problem of the Sign in Husserl's Phenomenology.* Trans. Leonard Lawlor. Evanston: Northwestern UP, 2011.

Flaubert, Gustave. *Correspondance.* Vols. 1–5. Paris: Gallimard, 1973–2007.

—————. *Oeuvres* 1. Ed. A. Thibaudet and R. Dumesnil. Paris: Éditions de la Pléiade, 1951.

Lacan, Jacques. "Seminar on 'The Purloined Letter.'" *Écrits.* Trans. Bruce Fink. New York: Norton, 2002. 6–48.

Rousseau, Jean-Jacques. *Émile, ou de l'éducation. Oeuvres complètes.* Vol. 4. Paris: Gallimard, 1969. 239–868.

Schor, Naomi. *Bad Objects: Essays Popular and Unpopular.* Durham: Duke UP, 1995.

—————. *Reading in Detail: Aesthetics and the Feminine.* New York: Methuen, 1987.

Svenbro, Jesper. "Archaic and Classical Greece: The Invention of Silent Reading." *A History of Reading in the West.* Ed. Guglielmo Cavallo and Roger Chartier. Amherst: U of Massachusetts P, 1999. 37–63.

On the Lapidary Style

Defining the Lapidary

*T*he relatively rare word *lapidary* may well puzzle a native English speaker. It can be a noun—a *lapidary* is someone who's a sort of jeweler, a worker with precious stones—or it can mean a book on such practical studies. It's more common in contemporary French; a *lapidaire* means a professional worker with gemstones, while a *dépôt lapidaire* is somewhere that stores fallen, often carved, chunks of masonry, the remains from ruined chapels or cathedrals. A *lapidaire* also names a medieval treatise on the curative properties of particular gemstones.

But it's as an adjective that I'll be concerned with it. So, to the dictionary definitions, which severally announce: the lapidary style is suitable for engraving in stone, and a lapidary inscription is one actually carved in stone, while a style of writing, especially in verse, is called lapidary if it has dignity and concision. The word comes from *lapis*, the Latin word for stone. It could apply to epitaphs on gravestones or to inscribed obelisks or monuments. More broadly, any writing that's extremely concise, and tersely expressive, may be described as lapidary.

Volume 28, Number 1   DOI 10.1215/10407391-3821676

© 2017 by Brown University and d i f f e r e n c e s : A Journal of Feminist Cultural Studies

So far I can't find any history of the "lapidary style" used as a literary-critical term. But then, there's surprisingly little by way of histories of literary criticism in general. Instead, here's an admirably pragmatic eighteenth-century explanation in "On Inscriptions and the Lapidary Style" by Vicesimus Knox, an English essayist and pacifist minister:

> *As the space on monuments, columns, and sepulchres, which admits of inscription, is usually too little to contain many words; it is necessary that the words which its limits are capable of receiving should be expressive of as much meaning as words are able to convey, and be couched in a style as forcible as rhetoric can devise.*
>
> *The smallness of the space devoted to the writing, and the trouble and difficulty of writing on stone, marble, and brass, were the reasons why abbreviations abounded on the ancient inscriptions, and, indeed, furnish the principle of that rule which prescribes for them a laconic brevity of style.*
>
> *Indeed, if these causes for brevity had not existed, it would have been still very desirable, since inscriptions were to be read by the passenger as he journied on his way, to whom it might not be convenient to be detained [. . .].*
>
> *But brevity alone would be a poor recommendation of the lapidary style. It admits of point, antithesis, harmony, and sublimity. It is a style, participating of prose and poetry; in a due mixture of which consists its peculiar character. The cold, the dull, the humble, and the mean, it rejects with contempt. Whatever is noble in sentiment, or forcible in expression, whatever is lively, animated, nervous, and emphatic, forms an essential ingredient in the lapidary style.*
>
> *The churches, and church-yards of England, furnish many examples of sepulchral inscriptions, which would do honour to the best ages of antiquity. At the same time they exhibit others, which excite sentiments very unnatural in a church or church-yard; those arising from the absurd and the laughable.* (161–62)

It's this link between the functional and the expanded senses of the lapidary, and its style, that the following reflections have in view: the ways a literally material surface permits, or heavily influences, the style and then how that style profoundly inflects or dictates the meaning. Mainly I'll be referring to the "lapidary" as that which is cut in stone, where its habitual use is in lettering. That the lapidary usually refers to the literal "letter," or by derivation to a literary style, is itself striking; you might expect it to apply to any incised sculptural ornamentation. But no; it means more than even the finest striations and ribbings on the surface of stone of the kind found on early Ife sculptured heads from Nigeria.

The lapidary style holds a promise to be taut and incisive. But the dictionary also says that the word *lapidary* can refer to the "gem-like" itself, not just to the results of cutting a surface as if with a hard gemstone. There's an oscillation of meaning here between the brilliant gem and the unbright solid stone. This is strange insofar as stone's density is hugely different from the light-refracting and translucent properties of precious stones such as emeralds or sapphires—and is different again from the semiprecious and semiopaques like hematite, agate, malachite, opal, quartz, topaz, and moonstone (all of which carried their own connotations in some nineteenth-century novels, much like the "language of flowers"; there is indeed a literary gemology, including studies of how Victorian jewelry has cropped up in fiction [see Arnold]). And then lapis lazuli, that opaquely blue gemstone, comes from the rock called lazurite. In any event, there's a curious indeterminacy as to what counts as lapidary: is it decided by the surface on which the style is inscribed (on stone or on gem, the stony so very far from the gem-like)? The wide spectrum of variation is striking: the light-refractive gem versus the densely unyielding stone.

Applied to a style as "lapidary," the term borrows the qualities of stone, or of gems, in a kind of metonymy. But the whole notion of any evident lapidary style will, on closer inspection, tend to slip into an indistinctiveness, only of interest to anyone driven to promote an aesthetics of blurriness. When we get to an end of seeking the nature of the lapidary style, a large blur is what we shall find. Then why ever pursue so hopelessly archaic a topic? But its interest includes this: it suggests that a literary style is bound in part to the controlling dispositions of the writer but bound in part, too, by the sway of its materials and by what will suit those restrictions. The so-called materiality of the word is here rendered almost literal. It is a grounded manner where its inescapable "materiality" isn't a restriction, but an aesthetic virtue. Still, it turns out that material per se is only one aspect. Any weighting toward the material ground can sound old-fashioned, especially now, when the word is overwhelmingly digitalized, capable of being endlessly duplicated and dispersed online, and this flatness necessarily dominates. What has this ubiquitous digitalizing brought about for its viewers, now that any tactile or gestural presence of the word has largely gone? It's without tangibility, palpability. Incised lettering is limited to rarity, put only to exceptional uses. We're used to characterizations of the word as evanescent, marked by its aural and oral qualities, by its reception and its transmission as fleeting. Perhaps the thought of "traces" is better liked by today's readers than is permanence: lament, for instance, figured as a breath of wind among the leaves or the passage of language as only rustling, whereas the lapidary owns a violently different aesthetic—monumental, declarative, and admonitory. Its tone holds assertive fullness.

Nevertheless, an intelligible phrase that has been carefully incised in stone is not neutrally impersonal, nor is it some warm track of a human gesture. It is far from handwriting, but it is not calligraphy. It aims at legibility, yet it's not mere legibility, but carries with it a certain authoritative overlay. The silent address of such inscriptions is taken up by the reader's work of retracing the engraved word. This action can multiply the qualities of the "read voice"—that reanimation, inside its reader, of what he or she hears as the voice of the text, so to speak. Even the painted lapidary can carry a sonorous import on its face. Nicolas Poussin made two paintings, both titled *Et in Arcadia ego* (in 1627 and again in 1637–38), in which shepherds and maidens gather around an inscribed tomb or stone, pointing closely to its lettering as if following it by hand. "Vision is a palpation with the look" (134), writes Maurice Merleau-Ponty, and here the pastoral touch traces out the sentiment of mortality, even in rural contentment. There's another *Et in Arcadia ego* by Guercino, painted earlier, between 1618 and 1622, in which a skull sits emphatically on an incised stone plinth. These works have accrued their densely rich interpretations by Erwin Panofsky and other art historians. It's notable that these are also speaking inscriptions, whichever iconographic interpretation you favor: "I, too, am here in Arcadia"—the speaking voice of death itself—or, in a more human rendering, "I, too, who am now dead, lived in Arcadia." In this most celebrated of lapidary admonitions, "Et in Arcadia ego," what, or who, calls out to the passerby? It is death's vivid and admonitory presence. This is the darker cousin of carpe diem. Many instances of the lapidary style exhibit this same tendency to function as knowing, if quiet, speakers engaged in mutely addressing their onlookers. On the other hand, here is another talkative stone: the Obelisk of Emperor Theodosius in Istanbul (see fig. 1). It's a relic of the last ruler of the eastern and western Roman empires and was itself an ancient Egyptian monument. Its base declares, "All things yield to Theodosius and to his everlasting descendants. This is true of me, too; I was mastered and overcome in three

times ten days and raised toward the upper air, under Governor Proculus."
It's another inscription that is directly speaking out toward its reader, the
casual passerby. While evocative, it lacks the terseness of "Et in Arcadia
ego"; long winded, it would never make a candidate for the lapidary style.

Once it's allied to the terse, the magisterial sentiment can become
fully declarative. There may be overlaps between the laconic, the epigram-
matic, and the lapidary, but the ideal of the lapidary is anchored in the
notably concrete and decisive utterance. Let's take a promising candidate:
"In the beginning was the Word, and the Word was with God, and the Word
was God" (John 1.1). This enigmatic and alluring pronouncement has that
concentrated quality of the true lapidary. As for the lapidary style's commitment to brevity, we'll often find it runs very close to the laconic. This is
exemplified in the punch line of the tale of Philip II of Macedon who, intent
on capturing Sparta, sent this message to its leaders: "If I win this war,
you will be slaves forever. You are advised to submit without further delay,
for if I bring my army into your land, I will destroy your farms, slay your
people, and raze your city." To which the Spartans replied in one word: "If"
(Plutarch 446).

This ideal of a brevity that steers clear of any tinge of bathos recurs in "On Conciseness of Style in Writing and Conversation," when Vicesimus Knox elaborates:

> *A celebrated French writer, remarkable for conciseness of style, in a letter to a friend which he had made rather longer than usual, apologizes for its prolixity, by saying, that he had not time to write a shorter. [. . .] Brevity of expression is sometimes the mark of conscious dignity and virtue. It was manliness of sentiment and haughtiness of soul which gave rise to the laconic style. [. . .] Military harangues derive their chief beauty from expressive brevity. [. . .] But ancient history scarcely affords any instance more striking than that of a French king, who thus addressed his men immediately before an attack—"I am your General—you are Frenchmen—there are the enemy." (48)*[1]

Any candidate for the lapidary's terse brevity needs to be capable of being inscribed within a small compass, and so to be tightly composed, for instance, "Quod scripsi, scripsi," Pontius Pilate's taut insistence that "what I have written, I have written" (John 19.22). (His retort concerned Christ's standing as "the King of the Jews.") Thinking of the lapidary as embodying an aesthetics of incision can conjure up an ideal of elegant lettering, and then there's a risk of slippage from an assumed standard of taste into a dubious "tastefulness." But the lapidary style carries an aesthetic that merges into a virtue; it encompasses a notion of a sharpness of thought and an economy of expression as together enabling clarity. That's the argument of George Orwell's "Politics and the English Language" essay of 1946. A neat example of the contemporary lapidary as political wit is the coinage of "Bliar" for the surname of Tony Blair. Such brilliantly sardonic concision could lend itself easily to being engraved in stone.

On the other hand, brevity—per se—does not guarantee incisiveness. It can be infantile, as with the current vogue for contracted words, such as the recent use of "poo" for shampoo in the "No-Poo Movement." As if our time's too short to allow us to use a two-syllable word. Nor will admonition alone suffice to constitute the lapidary, however delightful to passersby an announcement may be (see fig. 2).

Figure 2
First Baptist Church
of Providence, Rhode
Island

Photograph by
Denise Riley (2009)

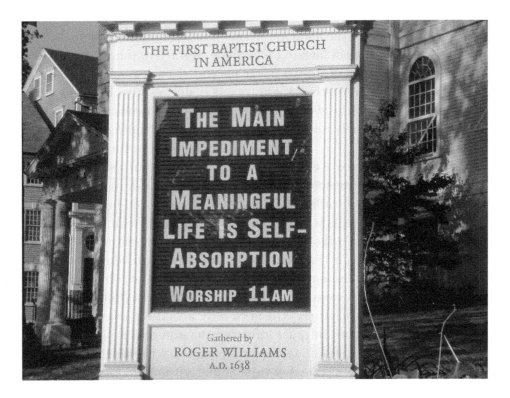

The Lapidary in Practice

The stony aspect of the lapidary emphasizes its desired overtones of dignity, gravitas, reliability, and endurance. Its gemlike aspect, however, emphasizes, in its faceted nature, the lighter worth of some highly wrought artifice. (If these aspects are applied to the imagined writing of a poem, both the chiseling of verses and a longing for the enduring, hard, jewel-like quality in them are found sanctified in Walter Pater's lapidary aesthetic, where to burn with a "hard gem-like flame" is his ideal of an ecstatically lived life [152].) Age-defying artifice triumphs in W. B. Yeats's "Sailing to Byzantium," where the declarative poet announces his longing to pass "out of nature," to become a decoration, an artificial bird set on a bough:

> *Once out of nature I shall never take*
> *My bodily form from any natural thing,*
> *But such a form as Grecian goldsmiths make*
> *Of hammered gold and gold enamelling*

The life of a professional lapidary works, however, not with such precious metals but with precious stones—distinctive because they admit light. To read the manuals of a modern lapidary introduces us to a whole new vocabulary: of faceting technique, refractive index, dispersion, pleochroism. The work of cutting has to maximize each gemstone's color, brilliance, fire, and scintillation. Light travels inside a stone, but the optical characteristics of each kind of stone will differ, so each needs its particular mode of fashioning, whether of sawing, shaping, facet grinding, or polishing (see Kunz).

Lapidary manuals deal in alluring terms like *chatoyancy* (the cat's-eye effect) and *asterism* (as seen in a star sapphire), both related to the play of color in the dispersion of light—how it may split inside the gemstone and be affected by its pavilion angles. So beryl, corundum, and tourmaline crystals will splinter light into two rays at right angles: the quality named *birefringence*. And *pleochroism* means the differentiated colors in these split rays, as happens in the gemstones andalusite, axinite, corundum, iolite, spodumene, tourmaline, and tanzanite. The professional lapidary will cut each stone accordingly to get its most productive faceting. Dark garnets, for instance, will need only a shallow cut for the best dispersion of their limited internal light. But the differing properties of gemstones mean that only certain types can be faceted, whereas the *cabochon* cut is a smoothing, domed style that suits amber, cornelian, and onyx, for instance.

It's needless to labor the parallels between the activities of the professional lapidary, described in technical textbooks, and those of the poet; enough to say that the writing of poetry can demand extreme compression and the dispersal of as much internal light as possible. It can be experienced as a working technique of chipping verbal matter into shape. An aesthetics of translucency may be invoked:

> *TRANSPARENCY*
> *IS THE GAUGE*
> *OF ALL VALUE*
> *WHEN CUTTING*
> *WHEN WRITING (78)*

So writes Christian Bök in his chapbook, *Crystallography*. Yet, what is really "transparent" about an intaglio mark, which is an incision into a surface, as in etching or engraving? How is it that the exactness of some fine cutting comes to be associated with being admirably see-through? There's a curious sort of synesthesia here. What, then, could count as a modern "lapidary verse"? Perhaps Marianne Moore's "The Fish": "wade / through black jade." Or Lorine Niedecker's "A monster owl." Or some of George Oppen's or Louis Zukofsky's writings. Only occasionally, though, will Imagism itself fit the specifications of the lapidary, as in some fragments by HD. But James Schuyler's ultra-lucid hospital poems, not composed under the banner of any movement, almost do.

We might anticipate that some twentieth-century art forms would have investigated this question of concentratedness and of "implication" (to use Moore's term) in relation to the physicality of words. The artist Cy Twombly was deeply susceptible to the charms of ancient graffiti. And he often painted the proper names of classical figures in trailing brushstrokes, like handwriting in veined marble. But an antiquarian "content" alone does nothing to guarantee a truly lapidary style. Then, is the lapidary in practice particular to Roman lettering? The Roman script is, though, hardly universal. How would some very different system of lettering be sensed by those who grew up inside its own physical shapes? For instance, Arabic, Laotian, Cambodian, Japanese, and Vietnamese engraved characters all possess their varied effects that, while differently alluring to this Western eye, feel very different from reading the Roman script. This isn't a matter of comprehension alone. What is found to be "numinous" or "authoritative" must depend on a known language incarnate in a known script, one that you can recognize to be weighty. So the notion of a "pan-linguistic lapidary style" would seem implausible.

Although the choice of typography isn't the only determinant of the lapidary, it's clear that within twentieth-century art, Bruce Nauman's work, which can involve the prominent exhibition of terse phrases or single words as signs, wouldn't conceivably count as lapidary. The medium of light in his neon signs is far removed from that quality of chaste excision on a hard ground but is usually mobile, brilliantly colored, satirical, bossy, and parodic. But the work of the late Scots artist Ian Hamilton Finlay could. He's exemplary among those who've developed a contemporary lapidary style. This includes his displayed fragments of stone incised with Roman capitals, bearing legends such as "THE WORLD HAS BEEN EMPTY SINCE THE ROMANS." Or with engraved quotations from Saint-Just. Or a medal engraved with one bisected word: VIR||TUE. The split between the two syllables makes evident both the "vir" as the Latin word *vir*, or man, and the "tue" as in the French "he kills," or *il tue*. Indeed, the other side of that same coin, literally, is the word *terror*, where the image is of a guillotine bisecting the word. Do we call this "concrete poetry"? But that seems an inept term for the work of Hamilton Finlay, an admirer of the stony aesthetics of the severest French revolutionary. His production has the authority of the hard line that stands over and above the semantic content to exploit its components. It uses the lines' incisions, not just the Roman capitals' angularity.

For lettering in relief alone doesn't carry the same affect as that which is incised. The letter that stands proud, or is embossed, isn't nearly so impressive despite its theatricality or clamor. Superscription has a very different tone from inscription, or gouged-out work. As, of course, does font. Let's think back for a moment to Poussin's painting. Could we imagine its injunction, "Et in Arcadia ego," set in a sinuous copperplate? Its affect would be quite different. For as it stands, what, or who, speaks to the passerby? It is an announcement of death's presence: "I am here, too." This inscription, on the tomb, is itself the subject of the painting. Yet it's not only what the lettering alludes to. It is also the uttering spirit of these admonishing letters. And it's this spirit that seems central to the attraction of the lapidary.

Why is this, though? I'm inclined to think there's something highly specific about the letter that's incised: if so, what is it? Perhaps it is its invitation to belief or consent through its call to follow the lines. There's almost a lure to the spectator to trace out what's incised, as if to demonstrate this power of the tangible—to involve a fingertip or a hand's touch, as in Christ's instruction to his skeptical apostle "Doubting Thomas" after the resurrection: "Then saith he to Thomas, Reach hither thy finger, and behold my hands; and reach hither thy hand, and thrust *it* into my side: and be not faithless, but believing" (John 20.27). Thomas was only ready to be convinced via this demonstration. To run over the chiseled letter with the fingertips enacts a similar tracing in order to establish its truth: touching the hollow of the letter, as if an open wound in the flesh.

This hollowing out of the letter into the stone is like a literalization of that much-invoked phrase, the "materiality of language." The incised shape is a scooped-out letter, standing in for its full form. Its outline offers the petrified memory of an act of carving. A V-shaped incision casts an elegant and clean shadow in the middle of the Roman letter, in effect bisecting it. And yet, even when we speak of incised Roman capitals on stone, we find we need to specify the font. The inscribed slab shown in figure 3, cut at the base of a stone female figure of the rising spirit of the resistance, stands as a war memorial in a public garden in Menton in the South of France. But, stony as it is, its curly serifs let down its candidacy for the lapidary style.

Such practicalities of the lapidary style are those of epigraphy in general. Epigraphy, the study of inscriptions, is often considered a thoroughly antiquarian knowledge, though it's still, of course, practiced. Indeed, its resources have been revitalized by new online archives of inscriptions, including the Cornell Greek Epigraphy project. While digital lettering doesn't require a capacity to bite deep into the surface that bears it, epigraphy

Figure 3
Resistance
Memorial. Menton,
France

Photograph by
Denise Riley (2009)

must always consider the actual material, the stone or marble, and its historical production. The Greek prefix *epi* means "upon," which immediately asserts it as a kind of "writing on." (An *epitaph* is, literally, "a writing upon a tomb"—while the Greek *epigramma* is an inscription or a "writing into." Hence our word "epigram.") So the etymology of epigraphy announces its own physicality. It is writing on a ground.

This phrase "the materiality of language," would customarily imply that language owns its histories of force. It has political effects as it carries its own affect. But for epigraphy in general, and for the lapidary inscription in particular, the literal ground on which it's inscribed is crucial. That ground must be receptive to being incised, but it mustn't tear, sag, or splinter under the physical pressure of the inscription. And its material also enables—or hinders—what can be said. This statement is from the stone letterer Fergus Wessel: "In many ways, with lettering in stone there is more flexibility than in type, where one is restricted by the piece of type. Again it depends on the material; a coarse and open limestone only really lends itself to big, bold lettering. Slate, on the other hand, is very fine to cut and one has complete control over the material—one's chisel being like an extension of the hand."

These technical constraints include the font that can be used, which will be limited because physically constrained by the ground. For example, a modern roman font like Perpetua, designed by Eric Gill, might lend itself especially well to slate carving. And while you couldn't really carve a sinuous copperplate into wood or stone, on metal it is feasible. This is shown by examples of Arabic calligraphy. The word *calligraphy* means, literally, "beautiful writing"; it is an art determined not only by the styles of its lettering but by its reception on a particular material ground.

> *Whence did the wond'rous mystic art arise,*
> *Of painting SPEECH and speaking to the eyes?*
> *That we by tracing magic lines are taught,*
> *How to embody, and to colour THOUGHT? (3)*

That's William Massey, the eighteenth-century author of "Calligraphic Exercises." But because Arabic is a cursive script, it was hard to adapt to the invention of the printing press. So the Arab world continued, for some centuries after Gutenberg, to rely on handwriting for making books and legal documents. The art of calligraphy was more than just retained; it flourished.

The Staged Lapidary

Inscriptions, as the vehicles for theological precepts or exhortations, are such ordinary sights that John Ruskin, in his "The Stones of Venice," wrote about inscribed churches: "Our eyes are now familiar and wearied with writing; and if an inscription is put upon a building, unless it be large and clear, it is ten to one whether we ever trouble ourselves to decipher it. But the old architect was sure of readers. He knew that everyone would be glad to decipher all he wrote" (123). When we turn his remark on the instance of the cathedral at Pisa, then instead we'll find surprises. These inscribed slabs are certainly "large and clear," prominent on the outside walls, but the lettering is upside down or sideways (see figs. 4 and 5).

There's been intense speculation as to why these letters are displayed askew. Some argue that a desired air of gravity was bestowed on the walls, whichever way up the early masons had laid the slabs. Montaigne commented in his journals that these were fragments taken from an old site of the Roman Emperor Hadrian, as they are still thought to be. ("Borrowing the spoils of the ancients" became a trope for an embellished literary style.) Others have interpreted the scenario as a deliberate demonstration of Christianity's conquest of, and indifference to, the declarations of the

Figure 4
Inscription. Pisa
Duomo, Italy

Photograph by
Denise Riley (2012)

Figure 5
Pisa Duomo, Italy

Photograph by
Denise Riley (2012)

old Roman political world. Others have put it down to the simple illiteracy of the stonemasons (but that interpretation's been found unconvincing by other historians). It's been discovered that Pisa imported such stones in great quantities from Ostia and Rome, so it was not simply an action dictated by what happened to lie handily around on the spot. So, what kind of lapidary gesture was being enacted at Pisa through these mislaid stones? No one account seems exhaustive. It's as if these inscribed slabs embody a gesture of authority that's in part a travesty or a parody, in part rendered more powerfully mysterious.

The nonironic lapidary can incarnate the most well known of admonitions, as in the scriptural tale of "the writing on the wall." At his drunken feast, the Babylonian King Belshazzar had used looted holy vessels to praise "the gods of gold and silver, brass, iron, wood, and stone." Soon afterward, disembodied fingers appeared to write on the wall of the royal palace these words: "Mene, Mene, Tekel uPharsin." They were decrypted by Daniel to signify "numbered, weighed, divided" (Daniel 5.25–28). Interpreted, the writing on the wall announced: "[Y]ou've been weighed in the balance and found wanting." On that very night Belshazzar was killed. There's a well-known Rembrandt painting of this episode, in which the painter has mistranscribed one of the characters and arranged them in columns, rather than from right to left as Hebrew is written. So, rather like the cathedral at Pisa, the announcement is not right. It's another miswriting, in what's no doubt a venerable history of error. But what's universally comprehended is the inscribed admonition's gravity, drawing attention to its declarative self.

The stiff immobility of the carved letters throws the word into relief, so to speak. It's this very petrifaction—a literal "turning to stone"—that lets any aspect of irony come to the fore. Irony will establish itself in the self-noticing word, the word made prominent as such. There's a delightful granite tombstone by the British artist David Shrigley; carved with Roman letters in gold leaf, it's actually an imagined and determinedly dull shopping list: "BREAD / MILK / CORNFLAKES / BAKED BEANS / TOMATOES / ASPIRIN / BISCUITS" (see fig. 6). The effect is both comical and grave: it's the banality of daily consumption that will see you out eventually. Its dark wit turns completely on the incision of this cheerily plain content in the monumental stone. It gives to the plainest shopping the *sub specie aeternitatis* weighting of the lapidary.

This "feeling of the lapidary" is a sensation for which maybe only that great elaborator of ambiguity, William James, could supply an apt

Figure 6
David Shrigley.
Gravestone, 2008.
Gold leaf on granite

Stephen Friedman
Gallery, London

term. It wouldn't be a purely psychological characterization, although the lapidary does radiate a kind of feeling: an aesthetic emotion of its own, a sort of indication or a pointing toward. To return to Vicesimus Knox, who finds the elusive and the allusive to be the keys to concision's attraction:

> *Were the causes of the pleasing and powerful effects of conciseness to be investigated, one of them might perhaps be found to be the pleasure which a reader, or spectator, takes in having something left for his own sagacity to discover. The mind greedily snatches at a hint, and delights to enlarge upon it; but frigid is the employment of attending to those productions, the authors of which have laboured every thing into such perspicuity, that the observer has nothing to do but barely to look on. ("On Conciseness" 51)*

There's an intimacy between the lapidary and the ironic, which lies partly in their common capacity to "stage" the word as such. Mere display can expose an ironic undertone. The repetition of a word will make its thinghood prominent, often to comical effect. But sometimes an intended and controlled irony can lapse into drained-out restatement—for instance, those Barbara Kruger posters used by Selfridges, the London department store, in collaboration with an advertising agency and with the artist's full involvement. The intention of slogans such as "I shop, therefore I am" is to satirize the emptiness of a life validated by buying. Another Kruger poster slogan runs, "You want it, You buy it, You forget it." This comes close to being a critique of the store's inevitable failure to realize the consumer's hopes, for the psychology of buying will habitually end in dejection. Yet another poster has the sardonic instruction "Buy me, I'll change your life." These posters deploy her distinctive, slanted Futura Bold typeface, the font of brash postwar advertising. The sentiments here are certainly terse; but their means of exhibition is not lapidary.

The Lapidary and Time

A vaguely Kleinian psychosocial term, "object loss," denotes the experienced absence of an emotional center of attachment. It's a curious phrase if taken too literally, for these are precisely objects that won't get lost, insofar as inanimate things stay, somewhere or other. People go. Then the graven word may fix their trace, offering to the onlooker some suspended or arrested thought.[2] Their longed-for but frustrated permanence comes to dwell, instead, in a reliably incised mark. Lapidary inscriptions function, too, as a way of "stopping time." The lapidary has already done its coming to being. It's the triumph of what has already become, has settled, and can now be proclaimed. The lapidary style turns on a kind of confident singularity. Here, the word stands to present itself to itself, so to speak, *as* the word.

In fact, a writer can exploit this quality of useful estrangement, through self-contemplation, for her own writing. What happens when you put a draft away and then fish it up a week later to look again at it? You'll suddenly see it clearly "as it is," with all its weaknesses. It has cooled down during its separation from its author; it's stepped away from being an emanation of you and has gone toward becoming more of a thing for itself. It can now expose its formal qualities to be scrutinized. (One way of "seeing what you've written," if you're struggling with the draft of a poem, is to throw it into a huge typeface. This, strangely enough, reveals more to you of what you'd put down, which then lets you edit it accordingly.)

But to speculate about the lapidary inscription's capacity to freeze time would need a return to the topic of concision. There's undoubtedly a pleasure, an aesthetic value, in concision, but what kind of value is this?

Why should less be more, unless you're short of space? Yet compression is often admired, even where there aren't any pragmatic needs for it, such as those imposed by the spatial limits of a gravestone. We might wonder, what's the nature of the beauty of the taut, the incisive, and what particular kind of brilliance exists in this highly compressed and specific gesture?

The link between *incision* and *concision* holds strong at the level of etymology. So in the late fourteenth century, the word *concision* was synonymous with "cutting away" or even with "mutilation." We recognize the gradations of the lacerating or cutting remark (we even speak of someone having a "sharp tongue"–a peculiarly pointed figure of speech, because what could be less "sharp" than an actual tongue?). If we pursue the figure of the sarcastic speaker, we'll find that sarcasm's own etymology is surprising in that it shows its fleshy origins: it comes from the Greek *sarkasmos*, "a taunt, mockery," from the verb *sarkazein*, "to speak bitterly, sneer." And that word in its turn means literally "to strip off the flesh," from *sarkos*, "flesh," as in "sarcophagus"–or, like the modern phrase, to "tear someone off a strip," which comes from "to tear a strip off them."

In brief–to return to concision's historical closeness to incision– the lapidary style is a perfect blend of these two related nuances of cutting. It cuts away, gouges out, as its way of compressing. But these elements of incisiveness are saved from the taint of destruction, even of sadism, by the stillness of the lapidary style. In this, the lapidary harmonizes with the monumental and funerary mode. Perhaps this quality stems from that air of timelessness embodied in the hard lettering on hard stone. Speech is being rendered numinous by means of a durable inscription. Its immobility becomes a virtue here, expressive of the precise element "fixed in time." This suits a possible feeling of atemporality in the living, in their feelings of the suspension of time's flow that may follow from a sudden death.

Death and the lapidary style make easy companions; the latter's stillness settles the conceptual tension between the physical thing, or body, and its animation. Engraved words are at home on graves. Their final interpellation is that calling-out to the passerby, "Someday you too will be like me, entombed." This sentiment is monumentalized as the words are held in display. The naturally mobile timing of language gets suspended for the eye as the lapidary inscription. The word is no longer fleeting or gestural. It is literally "set in stone." This very material of stone itself conveys the duration of time as endurance, as hardening. It also marks the evanescence of human temporality. "Time, how short," it says. The mark of meaning also becomes a calcified gesture. As such it defies time's

Figure 7
Tomb of J. R. Green.
English Cemetery,
Menton, France

Photograph by
Denise Riley (2009)

eroding powers as it also defies human amnesia. It's the very opposite of a "mystical writing-pad," the toy on which any writing will easily let itself be wiped away (Freud 230).

So the "lapidary" also touches on our styles of remembering. Do we think of ourselves as being "impressed" with our memories, as if we are a softer kind of stone? Or we might understand ourselves to be sharply incised by remembering. To be, as we say, "deeply marked" by some distressing experiences. Conversely, we might feel relieved joy in being somehow "unmarked" by them. That they were "water off a duck's back" means that they slipped easily and harmlessly over our well-protected surfaces.

Then could "the lapidary style" even function as emblematic of some human recovery from an attack—as a recording gesture on a marked rather than an unscarred surface? The cutting of stone has, in common with cutting into flesh or with tattooing, the will to permanence. Some bereaved mothers, for example, will decide to wear, tattooed, the names of their dead children. These will indeed prove to be longer-lasting inscriptions than the names of transient lovers—as in those cartoons of a sweetheart's name crossed out on a shoulder, another substituted, and then a whole run of erased names down to the forearm. Perhaps it is more plausible to hope to live on as an inscribed, if lacerated, pillar, rather than as a surface carefully sandblasted by some willed amnesia into smoothness.

The lapidary, in short, is an instance of a style that in practice is doubled between asserting its aesthetic values (of tautness and clarity) and its material values—the constraints and potential of the cut stone or the faceted jewel. It is the *cutting gesture alone* that pulls together such disparate objects: the jeweler's lapidary to the grey stone to the writing style. It's a triumph of the enacted verb of incising. Different sorts of "materiality" are worked up into a style that's intensively wrought and highly fashioned. That notion of "style," extended to literature, runs closer to control and craft than to style considered as a demonstration of its author's sensibility or persuasions. Such a writing style can only be willed to a limited extent; it tends to escape intention and to slip beyond management. If the lapidary holds an ideal of restraint that is difficult to sustain for long, its principled commitment to brevity is underscored by its material limits.

A last lapidary inscription, found in the so-called English cemetery in Menton in the south of France, marks the tomb of the historian J. R. Green, who'd been dogged with ill health and had gone in the hope of recuperating there, as did so many nineteenth-century invalids with weakened lungs (see fig. 7).

DENISE RILEY is a critically acclaimed writer of philosophy and poetry. She is currently a professor of poetry and of the history of ideas at the University of East Anglia. Her visiting positions have included A. D. White Professor at Cornell University, Writer in Residence at the Tate Gallery in London, and Visiting Fellow at Birkbeck College in the University of London. Her most recent collection of poetry is *Say Something Back* (Picador, 2016).

Notes

1 Here, Knox has Pascal in mind as the "celebrated French author," while the King mentioned is Henri IV.

2 Adrian Stokes says of the completed art object: "It is as if the various emotions had been rounded like a stone" (406).

Works Cited

Arnold, Jean. *Victorian Jewelry, Identity, and the Novel: Prisms of Culture.* Farnham: Ashgate, 2011.

The Bible. King James Version. 1611. Oxford: Oxford UP, 2008.

Bök, Christian. *Crystallography.* 2nd ed. Toronto: Coach House, 1999.

Freud, Sigmund. *A Note upon the "Mystic Writing Pad."* 1925. *The Standard Edition of the Complete Psychological Works of Sigmund Freud.* Trans. and ed. James Strachey. Vol. 19. London: Hogarth, 1961. 227–34. 24 vols. 1953–74.

Knox, Vicesimus. "Essay 7: On Conciseness of Style in Writing and Conversation." *Essays, Moral, and Literary.* 2nd ed. London: Edward and Charles Dilly, 1779. 44–51.

————————. "On Inscriptions and the Lapidary Style." *The Works of Vicesimus Knox, D. D. with a Biographical Preface.* Vol. 3. London: J. Mawman, 1824. 232–36.

Kunz, Sandrine. "A Brief Review of Gemstone Optical Properties from a Lapidary's Perspective." June 2000. https://www.cigem.ca/pdf/sandrine.pdf.

Massey, William. *The Origin and Progress of Letters.* London: J. Johnson, 1763.

Merleau-Ponty, Maurice. "The Intertwining–The Chiasm." *The Visible and the Invisible.* Trans. Alphonso Lingis. Ed. Claude Lefort. Evanston: Northwestern UP, 1968. 130–55.

Moore, Marianne. "The Fish." *Complete Poems.* New York: Penguin, 1994. 32–33.

Pater, Walter. *The Renaissance: Studies in Art and Poetry.* New York: Oxford UP, 1998.

Plutarch. *The Life of Alexander.* Part 1. *The Parallel Lives.* Loeb Classic Library Edition. 1919. http://penelope.uchicago.edu/Thayer/e/roman/texts/plutarch/lives/alexander*/3.html (accessed 31 Oct. 2016).

Poussin, Nicolas. *Et in Arcadia ego.* The Louvre, Paris.

Ruskin, John. *The Stones of Venice.* Vol. 2. London: Blackfriars, 1900.

Shrigley, David. *Gravestone.* 2008. Stephen Friedman Gallery, London.

Stokes, Adrian. "Form in Art." *New Directions in Psychoanalysis: The Significance of Infant Conflict in the Pattern of Adult Behavior.* Ed. Melanie Klein, Paula Heimann, and R. E. Money-Kyrle. New York: Basic, 1955. 406–20.

Wessel, Fergus. "Letters and Stone." *I Love Typography.* 9 Mar. 2012. http://ilovetypography.com/2012/03/09/letters-stone-interview-fergus-wessel/.

Yeats, W. B. "Sailing to Byzantium." *The Tower.* London: MacMillan, 1928. 80.

The Novel Comes of Age:
When Literature Started Talking with Children

*V*irtually all of us who write about the eighteenth century observe at some point that three now often distinct ways of thinking about human experience developed with particular intensity in the period and went on to become separate subjects in publishing catalogs and university curricula. Education absorbed attention and concern, attracting the notice of philosophers such as John Locke, Jean-Jacques Rousseau, and Immanuel Kant and the practical plans of Joseph Priestley, Anna Laetitia Barbauld and her brother John Aikin, Mary Wollstonecraft, and Maria and Richard Lovell Edgeworth. The effort to identify the standing of what we now call aesthetic experience came to be considered on all sides, with Kant's third *Critique* laying out the possibility that apprehensions could be taken seriously even when they could not resolve themselves into clear concepts. And the novel in Western Europe commanded such a substantial audience that commentators felt the need to explain what that audience was seeing and responding to when they demanded more novels.

      With various different degrees of obviousness, the discussions of the novel, aesthetics, and education revolved around the question of

Volume 28, Number 1 DOI 10.1215/10407391-3821688

availability—the ease of use that various experiences carried or might carry. The novel, as a writer such as Barbauld suggested in her essay "On the Origin and Progress of Novel-Writing" (1810), was a form that even children—and certainly adolescents—could read and understand. It may sometimes have been castigated precisely on those grounds, but the argument for strenuousness had to yield in the face of clear popular enthusiasm. Comparatively untrained readers were able to feel the pleasure of understanding and could do so without catching every erudite allusion to Homer or Horace. Aesthetic experience, especially in Kant's description of it, gave standing to pleasure in both natural and artistic objects without needing to justify that pleasure in highly cultivated taste. And educational writers increasingly tried to identify what their pupils could learn easily, in the conviction that what was taken up most readily was best learned. Of the writers most deeply concerned with these questions, Barbauld was arguably the one most actively engaged with their full range.

As she provided an overview of late eighteenth- and early nineteenth-century examples of the novel in a survey that reached back to classical antiquity and ranged across continents, she highlighted features of the genre that showed it to be a near relation to her writings for children and to the essays and poems in which she highlighted conversation. Conversation, as she depicted it in the imaginative and actual conversations that she carried on and transcribed for her adoptive son, Charles, was not merely a way of conveying information—though it partially served that purpose, as Michelle Levy has suggested in describing Barbauld's pedagogy as "instructive conversation" (133). At least as much a way of inducting a child into society as an expression of sociability, Barbauld's version of conversation assumed that the personal interchange represented an understanding that embraced both parties to it and was not a matter of one person's having a meaning that the other party might or might not catch. Moreover, it did not revolve around the kind of exchange and debate that Jürgen Habermas associated with coffee house culture. Rather, Barbauld's account of conversation as a general form accommodating a variety of different speakers and a variety of different understandings bypassed any demand that interlocutors lay out their positions and defend them. I want to argue here that it is this presentation of conversation as a way of forwarding thought in those who are not demonstrably scholars and thinkers that helped Barbauld to a distinctive and important understanding of the novel, one that allied the novel with both her own educational writing and aesthetic thought current in the period.

Emphasizing the contemporaneity of novels—their taking "a tincture from the learning and politics of the times" and serving "successfully to attack or recommend the prevailing systems of the day" ("On the Origin" 2)—Barbauld lays out a series of implications. She notes the affinities among the fictitious adventures that the novel documents and those of other genres: "Adorned with the embellishments of Poetry, they produce the epic; more concentrated in the story, and exchanging narrative for action, they become dramatic. When allied with some great moral end, [. . .] they may be termed didactic" (1–2). Novels may, in her view, overlap with those other genres; she is happy to admit some verse narratives into the category of the novel. But identifying transhistorical commonalities between ancient novels and contemporary ones ultimately makes it possible for her to lay out a way of imagining the availability of actions to modern characters, to suggest how the novel of the eighteenth and early nineteenth centuries made itself accessible to modern readers, and to draw a sharp contrast between ancient and modern emotions.

In 1810 Barbauld tried both to meet the demand for novels and to examine the impulses it represented. For the publishing house of F. C. and J. Rivington and its associates, she selected some twenty-eight novels by twenty-one novelists for a fifty-volume set (Toner 172; McCarthy, *Anna* 422–30). Laying out eclectic principles of selection in the essay "On the Origin and Progress of Novel-Writing" with which she prefaced the collection, she said that she aimed to present "a series of some of the most approved novels, from the first regular productions of the kind to the present time." Her essay ranges widely across ancient and modern national literatures before addressing the British novel. Singling out "that truly original genius De Foe" as the "first author amongst us [in Britain] who distinguished himself by natural painting" (35), she points to one particular era, the reign of George II, as having consolidated the consciousness of the importance of the genre: "Richardson, Fielding, and Smollet [*sic*], appeared in quick succession; and their success raised such a demand for this kind of entertainment, that it has ever since been furnished from the press, rather as a regular and necessary supply, than as an occasional gratification" (36).

Having noted the importance of these four novelists, however, Barbauld is decidedly reticent about offering strong recommendations: "A few of superior merit were chosen [for the collection] without difficulty, but the list was not completed without frequent hesitation" (58). She needs to consider "the taste and preference of the public," because the publishers' only hope to cover the "expense and risk of the publication" lies in the popularity of the collection (59). She is unable to intrude upon copyright, and the booksellers limit the number of volumes they allow her. The very specific and practical concerns about the literary market for the collection, however, provide merely one strong restatement of a view that she presses throughout the essay. Noting both that "no two people would probably make the same choice, nor indeed the same person at any distance of time" (58), she goes on to lay down her famous final judgment on the novel as a genre: "Let me make the novels of a country, and let who will make the systems" (59).

In an article she titles with that line, Claudia Johnson observes that Barbauld claims a convergence between the systems of a country and its novels—and in ways that reflect well on both. Johnson rightly highlights the importance that Barbauld attaches to the public appetite for novels. Rather than disparaging the novel as if one could and should dismiss it as an encouragement to idleness and a corrupter of morals, Barbauld writes almost as if she were an anthropologist, someone trying to figure out the significance of the behavior she is seeing without having recourse to the systematic statements that people make about their behavior. The systems of a country—literary as well as legal—convey a great deal of information about it and its inhabitants, and the behaviors they enjoin and prohibit, Barbauld insists. In her survey of specific instances of the novel, Barbauld paints the taste for certain novels as unlegislated and relatively quiet state- ments of the manners of any country in any particular era. Novels may be "condemned by the grave, and despised by the fastidious: but their leaves are seldom found unopened" ("On the Origin" 1). Analyzing how people spend their time rather than how they say they spend their time—and rather than how the grave or fastidious say they should spend it—she takes the same approach to the novel that she had earlier done to education in advising a friend about his son. Examples, she says, speak more loudly than precepts: "[Y]ou must *educate* [your son] yourself. You not only ought to do it, but you *must* do it, whether you intend it or no. [You must] trust that [children's] characters will form themselves from the spontaneous influence of good examples, and circumstances which impel them to useful action" (*Anna* 331). As if she were in conversation with M. M. Bakhtin before the fact, she sees literature providing evidence about the history and social conditions of its worlds. Moreover, she seems, again prophetically, to be endorsing his claim that the novel's signal contact with the contemporary world in which it appears militates against the identification of a canonical list of novels (Bakhtin 3, 39). Her survey and suggestions in "On the Origin and Progress of Novel-Writing" yield no required curriculum, but only a series of lightly urged recommendations. These call attention to aspirations toward encyclopedic comprehensiveness in order to suggest their futility.

Barbauld thus deploys literary history in two different directions. On the one hand, she surveys historic examples of the novel to claim a distinguished genealogy for "[f]ictitious adventures, in one form or other" in the polite literature of "every age and nation" ("On the Origin" 1). She legitimates the ancient novel with anecdotes about its loyal partisans and instances in which readers and writers of novels displayed their strong commitments to their novels: the Romans were such avid novel-readers that "the Parthian general who beat Crassus took occasion [. . .] to reproach [the Romans] with effeminacy, in not being able, even in time of danger, to dispense with such an amusement," and Heliodorus resigned his bishopric rather than burn his book *Theagenes and Chariclea* (4). On the other hand, she notes how little certain modes of behavior are available to a modern audience. They are historically interesting but remote from the experience of people living in the nineteenth century—nearly as remote as the closed system of the epic that Bakhtin contrasts with the novel. And she applies the test of contemporary availability even in acknowledging the popularity of such recent novels as John Buncle's *The Memoirs of Several Ladies* and *Chrysal; or, The Adventures of a Guinea* even as she gives them clipped sardonic tags. (Of Buncle: "The ladies, whose memoirs he professes to give, are all highly beautiful and deeply learned; good Hebrew scholars; and above all zealous Unitarians. [. . .] Many of the descriptions are taken from nature; and, as the book was much read, have possibly contributed to spread that taste for lake and mountain scenery which has since been so prevalent. The author was a clergyman" [37–38]; of the anonymously published *Chrysal*, "It described real characters and transactions, mostly in high life, under fictitious names [. . .] the generation it describes [is] passed away" [38]). Evidence that substantial numbers of people have enjoyed these novels makes them worth talking about, even while she herself reads them at a virtual arm's length in the consciousness that they have lost their audiences.

Yet while Barbauld rejects the idea that novels should conform to a particular model, she expresses clear admiration for Richardson's way of "carrying on a story" in letters (*Anna* 362). She sets up the usefulness of the epistolary novel by comparing it and contrasting it with two earlier modes. First, in the "narrative or epic as it may be called," "the author relates himself the whole adventure" and "is supposed to know everything; he can reveal the secret springs of actions, and let us into events in his own time and manner" (362). In the second mode, the memoir, "the subject of the adventures relates his own story" (362) and is confined to what he knew and to what he might be supposed to remember at a distance of years. The "third way [. . .], that of *epistolary correspondence*, carried on between the characters of the novel" offers many of "the advantages of the other two," as it "gives the feelings of the moment as the writers felt them *at* the moment. It allows a pleasing variety of stile [. . .]. It makes the whole work dramatic, since all the characters speak in their own persons" (364).

For all the advantages that Barbauld attaches to the epistolary mode, she recognizes the disadvantages of its "fictitiousness"; it is simultaneously "the most natural and the least probable way of telling a story," for a variety of reasons that commentators on Richardson's novels have reiterated through the years (*Anna* 364). It sometimes requires an "insipid confidant to tell the circumstances that an author cannot relate in any other way"; it obliges characters to say of themselves things that candor would not require and modesty would prefer to leave unsaid. Furthermore, it makes memory look improbably durable when a character repeats a long conversation (364). These disadvantages, however, are swallowed up by the characteristic effect of the epistolary novel—that it tracks the progress of conversation and registers what characters understand as their understandings develop. For a novel such as *Clarissa*, she maintains, this identity between letters and conversations contributes to the overriding sense of the novel's unity. Even when some letters do not immediately reach their destination, *Clarissa* presents characters—and one character in particular—so circumstantially and so conversationally that Richardson can "[found] a most pathetic tale" on a "slight foundation, and on a story not very agreeable or promising in its rude outline" (*Anna* 365): "No digressions, no episodes. It is wonderful that without these helps of common writers [Richardson] could support a work of such length. With Clarissa it begins—with Clarissa it ends. [. . .] We see her fate from afar, as it were through a long avenue, the gradual approach to which, without ever losing sight of the object, has more of simplicity and grandeur than the most cunning labyrinth that can be contrived by art" (365–66). *Clarissa* stands as an example of the greatest possible approximation of character to plot, with the incidents of the novel appearing as events in an unfolding conversation.

The novel thus comes to seem a series of acts of attention, and specifically attention to the movements of conversation itself. Neither war nor continually renewed epic wrath has any place in the world of the novel that Barbauld recognizes as proximate to her own time. What is realistic about the novel is not that it describes reality but that it offers ways of attending to the world of a character's experience. The events of the novel, such as they are, Barbauld characterizes as moments in a game: "After Clarissa finds herself, against her will and intention, in the power of her lover, the story becomes, for a while, a game at chess, in which both parties exert great skill and presence of mind, and quick observation of each other's motions" (*Anna* 367). It's that particular characterization of *Clarissa* that I want to flag as crucial to Barbauld's sense of the importance of conversation in education and in the novel generally. Much as she values Madame Genlis's *Adèle et Théodore* for representing a "preceptive" novel with "a system of education, the whole of which is given in action," with "infinite ingenuity in the various illustrative incidents" (*Anna* 393), she objects to its being (like Rousseau's *Émile*) "much founded upon deception" with "the whole of [a pupil's] education [. . .] a series of contrived artificial scenery, produced, as occasion demands, to serve a particular purpose" (*Anna* 395). Such preceptive novels do not lecture their young charges; they construct stage sets that dictate the ideas that will emerge. Thus, although Rousseau's and Genlis's novels move in the direction of example by rendering all the lessons as experimental actions, Barbauld calls attention to the way they develop their examples so tendentiously as to become preceptive.

Barbauld's preference for the centrality of conversation over even the action-oriented systems of Rousseau and Genlis is summed up in the remark I quoted earlier: Clarissa and Lovelace's interaction resembles "a game at chess, in which both parties exert great skill and presence of mind, and quick observation of each other's motions." Conversation is, in other words, key to her description of the novel as a genre because it involves the parties to it in a series of improvised responses. Unlike catechisms that represent both questions and answers in the form of a mock dialogue, conversations develop directions of their own. Unlike Rousseau and Genlis's stage sets, Barbauld's conversations are continually affected by the characters participating in them and the setting in which they find themselves. Characters—or, rather, the conversation that recruits them—become part of one another's environment.

Pointing out the fluidity of Barbauld's account of conversation, however, runs the risk of making it seem as if the novel were nothing but an open form that never knows when to stop and that can seem as virtually unending as life itself. Precisely that question has led Anne Toner to point to Barbauld's concern with form, a concern that Toner sees manifest in Barbauld's attention to novelistic endings. Endings give a shape and finality to novels of a kind that only comes to ordinary persons with the epitaphs and obituaries that characterize them on their deaths. For a novelist such as Richardson, Clarissa's death was not only moving but an almost inevitable way of rounding out the novel that bears her name. And we might add that much of the force of the marriage plot and the detective story alike is to make the entire plot of a novel look as though it has all along had one principal aim in view. But characterizing the difference between the novel and actual life as a difference between finite and infinite description puts more exclusive emphasis on novelistic closure than I think Barbauld would allow. For her suggestion that Clarissa and Lovelace participate with "skill and presence of mind, and quick observation of each other's motions" brings out the extent to which many of the realist novels with which Barbauld was familiar—and many of the realist novels that she might be said to predict—include under the umbrella of their overall plot structure a series of micro games, moments in which characters register themselves as having solved a puzzle and answered a riddle. Barbauld may see the limitations in episodic plots in which characters move from one place to another, picking up a new set of concerns as they go. Yet her characterization of *Clarissa* as unified points us to her interest in episodes of thought, moments in which a novelistic character is shown thinking differently from the way they had thought before. Such moments represent discontinuous irruptions of a fresh consciousness in the continuous life of a character and appear almost as if they were a spontaneous physical reflex. Like Dorothea Brooke's early morning realization of her situation in Rome after her marriage to Casaubon, they appear almost in the form of an answer to a riddle.

Following Claudia Johnson's lead in seeing the affinities between Barbauld's thinking and Jane Austen's practice, we can see in *Emma* a highly explicit handling of just such a way of understanding riddles as local versions of form, landing places for consciousness that need not be as definitive as the full-stop conclusion to the novel. Thus, Harriet Smith, in *Emma*, is "collecting and transcribing all the riddles of every sort that she could meet with" (54). Austen frames Harriet's undertaking with a series of descriptions that carry substantial evaluative weight. Harriet's collection, "the only mental provision she was making for the evening of life," looks like a low-balance retirement account. And setting Harriet's effort into general social context does not remove the sting: "In this age of literature, such collections on a very grand scale are not uncommon. Miss Nash, head-teacher at Mrs. Goddard's, had written out at least three hundred" (54). Harriet is the principal here, but even the production of the collection is a social activity. Harriet may be inspired by Miss Nash, but Harriet and Emma continually enact an easy collaboration: Emma supplies "invention, memory, and taste" and Harriet writes "a very pretty hand" (54). All three young women command the rules of the genre, and Austen suggests that the three practitioners of the art of the riddle are part of a veritable community of understanding. Even though we have no reason to suppose that Emma knows Miss Nash directly, Harriet's undertaking links all three women as persons who recognize and practice the art of the riddle, if only by being connoisseurs proficient enough to collect examples.

The charades that Austen deploys in *Emma* have a slightly more complex form than the classic riddle form favored by the Sphinx who addressed Oedipus. In charades, the riddle takes an artful turn. It presents lines of verse that identify single-syllable words before going on to introduce a description that can be resolved into a two-syllable word. The "affliction" of one line is combined with "man" in the second to yield "woman" (55). Mr. Elton contributes a charade that links "court" with "ship" and unriddles it to supply the word "courtship" (56). As the novel's readers will remember, Austen introduces a central complication among the characters at this point: Elton takes himself to be announcing his hope that Emma will favor his address, but Emma thinks that he is professing love to Harriet.

Because the misunderstanding that arises from Elton's charade represents a crucial turn in the action, it is easy for us to pass over the function of the riddle in the structure of *Emma* and, I want to suggest, other novels and novel forms. The solution to a riddle locks certain words in place and represents them as something akin to a mathematical equation. In that sense, riddles starkly introduce facticity and help to create the realism of the realist novel—not because they are referring to an external world, but rather because they achieve a solidity that suggests the solidity of the world behind it. Moreover, the riddles of the novel—and riddles in general—are a supremely democratic form. They depend on a cryptonomy that almost instantaneously opens itself up to the light. Even though Austen notes Emma's "invention, memory, and taste," solving the riddle scarcely demands such exalted talents.

In fact, riddles as a form so nearly approach proverbs that it is hard for a character to feel ashamed of not having solved them. Any adult being quizzed by a child reading from a riddle book can easily feign ignorance without loss of face. A question such as "What's black and white and red all over?" seems so readily to resolve itself into the word "newspaper" that it feels like something anyone, everyone, has always known so that someone can fail to produce the answer and still give themselves more than half credit: "I knew that." A collection of riddles may seem an adolescent activity, one that Harriet Smith may, and Emma Woodhouse certainly will, outgrow. But it is also a practice that is so widely dispersed through their society as to count almost as elevator music or ambient noise. Though riddles do not rise to the level of high art, they are so generally known that no one is to be blamed for having heard them and remembered them.

 Cleverness at solving riddles may not be any more a help to Emma than it was to Oedipus, but recognition of the distribution of riddle-solving is crucial to the recognition of stories as such. Although there may be various different contenders to fill in the blank that Sophocles left for the Sphinx's riddle, it's easy to see why the most common form of the question has come to be "What goes on four feet in the morning, two feet at noon, and three feet in the evening?" and the all but inevitable answer, "Man." Once the riddle is presented in a form that makes the answer look virtually given, we are all solvers and connoisseurs of riddles, with superiority more a function of the accidents of timing and situation than of extraordinary cleverness.

 Austen's riddling pays homage to common knowledge while also awarding special prominence to particular individual characters. The work that the riddle does is not so much to highlight the superior knowledge of a particular character but to award him or her a special place in the narrative. In the crowded space of a populous world, one that includes readers as well as characters, Austen ties Emma especially closely to riddles and charades, making her look like the one most adept at solutions. Emma, like Oedipus before her, is narratively credited with being first to provide what seems like a simple answer. Oedipus's success with the Sphinx's riddle might scarcely look like an accomplishment in actual life because it is hard to imagine the answer being hard to come by. Imagining that there was ever one person who could plausibly be said to have been the *first* to hazard that "man" is the answer to the Sphinx's question is less a realistic gesture than the means of awarding narrative merit to Oedipus, of singling him out as a character and setting up his story as one worthy of being attended. Seeing Sophocles and Austen together is to see the pressure of narrative in its various forms and to see how two different movements combine in the formation of the realist novel in the eighteenth and nineteenth centuries. For the realist novel does not achieve its sense of realism from referring to many places and things from the actual world. The riddles and charades of the novel likewise stabilize the fiction and put characters and readers on the same page—participating in obviousnesses together. And even as the availability of riddle and its solution expands the novel's community to virtually democratic proportions, the placements of the riddles and their solutions create that profoundly undemocratic creature, the hero or heroine.

Aspects of these dual and opposed impulses in the novel attract Barbauld's notice when she collects specimens of the novel in *The British Novelists* and introduces the collection with "On the Origin and Progress of Novel-Writing." Her concluding statement might be taken as a simple expression of personal preference: "Let me make the novels of a country, and let who will make the systems" (59). That sentence contains more than a mere evaluative judgment. Already contained in it is an observation that earlier genres such as epic and tragedy resemble legal codes; they clearly create standards by which to judge individual performances.[1] Barbauld's claim on behalf of the novel as a literary form is that the novel is the literary form of her era that participates most closely in philosophy of mind. It's this aspect of Barbauld's account of the novel that has prompted Claudia Johnson to term her an early narratologist and that has led Anne Toner to call attention to Barbauld's interest in form as such. Although Barbauld's account of the novel would have to be updated in various ways to account for subsequent specimens, she anticipates the kind of thinking that Vladimir Propp did in identifying heroes in folk tales. The hero or heroine of a tale is picked out when the action of the tale or the novel has scarcely begun. The lack of reliance on already extant popular history or legend helps to dramatize a reader's ability to recognize a principal character when there is scarcely anything other than an interesting situation to commend them: a person leaves home (as Propp would say); a person is, whether avowedly or not, a participant in the marriage sweepstakes (as Austen would say). These are characters who are awarded their central place in the narrative by the narrative itself, and Barbauld calls attention to the way this election offers them considerable protection. "It was very probable, at some periods of his history, that *Gil Blas*, if a real character, would come to be hanged; but the practiced novel-reader knows well that no such event can await the hero of the tale" (53). Although Barbauld mentions novel upon novel and comments on the distinctive features of the twenty-eight novels she includes in her collection, she is particularly alert to the ways the novel achieves coherence by following through on what it foreshadows and avoiding digressions. Barbauld's account of the novel, then, offers up a picture of the novel that represents its plots as large-scale riddles. She favors least digressive plots for sustaining the basic questions "What is . . . ?" and "Who is . . . ?" without making them unanswerable.

While Barbauld has often been praised for the range and intellectual seriousness of her literary career, the various aspects of her writing and thinking have only infrequently been linked with one another. The criticisms that Charles Lamb and Samuel Taylor Coleridge lodged against her writing for children have obscured the importance of that work and the significance of that work for her account of the novel. Her critics railed against what they saw as writing that attended to realities and reined in a child's imaginative freedom, a freedom that they saw epitomized in fairy tales that featured children who were heroic because of their outsized exploits. "The cursed Barbauld crew," Lamb suggested, delivered doses of actuality that compromised children's imaginative contemplation of extraordinary possibilities and restricted their ability to cast themselves in heroic roles.[2] What I think her detractors failed to appreciate is the extent to which she was providing a new understanding of heroism and of literature's relation to it.[3]

The riddle is at the heart of Barbauld's literary project when she writes for children. Her *Lessons for Children (of Two to Three Years Old* [1778]; *of Three Years Old*, part 1 [1778]; *of Three Years Old*, part 2 [1778]; and *of Three to Four Years Old* [1779]) follow the movements of conversation between a mother (Barbauld herself) and her child (her nephew and adoptive son, Charles). The books feature moments in which the mother points out various things to her son: the cat in the room with them and other elements of their domestic life together. And though the mother makes statements and imaginatively extends her pointing hand to these features of their shared experience, the book immediately sets up a question-and-response format. The first book is not an illustrated alphabet that asks the child to name objects for the various letters: there is no "'a' is for apple." Instead of laying out an alphabetic arrangement, the naming of various things makes the identification of those things continuous with the learning of language. The implicit question "What is this?" or "What is this called?" is continually being raised and answered. In *Lessons for Children of Three Years Old*, part 1, this naming practice takes up rather more abstract terms: "What is today . . . ?" And it's here, in the simplest sort of procedure, that one can see Barbauld deploying a technique that is fundamental to much of her writing: she draws out from Charles an observation that shows the pressure of his thought. Rather than simply asking Charles to list the names of the days of the week, she begins by asking an easily answerable question: "What day is it today?" Charles's continual responses lead to the question "And what will come after Saturday?"—to which the reply is "Why then, Sunday will come again." Moreover, subsequent lessons pick up on the same basic topics, recasting the days of the week in terms of past, present, and future: "I know a pretty riddle. 'What is that which was *To-morrow* and will be *Yesterday*?'" "To-day." "Yes" (*Lessons* 100).

Barbauld's *Lessons* were a domestic production, not just because they were written to be read in the home but also because they made a child's growing knowledge seem continuous with the home environment. A child engaged in the conversations in and around the books would have felt that he could not remember when he had learned a particular thing. The lessons progressed from simple sentences formed largely of words of single syllables to more complex descriptions and imaginative scenarios and were shaped by Barbauld's estimation of the developing capacities of her son, Charles. Some writers may have worried that Barbauld exaggerated a young child's capacities—thinking, for instance, that children could not be said to be real participants in the reading process before they had mastered the alphabet—but Barbauld insisted on pointing to the elements of a world that a child had already encountered, so that learning would proceed as a series of recognitions. Puss the cat is named both on the page and in the room with Barbauld and Charles so that learning is naturalized, and it seems as if a child cannot remember when he did not know what the little book makes him conscious of knowing.

Barbauld's books for children between two and four years old feature a child who exemplifies the heroism of ordinary life, who is singled out by the attention he receives and given only measured praise for attending to the world around him. He is someone whose education involves one effort after another to recognize elements of his world—not a character like William Wordsworth's little actor who "cons another part" in the attempt to gain recognition. He is a child who talks. From *Lessons for Children* through *Hymns in Prose for Children*, Barbauld continually asks a child to recognize himself as a speaking subject. Although Barbauld reserves her explanation that words are arbitrary signs of things for the four-year-old, she treats Charles's ability to speak as key to his nature. Babies do not speak; cats do not speak; and dogs do not speak. Charles, however, does.

The pressure of Charles's presence as an interlocutor makes itself felt even when Barbauld's speaker has the floor. Beginning with a dialogue of hide-and-seek ("Papa, where is Charles? [. . .] Papa cannot find him" [5]), Charles is a constant addressee. At times it even becomes difficult to sort out whether Barbauld or Charles is speaking in response to the question "How many fingers have you got, little boy[?]" At such moments, the questions lose their interrogative punctuation and are pointed as if they were declarative.

Solutions and answers appear almost as if they preceded the conundrums and questions that they address.

Indeed, Mary Wollstonecraft captured this aspect of Barbauld's thinking well in praising Barbauld's descriptions of the world in her *Hymns in Prose for Children* (1781) in saying how the hymns "contribute to make the Deity obvious to the senses" (Wollstonecraft 17)—and thus seeing them as a direct continuation of Baruch Spinoza's account of the democratic availability of the natural world. Moreover, Barbauld treats her conviction that the book of nature is equally open to all as imposing an obvious limit to the adult's ability to praise and blame. Whereas many other writers for children effusively praise children for their intellectual accomplishments, Barbauld treats them as expectable—the sorts of things that someone with human capacities would observe about the world in which they live. Charles is the hero of the piece, in that he is continually given the simplest possible riddles in the early stages of the series, so that he can answer "What is this?" with the various names that he knows without having been conscious of making an effort to learn them.

In the dialogue I mentioned earlier, Charles keeps naming days of the week until he arrives at a point at which he identifies a pattern; he hasn't just named eight different days, but rather a regular and recurrent cycle in which one Sunday and another stand as bookends. The mother's questions are all questions of naming, but they don't just ask that particular names be repeated. They issue in a recognition of an incipient order. It is as if Barbauld were here walking Charles through the kind of understanding that Priestley gestured toward when he observed in *A Course of Lectures on Oratory and Criticism* that we can't have a new word for every new thing—or, rather, for everything we newly encounter (184–85)—and that a crucial aspect of oratory, and of language-learning, is to contrive and recognize the arrangements that anyone is implicitly making in using the language.

The ability to compare "Sunday" with "Sunday" involves the most basic kind of matching. Yet the acknowledgment of the child's ability to make that comparison and introduce a new element into the discussion applies in increasingly complex situations. In *Evenings at Home, or The Juvenile Budget Opened*, Barbauld and her brother John Aikin create conditions for randomly assigning particular readings to particular children. The children who read the stories and the short discussions of minerals and trees are not matched with certain stories on the basis of gender or age or personality traits: no one is singled out, Claudius-like, by a story aimed directly at them. Instead, the discussions, which themselves appear as transcriptions of conversations, are drawn by lot, and they unspool in exactly the way that conversations do. George and Harry of some of the conversations, for instance, quiz their tutor about the various minerals and their properties, and the child who reads the story aloud is obliged to engage with it as if it were a part of the conversational education that Barbauld puts in place.

Barbauld's approach to education both honors the Lockean doctrine that all knowledge is derived from experience rather than innate ideas and also suggests why the experience of learning can feel as though it relies on a knowledge before one's knowledge. For conversation, as she presents it, is a distributive or attributive activity, in which being able to carry on the conversation is tantamount to learning as if one already knew. (Charles seldom feels impelled to say that he doesn't understand.) Her version of conversation thus represents something of an extension of her father John Aikin's pedagogical practice of "free, familiar conversation" (Janowitz 62). Yet her approach differed rather substantially from her father's. His was directed at pupils older than Barbauld's son, Charles, and it thus plausibly revolved around mutual questioning rather than the kinds of consonance that Barbauld pursued. John Aikin, Doctor of Divinity, was, like other pupils of Philip Doddridge, well trained in the art of reviewing various statements on particular subjects and assessing their merits. Perhaps, like some of his successors in the academies established by Dissenters or their intellectual allies, he took it as axiomatic that students should be encouraged to be on the alert for their teachers' lapses in even comparatively nonexperimental subjects such as Latin.

What I'm identifying as Barbauld's distributive or attributive account of conversation values conversation along different lines: it stresses the way a dialogue makes individuals into language groups of two or more and does not pause to calculate which of them has contributed the greater investment of thought. In the twentieth century, I. A. Richards would speak in mild disparagement of the looseness of our operations with language in ordinary social situations. But what looked to him like the imprecisions of ordinary social exchange appeared to Barbauld as statements of a small-scale collective consciousness, assignable neither to one party or the other. A common representation of what people do when they are talking to one another—or, rather, of what they ought to be doing when they are talking to one another—has it that mutual agreement on a common meaning is the goal. It appears, however, that Barbauld never subscribed to such a view, whether she was discussing conversations between a child and an adult or whether she was thinking of adults in company with one another in public worship.

Barbauld opened her *Remarks on Mr. Gilbert Wakefield's Enquiry into the Expediency and Propriety of Public or Social Worship* with the striking observation that "public or social worship" has never been defended because it has never previously been attacked (1). In the course of defending public worship—rather than lamenting its insufficiency in promulgating virtue—she accepts a situation that a Dissenter such as Wakefield found intolerable: the requirement that even Dissenting churches should, in their public worship ceremonies, read from the Common Version, the King James Version, of scripture. While a Dissenting theologian such as Philip Doddridge offered up his *Family Expositor* for the private use of families who wished to follow a translation of the scriptures cleansed of the doctrinal language of Anglicanism, Barbauld recasts the question of public worship so that it is scarcely a matter of religious doctrine. In answer to her own question, "What is public worship?" she responds, "Kneeling down together while prayers are said of a certain length and construction, and hearing discourses made to a sentence of scripture called a text!" (4). She lays out a minimal role for the place of the text and the specific form it takes. Against those, such as Wakefield, who would banish all observance of religion that smacks of ritual and denounce such observance as an overcoming of the proper consideration for belief that one can willingly subscribe to, Barbauld argues strenuously. She maintains that "Public Worship has this great advantage, that it teaches those to pray, who, not being accustomed to think, cannot of themselves pray with judgment" (9).

With this remark, she does not disparage those who are not "accustomed to think"—as many another might do. Rather, she accommodates the fact that children in particular and many adults may be hard pressed to have thoughts and opinions about certain topics and areas of knowledge. And she offers a view that strikes a contrast with Locke's tendency to treat education under the rubric of political representation and to argue that a parent, in his capacity as trustee for a child, must do the thinking and decision-making for him. She, rather, assumes that there can be collective thinking and that the various parties present to it need not contribute equally to its conscious explicitation. Public worship does not require thought that marks itself as a serious probing of doctrine. Rather, it appears as a very extended form of conversation, one in which only some need supply words to achieve the common purpose of paying homage to the deity they worship.

Here, again, Barbauld stresses the importance of a common language and augments its importance by pointing to the force of a shared social space. In suggesting that individuals cannot be allocated fixed portions of credit for conversation, whether it occurs on a small or large scale, Barbauld restates a position that one could have drawn from her *Lessons for Children*. One can only claim ownership of a conversation collectively and cannot assign it to one party or another. The corollary to this view is that one cannot use one's own understanding as a standard for what someone else should know. In illustration of just such a point, Barbauld imagines, in *Lessons for Children of Three to Four*, what it will be like for Charles and her to take a trip to France. Projecting moments in which people speak to Charles without his understanding them, she teases Charles about his incomprehension: he doesn't know French. But it is very much to her point that the superiority Charles might feel toward a French child who didn't know English is a mere artifact of geography. Some people will know one language as if by natural right, while others will know a different one by the same apparent natural right.

When Barbauld declares to Charles that he is better than Puss, because he can talk and read, it is easy to imagine that she is asserting human primacy and privilege. And she certainly sees talking and reading as capacities that set humans off from other creatures. Yet even as she is discussing Charles's abilities and Puss's with him, she mentions the cat's ability to do things Charles can't: "[Puss] can catch mice, which you cannot do" (*Lessons* 67). Moreover, she introduces this discussion by reminding Charles that he hasn't always known what he knows now: once, not so long ago, he was a baby and could neither read nor talk, and only "[a] little while ago, you know, you could only read little words" (68–69). She defines creatures of all kinds by what they do and thus manages to create an opening for an account of conversation so expansive as to embrace aspects of the natural world: "The Sun says, My name is Sun. I am very bright" (172). The action and attributes of the sun, as of other natural objects, become a language without benefit of speech and a language that Barbauld tasks the child with translating in her *Hymns in Prose for Children*.

Simple games of recognition—knowing that this is "Puss," that that is "Sun"—in the process become part of an extended conversation in praise of God:

> *I will praise God with my voice; for I may praise him though, I am but a little child.*
>
> *A few years ago, and I was a little infant, and my tongue was dumb within my mouth.* [. . .]

But now I can speak, and my tongue shall praise him.
(Hymns *1*)

In the earliest phases of Barbauld's work, naming figures as a way of picking out particular creatures and things and making them available for recognition. She introduces simple definitional attributes to explain how a name grasps a particular kind of creature in relative distinctiveness. In the kind of observation that Lamb lampooned, she identifies a horse as having four legs. Collecting strings of such descriptions, she enlists a child into an organization of his world. There are humans who walk on two legs, horses on four, birds on two. Then, by the time the child is three or four, she recasts the terms of identification, gathering up the four-legged, for instance, into the category of quadrupeds. As if she were thinking explicitly of Priestley's assertions that a metaphor is a renaming and that a metaphor brings new aspects into view, she confers new names on the creatures and things under discussion. A name, a description, and a categorization bring out different features.

Barbauld does not invoke Spinoza's precedent for treating the knowledge of the natural world as a version of the knowledge of God, but her ways of presenting that natural world clearly align with Spinoza's and, more proximately, Priestley's. The understanding of the natural world as essentially coterminous with divinity yields an acceptance of the various forms of life that occur in it. Snakes and mice and rats are not bad in and of themselves. They are not portrayed as enemies to man. Rather, they have their own place in the larger scheme of nature that Barbauld depicts, and she and the children who read along her *Hymns in Prose* together enter into a promise to the animal world. She and they "will not offer you in sacrifice, but [. . .] will offer sacrifice for you; on every hill, and in every green field, [. . .] will offer the sacrifice of thanksgiving, and the incense of praise" (*Hymns* 4).

Barbauld and her brother John Aikin share a vision of a demilitarized relationship between humans and animals. Even more, their short discussions of natural history in *Evenings at Home* establish a happy relationship between humans and the vegetable and mineral worlds, one in which Barbauld and Aikin replace the question of why there is evil in the world with the question of why there are poisons in the world. Barbauld and Aikin, like Priestley before them, continually depict a world that saddles neither humans nor animals with an indelible stain of evil. Writing from the capacious perspective of a natural economy, they represent human education as a process of figuring out how humans might accommodate other creatures of the natural world and of learning to estimate things by their proper uses. The dramatis personae of their only moderately fictional conversations are George, Harry, and their tutor, who walk in their neighborhood, observing the various plants and discussing a variety of minerals.

Barbauld frequently depicts animals in conflict with one another to illustrate situations in which aggression exposes its perpetrator to violence: the Chanticleer who is eaten by a fox after he has made himself vulnerable by pursuing another rooster (*Lessons* 122–25), the hog who announces his superiority over his fellow animals—the horse, the ox, the cow, the sheep, and the dog—only to be sent for butchering immediately after he has asserted his pride of place (Aikin and Barbauld 6: 113–17). But the emphasis on natural history enables her and Aikin to deliver pacific morals in an entirely practical mode—and with an unexpected application to plants. George, Harry, and their tutor, for instance, discuss the leguminous plants to build up an extensive catalog of the plants termed "*papilionaceous*; from *papilio*, the Latin word for a butterfly, which insect they are thought to resemble" (3: 83). The class, the tutor observes, includes such small plants as tares, and such large trees as the locust, the liquorice, and the tamarind. The conversation revolves around the tutor drawing out the things that one can learn from such simple things as the Latin (*papilio*) and the English names, descriptive terms (the standard, the wings, the keel), and memories of earlier mentions of them ("*G*: I have read of persons living on pulse, but I did not know what it meant before. *T*: It is frequently mentioned as part of the diet of abstemious persons. Of this kind, we eat peas, beans, and kidney, or French beans [. . .]. Other nations eat lentils and lupins" [3: 84–87]). The description of the "mischief" that tares do "among corn by twining around it, and choking it" (3: 88–89) yields to a question from Harry about what tares might be good for and an answer from the tutor: "They are weeds, or noxious plants, with respect to us; but doubtless they have their uses in the creation. There is a kind of tares, [. . .] which, when grown by themselves, are excellent food for cattle" (3: 89).

The discussions in "The Umbelliferous Plants," "The Cruciform-flowered Plants," and the two installments "On Metals" continue in this same mode, proceeding from what a child might have observed without entirely being aware that she had observed to the introduction of information that organizes and analyzes the untutored perception. Accounts of the poisonous qualities of hemlock yield to discussion of antidotes to its baleful effects, to distinctions between the toxic and the salubrious parts of a plant, and to the importance of human reason in matching animals' abilities to steer clear of plants that are poisonous to them. "[W]ild cicely, or cow-weed," we learn, is the name given to certain plants "because the cows will not touch them, though the pasture be ever so bare" (Aikin and Barbauld 4: 80–81). "What we call poisons are hurtful only to particular animals. They are the proper food of others, and, no doubt, do more good than harm in the creation." A metal such as lead receives a similar treatment. The dialogue opens by explicating the common association of the properties of lead with human personality traits ("Its colour is a dull, bluish white; and from this livid hue, as well as its being totally void of spring or elasticity, it has acquired a sort of character of dullness and sluggishness. Thus we say of a stupid man, that he has a *leaden* disposition" [4: 136]). The discussion touches on lead's uses in making glass before pointing out the dangers of lead paint and lead pipes to painters and plumbers and noting the allure of lead's sweet taste (which has prompted some to cure sour wines with it). The entire second dialogue on metals is devoted to remembering that George, Harry, and the tutor had talked about gold, silver, and quicksilver in an earlier dialogue and to extending what they had established then. Then, moving from a discussion of the weights of the metals relative to one another and to water, the conversation takes yet another turn, as the tutor says, "[N]ow I must tell you of an odd fancy that chemists have had of christening these metals by the names of the heavenly bodies. They have called gold *Sol*, or the sun." George, disappointed that the name Venus is given to copper ("Surely it is scarcely beautiful enough for that"), learns from the tutor that "they had disposed of the most beautiful ones before [on gold and silver]" (4: 144, 146).

Animals with four legs become quadrupeds and then the occasion for a story about the inability of quadrupeds on a farm to cooperate with one another, and conversations regularly include a reference to something a character knows or half-knows ("I had heard of pulse") and use it as the basis for further explanation. Barbauld, by herself and in collaboration with Aikin, continually lays out a variety of different names for the same things—as with gold and Sol and Jupiter—as if the language and the things that people have done with it over time were always metaphorical, always involving a renaming in which immediate observation and collective, inherited terms were continually being compared and coordinated with one another. And the patterns in the various strings of names prompt the interlocutors' own observation, such as the one about copper's not being beautiful enough to deserve to be called Venus.

Although John Aikin chiefly authored the botanical and min-eralogical discussions in *Evenings at Home*, Barbauld clearly recognized something important about the way in which those discussions worked. What is significant about the scientific conversations is not so much that they yield up invariable factual statements, results in the simplest sense of the word. Rather, those discussions point to the ways immediate experience and close observation of the natural world enable someone to take up a line of thought and continue it. Even when the tutor speaks and explains, he does not speak as someone who is repeatedly and merely automatically prompted by his dutiful charges. "Well observed" and "well objected" are recurrent phrases with which he acknowledges the ways his charges are taking up the points he's introducing and trying to figure out how they mesh with one another. Coordinating names and attributes of various natural terms makes scientific talk an exercise in posing riddles and tackling them.

Barbauld's story "Things by Their Right Names" represents a narratological version of such riddling, as Charles asks his father for a new story and asks that it be a story of "bloody murder." The story evolves in a genuinely collaborative way in that Charles is continually introducing new details. To the father's "Once upon a time, some men, dressed all alike—" Charles responds, "With black crapes over their faces" (Aikin and Barbauld 1: 150, 152). To Charles's suggestion, the father replies, "No; they had steel caps on," and the story continues in this way for virtually its full extent. Charles had been expecting and trying to dictate a story of robbers and potential murderers disguising themselves and stealing across the dark heath. Yet the father disappoints Charles's expectations when he introduces the detail that the men "murdered—twenty thousand men" (1: 152). As that information is added into the story, Charles protests that the story has become incredible: the victims would not lie still "and let these fellows cut their throats." When the father adds that "the *murderers* were twenty thousand," Charles exclaims "O, now I have found you out! You mean a battle" (1: 152). Through the sequence of twenty exchanges, the child dictates terms, only to have them redirected by the father who is telling the story. While the child imagines skulking villains, the father portrays these same protagonists as "[glorying] in what they were about" (1: 151), the final result being that the child no longer sees the story as an ordinary narrative, but as a riddle. The title "Things by Their Right Names" makes the story a name game, a way of claiming the realism of a world and a world view by focusing on the various descriptions and their combination.

The story is, of course, evidence of Barbauld's pacifism, a pacifism that fueled her most famous work, "Eighteen Hundred and Eleven," in which she represents England as a national version of the Chanticleer she had chronicled in *Lessons for Children*: its aggressions toward other nations were destructive to England itself. And it is of a piece with the observation, in the discussion of metals, that lead's deadliest use is in bullets (Aikin and Barbauld 4: 139). That pacifism appears as well in such stories as "True Heroism," which might be taken for her brother's as well as hers. Beginning with an address to the reader—"You have read, my Edmund"—the story calls up his knowledge of "the stories of Achilles, and Alexander, and Charles of Sweden" and explicitly assumes that he has "admired the high courage, which seemed to set them above all sensations of fear, and rendered them capable of the most extraordinary actions" (5: 85). In something akin to a reverse riddle, the story notes that "the world calls these men *heroes*" and offers to contest that claim.

In a rigorous redefinition of heroism, the story discredits Achilles, Alexander, and Charles of Sweden alike.

> *The first was a ferocious savage, governed by the passions of anger and revenge, in gratifying which he disregarded all impulses of duty and humanity. The second was intoxicated with the love of glory—swollen with absurd pride—and enslaved by dissolute pleasures, and, in pursuit of these objects, he reckoned the blood of millions as of no account. The third was unfeeling, obstinate, and tyrannical, and preferred ruining his country, and sacrificing all his faithful followers, to the humiliation of giving up any of his mad projects. Self, you see, was the spring of all their conduct; and a selfish man can never be a hero. (Aikin and Barbauld 5: 85–86)*

The account of heroism put forth in the discussion is one that holds up two examples: that of John Howard, "the reformer of prisons" and that of the son of a bricklayer. Howard's "whole life, almost, was heroism; for he confronted all sorts of dangers, with the sole view of relieving the miseries of his fellow creatures" (5: 86). Continually exposing himself to illnesses, and particularly to a "very fatal and infectious distemper, called the gaol-fever," and traveling across Asia and "almost the whole of Europe" to "gain knowledge of the state of prisons and hospitals, and point out means for lessening the calamities that prevail in them," Howard eventually died of a fever that he caught when he attended the sick "on the borders of Crim Tartary" (5: 87, 88). The bricklayer's heroism was domestic rather than international. Having a feckless father who spent all of his money on drink and left "his wife and children to shift for themselves" (5: 88), the son Tom worked to support the family and regularly led his father to bed, diverting him from his drunken fury. On being injured on a fall from a ladder, Tom did not lament his own pain as his broken thigh was set but reassured his mother that he would soon be well.

It might look as though the story discredits selfishness and applauds altruism in the most straightforwardly moral and moralistic way possible. But this representation of heroism in the ancient mode (even when it appears in the comparatively modern era of Charles of Sweden, who reigned between 1697 and 1718) involves a judgment that is literary and social as well. It chimes with a strong opposition Barbauld sets up in poems such as "Washing Day" and "The Caterpillar" between, on the one hand, the anger of ancient epic and, on the other, modern domesticity, for which the project of doing the household laundry and mounting a siege against caterpillars in the garden trees can call up a temporary archaic fury. These poems venture for a time into the mock heroic, less to follow Alexander Pope's lead in lampooning the triviality of contemporary life by dressing it in heroic terms than to mock the ancient representations of heroism. What Barbauld particularly focuses on—in both poems such as these and her essay on the novel—is the centrality of anger in fueling both deeds and epic descriptions of them. Epic is, she might have said, a hostile medium, and one that licenses forms of behavior that no longer have a place in the contemporary world. Barbauld's survey of the history of the novel from ancient times to the present is to make literature a source of information about historical and cultural differences, to document how "fictitious adventures, in one form or another, have made a part of the polite literature of every age and nation" and have been "grafted upon the actions of their heroes" ("On the Origin" 1). She thus finds it worth observing, of Heliodorus's *Theagenes and Chariclea*, both that it might afford modern readers the "pleasure of reading a genuine novel" (4) and that the "description of the manner of life of the pirates at the mouth of the Nile [. . .] shows that, as well then as in Homer's time, piracy was looked upon as a mode of honourable war," and that a pirate captain who behaved well to women, captives, and his men "did not scruple to rank himself with other military heroes" (5). Barbauld's quiet commentary: "[I]ndeed it might be difficult to say why he should not."

"Things by Their Proper Names" delegitimates a battle by pointing out that it is bloody murder no less bloody and no less murderous for taking place in the full light of day with the proud self-revelation of the soldiers. "True Heroism" repudiates the ancient heroes who were willing to see the hundreds of thousands—indeed, millions—of lives sacrificed to their own personal projects. It instead emphasizes the valor of persons who are more or less quietly risking their lives so as to ward off the deaths of other persons.

Barbauld lays out clear political positions in such statements. But perhaps the most important contribution that her writing for children makes to the realist novel is to pose the questions "What is a hero?" and "What is a villain?" in the distinctive way of modern fiction. Ancient epic, she might have said, allowed its heroes epic anger, announced its antagonisms at the outset, and measured heroism in terms of the numbers of persons whom one could treat as enemies. The conversationalism of the modern novel, by contrast, begins by treating sociable conversation as a solvent to such enmity. Yet, though an interlocutor such as a child like Charles may be accredited by the conversation even if he does not understand every aspect of it as fully as his elders, the novel identifies its villains only at its full extent. If, with Charles, the conversation allows for beneficent dissensus, Barbauld is perfectly willing to register the maleficent turn that dissensus can take. Defending Richardson's decision to represent Lovelace's appeal early in *Clarissa*, Barbauld maintains that he needed to appear good enough to attract Clarissa's positive notice. And when characters in the novel speak of the reformation of rakes, in obvious reference to Richardson's *Pamela*, part of what we're seeing is the novelistic attempt to find the circumstances that will enable even a deeply flawed character to count as good. By the same logic that finds the beneficial uses of the tares that otherwise destroy crops and that finds the medicinal and salubrious in the poison, novelistic conversation long indulges its characters in the possibility of discovering the role in which they can be marked as good.

The final formal requirement of the novel, then, is to banish certain characters from its precincts in the name of fictional justice when evil has, so to speak, gone underground and been absorbed in the apparent sociability of conversation. As Johnson has observed, this process is clearly at work in *Northanger Abbey* when Catherine Morland recognizes General Tilney as evil even as he operates in an entirely sociable world (176). While realist novels mark their heroes and heroines at the outset without benefit of any particularly impressive credentials, they also sort those heroes and heroines from the villains in a fashion that sometimes discloses them as unambiguously evil (as, ultimately, Lovelace) but more often identifies them as merely sociably hateful. Augusta Hawkins Elton, for instance, is banished from the world of novelistic concern late in *Emma* not for any momentous crime but merely for what we might think of as a violation of beneficent conversational dissensus. Her particular crime is to imagine that literary knowledge and social standing can be operationalized, conducted as if in a war. Her particular punishment is to be exposed to readers as someone who doesn't even understand her putative weapons. Yet the realist novel, as it evolves, will develop even less tolerance for the characters whom it banishes or sentences to death at the end. Think for instance of poor Emma Bovary. Although Jacques Rancière may ask why she had to be killed and may answer that Flaubert portrayed her as someone who wasn't an authorized user of literature ("Why"), I think that conclusion deserves a modest and friendly amendment. Emma Bovary, rather, stands as a classic example of someone who has developed such a belief in literature and art that she imagines they can become personal possessions, no longer subject to the same shifting of value that novelistic conversation brings forward. She leaves the world in which a poison might be medicinal through the means of a poison that is a poison, precisely so that she'll never have to have another conversation.

FRANCES FERGUSON is Ann L. and Lawrence B. Buttenwieser Professor of English and the College and the chair of English at the University of Chicago. Her current interests are on the rise of mass education (around 1800) and the history of reading and practical criticism. She has recently published essays on the work of I. A. Richards and D. A. Miller and on Jean-Jacques Rousseau's influence in Britain.

Notes

1   Jacques Rancière has recently made this observation with particular clarity in his *Mute Speech*. Rancière's account of distinct eras of French literature generally corresponds to the British literary eras frequently denominated classic and Romantic.

2   Lamb's remark in a letter to Coleridge of October 23, 1802, though often repeated, is worth quoting: "Knowledge insignificant and vapid as Mrs. Barbauld's books convey, it seems, must come to a child in the *shape of knowledge*; and his empty noddle must be turned with conceit of his own powers, when he has learnt that a horse is an animal, and Billy is better than a horse, and such like" (727).

3   William McCarthy has argued in "How Dissent Made Anna Letitia Barbauld, and What She Made of Dissent" that the spirit that impelled Barbauld's *Hymns in Prose for Children* was directly related to at least these important consequences: "Coleridge's poetry, New England's Unitarianism and Britain's First Reform Act" (66). While I understand the force of McCarthy's claim, I also think it worth noting that something has been lost between Barbauld's conversationalism and Coleridge's conversation poems: an interlocutor for the speaker.

Works Cited   Aikin, John, and Anna Laetitia Barbauld. *Evenings at Home, or The Juvenile Budget Opened.* 6 Vols. London: J. Johnson, 1792–96. *Eighteenth Century Collections Online.* http://name.umdl .umich.edu/004876861.0001.001 (accessed 31 Oct. 2016).

Austen, Jane. *Emma.* Ed. Frances Ferguson. New York: Pearson Longman, 2006.

Bakhtin, M. M. *The Dialogic Imagination: Four Essays.* Ed. Michael Holquist. Austin: U of Texas P, 1981.

Barbauld, Anna Laetitia. *Anna Letitia Barbauld: Selected Poetry and Prose.* Ed. William McCarthy and Elizabeth Kraft. Peterborough: Broadview, 2002.

——————. *Hymns in Prose for Children.* London: J. Johnson, 1781. *A Celebration of Women Writers.* http://digital.library.upenn.edu/women/barbauld/hymns/hymns-in-prose .html (accessed 14 Nov. 2016).

——————. *Lessons for Children.* 1778–79. London: Baldwin and Cradock, 1841.

——————. "On the Origin and Progress of Novel-Writing." 1810. *The British Novelists; with an Essay; and Prefaces, Biographical and Critical.* 2nd ed. Vol. 1. London: F. C. and J. Rivington et al., 1820. 2–59.

——————. *Remarks on Mr. Gilbert Wakefield's Enquiry into the Expediency and Propriety of Public or Social Worship.* 2nd ed. London: J. Johnson, 1792. *Eighteenth Century Collections Online.* http://name.umdl.umich.edu/004895897.0001.000 (accessed 31 Oct. 2016).

Janowitz, Anne. "Amiable and Radical Sociability: Anna Barbauld's 'free familiar conversation.'" *Romantic Sociability: Social Networks and Literary Culture in Britain, 1770–1840.* Ed. Gillian Russell and Clara Tuite. Cambridge: Cambridge UP, 2002. 62–81.

Johnson, Claudia L. "'Let me make the novels of a country': Barbauld's *The British Novelists* (1810/1820)." *Novel: A Forum on Fiction* 34.2 (2001): 163–79.

Lamb, Charles. *The Complete Works and Letters of Charles Lamb.* New York: Modern Library, 1963.

Levy, Michelle. "The Radical Education of *Evenings at Home.*" *Eighteenth-Century Fiction* 19.1–2 (2006): 123–55.

McCarthy, William. *Anna Letitia Barbauld: Voice of the Enlightenment.* Baltimore: Johns Hopkins UP, 2008.

——————. "How Dissent Made Anna Letitia Barbauld, and What She Made of Dissent." *Religious Dissent and the Aikin-Barbauld Circle, 1740–1860.* Ed. Felicity James and Ian Inkster. Cambridge: Cambridge UP, 2012. 52–69.

Priestley, Joseph. *A Course of Lectures on Oratory and Criticism.* London: J. Johnson, 1777. *Hathitrust Digital Library.* https://catalog.hathitrust.org/Record/008654519 (accessed 14 Nov. 2016).

Rancière, Jacques. *Mute Speech.* Trans. James Swenson. New York: Columbia UP, 2011.

——————. "Why Emma Bovary Had to Be Killed." *Critical Inquiry* 34.2 (2008): 233–48.

Toner, Anne. "Anna Barbauld on Fictional Form in *The British Novelists* (1810)." *Eighteenth-Century Fiction* 24.2 (2012): 171–93.

Wollstonecraft, Mary. *Thoughts on the Education of Daughters, with Reflections on Female Conduct in the More Important Duties of Life.* London: J. Johnson, 1787. https://archive.org/stream/thoughtsoneducaooounkngoog#page/no/mode/2up (accessed 14 Nov. 2016).

Wordsworth, William. "Ode: Intimations of Immortality from Recollections of Early Childhood." 1804. *Representative Poetry Online.* http://rpo.library.utoronto.ca/poems/ode-intimations-immortality-recollections-early-childhood (accessed 14 Nov. 2016).

Bating the Lobster

I seem to speak, it is not I, about me,
it is not about me.
—Beckett

"*E*verything was all set now and in order. Bating, of course, the lobster, which had to remain an incalculable factor" (Beckett, "Dante" 17). So reads a seemingly (literally) unassuming moment in Samuel Beckett's early story "Dante and the Lobster," first published in 1932 and later included as the opening story of the collection *More Pricks Than Kicks* (1934). *Bating* here, used as a preposition, derives from the aphetic form of *abating* (the unaccented opening vowel lost over time). *To bate*, as a transitive verb, meaning "to lessen in force or intensity; to mitigate, moderate, assuage, diminish," survives today chiefly in the phrase "to bate one's breath." Overlapping in its usage through time with *to abate*, *to bate* has named a range of ways to materially lessen or suppress, including "to beat back or blunt the edge of," "to lower in amount, weight, estimation; to reduce," "to strike off or take away (a part of); to deduct, subtract," and the now quite obsolete "to omit, leave out of account, except" (*Oxford English Dictionary*). It is from this last sense that the preposition *bating* derives its use, so that, at this point of "Dante and the Lobster," almost exactly its midpoint, what is being supposed by the character Belacqua Shuah is that, *barring*

Volume 28, Number 1   DOI 10.1215/10407391-3821700

the lobster, everything is all set now and in order. But is it? (The story's last words, in rebuke to another [different but related] hopeful thought, would be, famously, "It is not.")

What follows here will be a meditation on this "bating" that qualifies (or rather quantifies, and more precisely *dis*quantifies) not only the lobster but something like incalculable life as it makes its way through the story, unrecognized yet somehow not unthought. Whether the lobster can be kept out, that is, prevented from returning to disturb the count, will be the question. Another question, running under the first, concerns what kind of thinking, in a story, may happen in the bating.

First Lunch, Then the Lobster, Then the Italian Lesson

"Dante and the Lobster" relates a day in the life of Belacqua, the protagonist of all the stories of *More Pricks Than Kicks* (and likewise of Beckett's earlier novel *Dream of Fair to Middling Women*), who owes his name to a minor character from Dante's *Divine Comedy* with whom Beckett had confessed to being "fascinated" (Ackerley and Gontarski 47). Dante's Belacqua was a lute maker from Florence, in Purgatory for his indolence. Found, in *Purgatorio* 4, in the shade of a big rock, seated in a position of "embryonal repose," as Beckett would write later in *Murphy* (qtd. in Ackerley and Gontarski 47), Belacqua elicits a smile from Dante when, true to character, he argues against making any effort to head up the mountain or to strive for salvation (for surely he would be obstructed, so what would be the point?). That smile ("D[ante]'s 1st smile?" Beckett would write on a postcard [qtd. in Ackerley and Gontarski 48]), was Beckett's, too, who in one of his last texts, *Company*, would still remember "the old lutist cause of Dante's first quarter-smile and now perhaps singing praises with some section of the blest at last" (qtd. in Ackerley and Gontarski 48). Even more interesting than the presence of the character featured as such might be its orthopedic imprint on the oeuvre as a whole—indeed, Ackerley and Gontarski point out that Belacqua's "foetal posture" (a term appearing in the stage directions describing Estragon's demeanor in *Waiting for Godot*) would come to form the principle of the "closed space fictions" (47), texts starting in the mid-1960s featuring "barely perceptible movement" (99). Hélène Cixous, too, would single out Belacqua as Beckett's singular "survivor, his delegate, his residue, his spectre, his used-up double, his nilanticipator," a mediocre yet almost mythical being prefiguring multiple fetal and stagnating figures in the later works (24).[1]

Belacqua Shuah of the very early texts is not yet so fascinating; he is a misanthropic oddball of a "spavined gait" (Beckett, "Dante" 15) and consistently misplaced responses, the seat of an irritable, ratiocinating, alternatingly self-indulging and "self-loathing" stream of consciousness (Ackerley and Gontarski 47), so that critics concur easily that he is a murky alter ego of (early) Beckett himself: "[H]e was an indulgent bourgeois poltroon, very talented up to a point, but not fitted for private life in the best and brightest sense, in the sense to which he referred when he bragged of how he furnished his mind and lived there, because it was the last ditch when all was said and done" (Beckett, "Yellow" 161). Certainly the day related in "Dante and the Lobster," organized around "[f]irst lunch, then the lobster, then the Italian lesson" (Beckett, "Dante" 10), is one that unfolds principally in Belacqua's mind, with very few exceptions (one being a brief interlude governed by the grocer's point of view as he watches his "indignant customer hobble away" and feels "sympathy and pity for this queer customer who always looked ill and dejected" [15]). Allow me to summarize at some length this pithy tale, which opens with Belacqua "stuck in the first of the canti in the moon" (he has been reading Dante) and then remembering that he must start his day (9). First lunch, preparations for which occupy an inordinate length of the story, consists of two slices of burnt toast and a slab of stinky Gorgonzola cheese purchased with ill humor and fanfare at the local Dublin deli (provoking said grocer's sympathy and pity). While slicing his bread on an old newspaper, Belacqua sees the "rather handsome face of McCabe the assassin star[ing] up at him" (10). Later he will hear at the pub again of Henry McCabe, accused of murdering six people and condemned to be hanged the very next morning (a fact that has allowed critics to date the story to December 8, 1926)—indeed, "[his] food had been further spiced by the intelligence [. . .] that the Malahide murderer's petition for mercy, signed by half the land, having been rejected, the man must swing at dawn in Mountjoy and nothing could save him"; while "tearing at [his] sandwich and swilling the precious stout," he "pondered on McCabe in his cell" (17). But before the pub, Belacqua, having made his lunch arrangements, stops "to consider items two and three, the lobster and the lesson, in closer detail" (16). It is then that, among other thoughts about obscure passages in Dante and his charming Italian "Professoressa," he ponders thrice upon the variable that is the lobster in his otherwise tightly plotted-out afternoon (for the fishmonger would reopen at half-past two and any delay in securing the purchase would cause him to be late for his Italian lesson at three): "*Assuming then* that his lousy old bitch of an aunt had given her order [to the fishmonger] in good time that morning, with strict injunctions that it should be ready and waiting"; "*Always assuming, of course, that the lobster was all ready to be handed over*" (16; my emphasis), the series of assumings culminating in the "*Bating, of course, the lobster, which had to remain an incalculable factor*" some lines further (17; my emphasis). These are in fact the first substantive references to the lobster, till then the unexplained second item on a list ("one, lunch; two, the lobster; three, the Italian lesson" [10]). Belacqua's mind (and by extension the story), as it draws closer to the fishmonger's, seems to harbor a prescience that the lobster may signify a disturbance to the list, that is, to plans and to plot, not to say being and time.

 As it turns out, the lobster has been kept ready by the fishmonger, who produces it with alacrity:

> *"Lepping" he said cheerfully, handing it over.*
> *"Lepping?" said Belacqua. What on earth was that?*
> *"Lepping fresh, sir" said the man, "fresh in this morning."*
> *Now Belacqua, on the analogy of mackerel and other fish that he had heard described as lepping fresh when they had been taken but an hour or two previously, supposed the man to mean that the lobster had very recently been killed. (18)*

Belacqua then takes the "long knobby brown-paper parcel" along with him to his Italian lesson and places it on the table in the front hall before entering the room where he discusses with his teacher the finer points of Dante. Belacqua is intrigued by what he calls "a superb pun" in the twentieth canto: *qui vive la pietà quando è ben morta. . . .* His teacher, the admirable Signorina Ottolenghi, does not share his enchantment with the line and murmurs, when asked how it may best translate, "Do you think [. . .] it is absolutely necessary to translate it?" (19). The line, intended to signify that "piety lives only when pity is quite dead" or that "pity lives only when piety is dead"–words of caution (Virgil's) addressed to Dante, who is inclined to feel pity for the sinners suffering in Inferno–is indeed simultaneously enabled and irreducibly riddled by a homonymy (itself not elucidated within the story) at work in the Italian word *pièta*, signifying both pity and piety, so that Virgil can be understood equally as saying, more paradoxically, that piety only lives when piety is dead, or that pity only lives when pity is dead.[2]

 The Italian lesson is at this point interrupted by the school's French instructress, who enters "clutching her cat, her eyes out on stalks, in a state of the greatest agitation," to ask what was in the parcel left in the front hall. To which Belacqua composedly replies, "[A] fish." The text reads: "He did not know the French for lobster. Fish would do very well. Fish had been good enough for Jesus Christ, Son of God, Saviour. It was good enough for Mlle Glain" (19–20). Mlle Glain is "inexpressibly relieved" (20). After the lesson, Belacqua walks to his aunt's house, "gripping his parcel" and wondering, "Why not piety and pity both, even down below? Why not mercy and Godliness together?" (21). He thinks a last time of "poor McCabe" the Malahide murderer, wondering, "What was he doing now, how was he feeling? He would relish one more meal, one more night" (21). Thus we arrive at the last section of the story:

> *His aunt was in the garden, tending whatever flowers die at that time of year. She embraced him and together they went down into the bowels of the earth, into the kitchen in the basement. She took the parcel and undid it and abruptly the lobster was on the table, on the oilcloth, discovered.*
>
> *"They assured me it was fresh" said Belacqua.*
>
> *Suddenly he saw the creature move, this neuter creature. Definitely it changed its position. His hand flew to his mouth.*
>
> *"Christ!" he said "it's alive."*
>
> *His aunt looked at the lobster. It moved again. It made a faint nervous act of life on the oilcloth. They stood above it, looking down on it, exposed cruciform on the oilcloth. It shuddered again. Belacqua felt he would be sick.*
>
> *"My God" he whined "it's alive, what'll we do?"*
>
> *The aunt simply had to laugh. She bustled off to the pantry to fetch her smart apron, leaving him goggling down at the lobster, and came back with it on and her sleeves rolled up, all business.*
>
> *"Well" she said "it is to be hoped so, indeed."*
>
> *"All this time" muttered Belacqua. Then, suddenly aware of her hideous equipment: "What are you going to do?" he cried.*
>
> *"Boil the beast" she said, "what else?"*
>
> *"But it's not dead" protested Belacqua "you can't boil it like that."*
>
> *She looked at him in astonishment. Had he taken leave of his senses?*

*"Have sense" she said sharply, "lobsters are always
boiled alive. They must be." She caught up the lobster and laid it
on its back. It trembled. "They feel nothing" she said.*

*In the depths of the sea it had crept into the cruel pot.
For hours, in the midst of its enemies, it had breathed secretly. It
had survived the Frenchwoman's cat and his witless clutch. Now
it was going alive into scalding water. It had to. Take into the air
my quiet breath.*

*Belacqua looked at the old parchment of her face, grey
in the dim kitchen.*

*"You make a fuss" she said angrily "and upset me and
then lash into it for your dinner."*

*She lifted the lobster clear of the table. It had about
thirty seconds to live.*

*Well, thought Belacqua, it's a quick death, God help
us all.*

It is not. (21–22)

From Sea to Table

If this story has elicited a great deal of analysis and commentary
(and remarkably continues to do so), I find the most compelling pretext for
rereading it today in slight, oblique, hesitantly worded moments of recent
critical thinking on Beckett, as if such insights could not be beheld directly
or were places where commentary itself had reached an unfamiliar, far side.
Steven Connor, for instance, notes that in Beckett's treatments of objects and
animals language seems to be pushed out onto an "external scene" where,
especially in the later fiction, "the querulous, and sceptically self-conscious
reason of his narrators is stilled and the language takes on some of the exte-
riority of its physical subject" ("Beckett's Animals" 36). It is well known that
Beckett had struggled explicitly through his life and writing against what
Malone would describe as "that foul feeling of pity I have so often felt in the
presence of things" (*Malone* 248). "Indeed," writes Connor, "it is perhaps to
stand as examples of suffering which cannot be falsified by sentimental identification that Beckett uses animals most frequently" ("Beckett's Animals"
40). Jean-Michel Rabaté, in turn, speculating as to what Beckett might have
owed to the theories of his psychoanalyst Wilfred Bion (and notably Bion's
interest in "thoughts without subjects" or "wild thoughts" ["Think" 118]),
notes that Beckett's animals are both "objects of thoughts and subjects of a

different thinking: their very being in its often mute opaqueness provides the space for a different thinking, a thinking tempted by empathy for radical otherness, reluctant to reduce it to known categories" (123). The avoidance of "anthropomorphic insolence" (Beckett, *Watt* 202) will have drawn Beckett toward "a thinking-dreaming from the outside," suggests Rabaté who, citing Michel Foucault as he borrows this term ("thoughts from the outside"), offers it as "another name for writing" ("Think" 118, 123).[3]

I'd like to think about this insistence on an *outside*—and notably an outside to (human- or subject-friendly) recognition—by dwelling a little with the last movement of "Dante and the Lobster," most notable for its unsteadiness of narrative perspective as it veers between different locations. The dominant point of view is plainly and throughout the story Belacqua's, but here, through free indirect style, the perspective momentarily slides to that of the aunt ("Had he taken leave of his senses?" but also the earlier, "[She] simply had to laugh") as if to anchor in *her* still-intact common *sense* (the word itself uncharacteristically repeated from one line to the next) the simple and intransigent law regarding lobsters: they are always boiled alive; they must be (just as McCabe must die); they feel nothing; all this proclaimed even while the lobster trembles. There is something "fascinating and sickening" (*fascinant et écoeurant*), Gérard Genette wrote once (*Figures* 192), in the idiom of the "other" that free indirect discourse allows a narrator to speak "without being wholly compromised or wholly innocent" (*Narrative* 172; translation modified). But then, everything about this scene and the crawling in it of speech and thought across skins can be described so. No wonder Belacqua felt he would be sick (maybe even seasick). The lines that follow ("In the depths of the sea it had crept . . .") illustrate the radical distance from itself at which narrative can speak, where in a mode that is neither direct nor indirect nor in fact recognizably free indirect is described the lobster's journey,[4] how it made its way silently from deep sea into this kitchen (and this scene, this story), having survived and "breathed secretly" through "pot," "enemies," and "witless clutch"—that is, Belacqua's, as he carried it through much of the story in a brown paper parcel assuming it was dead. Then there are the extraordinary last words, as Belacqua's meek attempt at optimism regarding the time death takes is somberly "contradicted by a violent breach of narrative decorum, an intruding voice with no authority save anguish" (Ackerley and Gontarski 123). *It is not*. The narrative intrusion and regime disruption (a metalepsis, in Genettian terms) would appear, indeed, to suggest less a stable external knowledgeable or moral viewpoint, as Ruby Cohn, Sam Slote, and others have pointed out, than the difficulty of communicating by means of narrative time or recognizable subject consciousness the pain of death—literally, *peine de mort* in French.

A recent study bringing to light Beckett's relation to historical events of his time reads the "cultivated indifference" of Belacqua to the fate of McCabe as a reflection of the equivocal, alienated position in which a middle-class Dublin Protestant intellectual in a newly free Irish state would have found himself vis-à-vis the nationalist debate over the death penalty, a remnant of British colonial law (Gibson 35). In the 1920s, recalls Andrew Gibson, the Irish state was divided over how far to go in doing away with British law and other forms of allegiance to the Crown. To call into question the death penalty would have been to admit the destitution of the status of the Anglo-Irish class (Belacqua's and Beckett's) in a newly independent Ireland. For Gibson, "Dante and the Lobster" traces the near conversion of Belacqua over the course of the story to a nationalist position on the death penalty, bating an ultimate ambivalence, since the nascent empathy felt for the Malahide murderer is deflected onto the lobster, not to say "shrugg[ed] off." Gibson points out that "in the very last line, Beckett himself even has to correct Belacqua's [noncommittal] responses" (35, 37). In light of the ongoing publication of Jacques Derrida's later seminars, what might strike a reader more broadly here is that Beckett's lobster stands at that place where Derrida's thinking on animals, in *The Animal That Therefore I Am* and other writings, and his thinking on the death penalty, as laid out in the *Death Penalty* volumes, very exactly overlap. In both cases, Derrida points at the logic by which the sovereignty of a state (or indeed of the "I") is premised upon the continued possibility of a decriminalized, that is, legitimized, putting to death. Thus—and this argument is familiar by now—bodies dehumanized or deemed deficient in human properties become those condemned bodies from which a certain definition of human—as able to speak, to think, to know, to feel, to suffer—is continually produced. In both his work on the animal and his work on the death penalty Derrida expressed his stupefaction at the fact that not even the most lucid Western philosophy had yet known how to formulate arguments that might counter this sacrificial structure at the heart of humanistic thought. In both cases he deferred, rather, to literature as alone able to think differently the question of life.[5]

Derrida, as it turns out, had never been able to bring himself to write on Beckett: "This is an author to whom I feel very close, or to whom I would like to feel myself very close; but also too close. Precisely because of this proximity, it is too hard for me, too easy and too hard. I have perhaps avoided him a bit because of this identification," he had confessed in an interview in 1989 (qtd. in Royle 163). Nicholas Royle has rightly remarked on this "strikingly author-centered" confession, going so far as to suggest (even as he recognizes such a charge as "[c]omplete madness") that, with its recurrent, ritual deployments of "the identity-as-authority of an authorial 'I'" (even if then destined to be deconstructed), Derrida's work, when read "alongside or 'with'" Beckett, "*does not go far enough* with its deconstruction of the subject, and that a deconstructive resituating of the subject calls to be [even] further radicalised" (167–68). For the "unnamable" in Beckett is not the crisis of an "I" enjoying prior identity, writes Royle; rather, it "concerns an unnamability affecting entitlement itself, the very entitlement of and to identity" (165); indeed, *The Unnamable* from its very opening (the famous "Where now? Who now? When now? Unquestioning. I, say I. Unbelieving"), puts "the 'I' into play as always already dispossessed, the authority of identity always already cast into question, dislocated, beyond belief" (167). Royle here follows Maurice Blanchot in invoking Beckett less as a particularly radical practitioner of literature than as a practitioner of literature as something itself essentially radical: all authority and identity effects "are dissolved and dispossessed, obliterated in the space of literature," Royle writes (167); it is when held to this conception of literature that Derrida's writings "are marked by a kind of literary 'insufficiency,' a limiting of the 'literary'" (166). Royle quotes Blanchot from *The Space of Literature*: "The writer belongs to a language which no one speaks, which is addressed to no one, which has no center, and which reveals nothing. He may believe that he affirms himself in this language, but what he affirms is altogether deprived of self" (67).

La pensée du dehors, or "the thought from outside," Foucault would call this, adapting Blanchot's terms to describe the status of contemporary Western literature in the 1960s (and Blanchot's fiction in particular "as perhaps more than just a witness to this thought" [19]). "Literature," Foucault writes, "is not language approaching itself until it reaches the point of its fiery manifestation; it is rather language getting as far away from itself as possible" (12), that "returns thought to the outside" (25) and itself stands outside what it says, "for it undoes every figure of interiority" (31). Of or from the outside, literature thus understood presents a thinking that is not formed in our image, that "makes to draw one toward it," in Foucault's words, with an "indifference that greets [the person it attracts] as if he were not there" (28). As speech, it takes the form of a "continuous streaming of language. A language spoken by no one: any subject it may have had is no more than a grammatical fold" (54).

How, now, could I be preparing—twenty years after Pascale Casanova so competently denounced "literature's annexation by philosophers" (by which she meant chiefly Blanchot) and the insistence in critical scholarship in France, starting in the 1950s, on reading Beckett as "charged with the "prophetic, sacred mission" of "unveiling being," as the incarnation of "writing as testimony to the 'unsayable,' the 'essential,'" "lacking history, a past, an inheritance or a project" (11, 15)—a case for going Blanchot's way? But each critical period has its own bad objects,[6] and the risk today may rather be of forgetting (or losing confidence regarding) what it is that literature does. The question of the animal puts in focus and at stake again that of literature. One can work in sympathy with Casanova's interest in reading Beckett's writing not as timeless, essentially obscure, "radically strange in kind," nor as thereby determined by the "retrospective illusion" of his later, almost wholly abstracted works, but as a continual elaboration of literature's solutions to life's questions (13), even while continuing to insist on a denaturalized understanding of what those solutions may be. For if "thinking concerning the animal, if there is such a thing, derives from poetry" (or more broadly, the literary), if "it is what philosophy has, essentially, had to deprive itself of," if "[i]t is the difference between philosophical knowledge and poetic thinking" (Derrida, *Animal* 7), isn't it perhaps not because literature lends thematic, narrative, or figural force to our relations or homology with animals, nor because it offers us models for relating intimately or ethically to animals, but rather, quite on the contrary, because literature (in which indifference it is rather like life) is not really concerned with "us" at all, or only apparently or incidentally so?

Deleuze and Guattari's *becoming-animal* was indissociable, of course, from such a view of literature, neither representational nor metaphorical, but a "passage of life within language" (Deleuze 230). Claire Colebrook has recently returned to an "originally violent, disruptive and impersonal potential" that Deleuze had found expressed in its radical state in Plato, only to be "immediately covered over by normative images of the thinking and theorizing subject" (23). For Plato, writes Colebrook, "there existed Ideas that were beyond the lived experience of the self" and that were "at odds with the lived order of the world," but which he had then domesticated in favor of the arbitrary categories and constructions of difference and identity that thinking would impose on "undifferentiated life" (23–24). Invoking Deleuze's "return to the Idea" (24), Colebrook makes a strongly Deleuzian case for a practice of queer theory and reading that would not

be content with displacing, critically reusing, or even deconstructing con-
stituted identities, but that would fundamentally refuse the images of life
in which these thought formations trade. "[C]an we offer," asks Colebrook,
"Ideas to thought which are not our own?" (31). Truly queer theory, she
proposes, would be a taking of thought "beyond human recognition" where,
"aware of the essentially provisional nature of our grasp of our selves and
our world, we would always be compelled to consider the limitations and
locatedness of our point of view, never capable of appealing to life 'in itself'";
for life in its differentiated form results, rather, she writes, from a "strange
virtual potentiality which at once gives itself to be thought while always
violating and exceeding thought" (25, 28). "Queer encounters" would then
be "those in which bodies enter into relations where the mode of relation
cannot be determined in advance, and where the body's becoming is also
ungrounded." To heed Plato's/Deleuze's "liberation of the Idea from the
lived," proposes Colebrook, is to approach life continually with (and as) the
question of "what [. . .] might have occurred otherwise; what are the forces
of potentiality hidden in our experienced encounters?" (30–31).

    In the spirit of Colebrook's call, "How queer can you go?," I shall
be proceeding here as if the lobster might be a good hidden place to start.
Lobsters belong to a particular class of animals sharing what one could call a
weak phenomenological hold in our world (or a weak for-itself status): by their
curious, ancient anatomy[7]—chitinous carapaces, five pairs of legs including
three with claws (the first considerably larger than the other two), antennae,
mandibles, swimmerets, compound eyes mounted on mobile stalks—they
certainly discourage humanoid identification. Neither significantly bred/
farmed nor conventionally kept as pets (with the famous exception in French
literary history of the lobster of Nerval)[8] nor historically, when compared
to certain other species, massively displayed or represented or admired or
feared or chased, lobsters present the peculiarity, like certain other creatures
of the deep sea or deep forest, of living largely unseen lives and of entering
our sight and contemplation only when they have been profitably baited into
our world, where they lie, piled on each other, writhing, their pincers banded,
"in the midst of [their] enemies," waiting to be boiled (but is it all certain that
we see them even then?).[9] To "[c]onsider the lobster" (to borrow the phrase
from David Foster Wallace who, I feel, simply had to know Beckett's story) is
to risk opening thought to considerations "which are not our own."

    Now, of course, with Beckett, there is always the possibility that
"[e]verything—or virtually everything—there is to say about him has already

Figure 1
Provincetown, MA,
July 2016

Photograph by Tina
Tryforos

been said" (Casanova 12). Here, I shall contribute to this scholarship (if I'm lucky) two small footnotes. But these are, especially, two acts of reading. In both these readings—first of "the cruel pot," then of the "neuter creature"—I shall dwell on a small thing that does not add up and that has possibly been missed by readers and which to my mind has to do with the way the passing (or the missing) of an animal in a text is not only a big philosophical and ethical question but also a small question of hairbreadth differences in words.

Homonymy and the Pot

For Beckett's story is a queer tale indeed, with its heart located decisively in that passage uttered as if there were neither a person to speak it nor another to hear it, where the lobster creeps its way, unseen, toward us/its death, intercepted by the story even as (by the same paths by which) it is lured into a human comestible economy (or *foodways*, as social scientists today say). *In the depths of the sea it had crept into the cruel pot. For hours, in the midst of its enemies, it had breathed secretly. It had survived the Frenchwoman's cat and his witless clutch. Now it was going alive into scalding water. It had to. Take into the air my quiet breath.* In this afterthought, as it were, narrative consciousness seems to stand beside itself, as if host, indeed, to thoughts not its own. But if the lobster's final hours regained seem to belie (and make unreal) the story's distributions, premised till this point on seemingly realist allotments of body-perspective-voice-time, these six sentences have a tense, stitched-together-from-the-outside quality, relaying strictly nothing that cannot be inferred with certainty from the known facts (as if governed everywhere by the "It had to"), indisputable, unfalsifiable in this regard, yet seeming, in another sense (slight, a case hard to make and most interesting to me), to be very much the place where the story's accounting of itself, its own internal (temporal, narrative, imaginal, speculative) count, as it were, is disturbed: disturbed in the first instance by the time that it takes—time returning in the past perfect, analeptic, ghostly, time after thought, repaired and remounted to reanimate the lobster, or at least to conjure it again from the components of its capture (a "subject effect"), a telling that makes to hug the story's forms but by its stringing of verbs around an "It" already estranges them—to correct a mistake, to turn the assumed-to-be-dead lobster into a creature still living. I have already said something about the archaic use of the word *bating* early in the story; it is worth noting further that *bating* or *abating* in its sense of "excepting, omitting, exempting" comes from the old French form of the verb *abattre* that initially meant to take something down, as in a fortress, but soon came to mean to beat down or put down or kill, as in a person, and more often an animal. Belacqua may not know it yet (at that early stage of the story), but the very language of his thoughts, given in the free indirect style, does know that the lobster is "incalculable"—not because it is not certain that it will have been ordered or will be available for picking up at the fishmonger's, but rather because it may be yet alive enough to have to kill. The story is composed around the irony of knowing rhetorically (or retrospectively) what it is barred from knowing thematically (or contemporaneously): seen in these terms, it contains multiple modes and points of (inert) "knowing" (that the lobster is still alive) that both repeat and push to its ironic limit Belacqua's "witless clutch," whether structurally in the aligning of its time with the last day of McCabe or in smaller details such as Mlle Glain's unseemly "eyes out on stalks" as if transposed from the lobster (literally) to the French teacher (metaphorically).

But there is more to this riddled time. For *bating*, of course, keeps in play its homophone *baiting*, a word we might more naturally associate with lobsters, around which there is a thriving industry premised on bait, traps, and capture. Homophony (and homonymy as its limit case) is not to be underestimated, especially when it comes to the capture of animals. So with the "cruel pot" in the first sentence of that disquieting paragraph: "In the depths of the sea it had crept into the cruel pot." Critics reading the passage appear to at least implicitly link "the cruel pot" to the pot of "scalding water" in which the lobster is to be boiled,[10] even while the story does not feature a cooking pot as such, only more broadly, in the elliptical reference to the aunt's "hideous equipment," or logically, for the lobster would be boiled in something, of course; it had to. What recedes, however, in such a short-circuiting is the other "pot" known to lobstermen (and to lobsters) that is the trap lowered into the sea. Thus the "common lobster" entry in the *Encyclopedia Britannica* edition of 1911 mentions "traps known as lobster-pots, or creels, made of wickerwork or of hoops covered with netting, and having funnel-shaped openings permitting entrance but preventing escape." We know these lobster-pots (invented in the first decade of the nineteenth century in Massachusetts); traditionally wooden, they are more often today made of plastic-coated steel wire and lie many feet under the colorful lobster buoys that bob in the waters off Maine and Cape Cod, reappearing, when they have outlived their use, as pleasingly quaint *effets de réel* enhancing rustic seafood restaurant fronts. It makes more sense, of course, if there is a "cruel pot" into which the lobster "crept" in the "depths of the sea," that it should be not the cooking pot but the trap. Yet a communication between the pots is almost inevitable. On the one hand, the word *cruel* (technically a hypallage or case of a transferred epithet, since *cruel* more strictly describes the trapping or trapper—and by contamination further down the paradigmatic axis as it used to be known[11] [perhaps this problem, too, is resolved today by the word *foodway*?], the cook and the eater—than the trap) has the quasi magnetic effect of forcing "pot" back into the kitchen and into greater contiguity with cruelty's agents (humans); on the other hand—and this is something of an obscurer order that undercuts any apparent "ethics" of the first movement but is where homonymy does a queerer, more interesting work—the "cruel pot" effects a fantasmatic compression by which the cooking pot seems to somehow, however improbably, have been lying in wait for the lobster in the very depths of the sea, so that the lobster in effect creeps right into it, as if tricked by the fact that pot and pot carry the same name. This is complicated. One might object, what meaningful difference is there after all (and therefore what would be the sense in insisting on one) between trap and cooking pot for the lobster, given that a straight and inescapable path leads from one to the other? Behind one pot is only another crueler pot. Besides, isn't it in the "interest" of the lobster to "think" no further than the pot-trap and in the "interest" of humans to "think" no further than the cooking pot (disconcertingly now known in store catalogs as the lobster pot)?[12] One might say that the entire industry and trade of lobster fishing rests on this treacherous gap between pot and pot. But then, one interesting thing about homonymy is its directional indifference: whether you start from one pot or the other, the homonymic pull is the same. It is by this homonymic pull that the lobster creeps up into this story and so to its death, but by the same pull that the story (the story's pot, the story as pot) itself seems to descend into the depths of the sea to capture the lobster—with all the ungainly breaches of realism and of common sense that this could be imagined to entail (the cooking pot submerged in the sea could not contain "scalding water"; a lobster could not be lured even by bait into the second sort of pot; rather, one has to force it in;[13] "in the depths of the sea" there would be no one to cook the lobster nor to eat it, and if there were, it would be the person and not the lobster who would not be able to breathe—besides, lobsters do not breathe, not even "secretly," about which more anon). One way to read this passage then would be to say that to assume "the cruel pot" is the cooking pot (which may well be a confusion that Belacqua's own thought effects here) is to assume that there is a *metaphor* (one pot for another) where there isn't necessarily one; it is to refuse the difference (of words, of time, of fatality) between the pots and thus to annul the time in which the lobster still lives[14]—unless (to use one of Beckett's favorite words) it is to (pretend to) consider the lobster is still alive (enough that its death may have as little to do with oneself as its life, enough to creep into a pot, enough to feel for) when its appearance on the table has been preceded and conditioned by certain intents and processes (luring, trapping, storing, banding, subduing, selling, buying) that have long slated it for death, and to which one had agreed. (In this sense, here, pity lives only when pity is dead; it is a Schrödinger's lobster that troubles the text just as it might trouble us in life.[15]) Another way to approach the homonymic resistance of "the cruel pot" would be to consider that it (the homonymy) is in fact located earlier and more troublingly still, in the *the*, which, promising familiarity, then lures us into the pot, at this point cruel (also) to us, because we have been tricked into falling in with the lobster.

Whether Beckett would have intended such ambiguity in "the cruel pot" or not, in this story that is partly about the "superb pun" of piety/pity in the *Purgatorio*, it should not be surprising to find other (related) distinctions for which language affords no guarantees. "In the beginning was the pun," Murphy would proclaim some years later (Beckett qtd. in Ackerley and Gontarski 469). Homonymy is the lure of language, its unfalsifiability, a potential for switch and bait whose last prey may well be humans. "Do they believe I believe it is I who am speaking?" the narrator of *The Unnamable* would ask some years later. "That's theirs too. To make me believe I have an ego all my own, and can speak of it, as they of theirs. Another trap to snap me up among the living. It's how to fall into it they can't have explained to me sufficiently" (Beckett, *Unnamable* 348). Reading Beckett's writings from the years following *More Pricks Than Kicks*, I cannot help wondering whether in that last movement of "Dante and the Lobster" certain lines had not crossed between the lobster and the "I" ("Take into the air my quiet breath") that were to remain irresolvably crossed. Indeed, a few years later Beckett's character Watt would mull obsessively—and eerily for anyone stuck in the pot of the earlier story—over pots:

> *Looking at a pot, for example, or thinking of a pot, at one of Mr. Knott's pots, of one of Mr. Knott's pots, it was in vain that Watt said, Pot, pot. [. . .] It resembled a pot, it was almost a pot, but it was not a pot of which one could say, Pot, pot, and be comforted. It was in vain that it answered, with unexceptionable adequacy, all the purposes, and performed all the offices, of a pot, it was not a pot. And it was just this hairbreadth departure from the nature of a true pot that so excruciated Watt. For if the approximation had been less close, then Watt would have been less anguished. For then [. . .] he would have said, This is something of which I do not know the name. And Watt preferred on the whole having to do with things of which he did not know the name, though this too was painful to Watt. (81–82)[16]*

The furthest effect of homonymy is in a cleaving away at words from their inside, so that they may no longer be accountable to themselves. At such points language, instead of referring back to the self or the real, assumes its own unreality and unconcern for worldly contours. Note that the line following the cruel pot (once one has begun to read in this way) is equally thick and tense with indeterminacy: *For hours in the midst of its enemies, it had breathed secretly.* Whether "enemies" refers to humans (including Belacqua and the Frenchwoman and her cat) or to other lobsters,[17] and thus whether the time sequence captured in the line is that of the lobster's journey in Belacqua's "witless" hands (replayed now, corrected, in his witful, fitful mind) or of its prior captivity in a tank with other members of its species (a scene not included in the story and with the most potential for unsettling its temporal and pathic count) is impossible to say for sure. "Enemies," too, then, like the pot, is affected by a "hairbreadth departure," whereby time and matter bifurcate, divide subtly away from themselves, almost as if language had been infiltrated by a/the lobster, whose world, whose time could be expressed only homonymically, equivocally, through the only means left it (pot words designed for us to deliver reasonable or comforting things to ourselves). To "speak" under such cover is to risk merging with (melting into) language. But peering more closely, one may be able to see that this is language reaching a no man's land, a remote outpost where words no longer know, or do not know yet, that they are not a lobster's. In a conversation with Patrick Bowles two decades later, Beckett (now the author of *En attendant Godot* and the trilogy *Molloy, Malone meurt, L'Innommable*) would reflect: "It is as if there were a little animal inside one's head, for which one tried to find a voice; to which one tries to give a voice. That is the *real* thing. The rest is a game" (qtd. in Knowlson 111).

How much would the "*real* thing" have owed to an early lobster? For me this is a real question. A "little animal inside one's head" would seem to etch its entrapment and unease through so much of Beckett's later prose, even while being unable to escape the suspicion that another was feeding it its lines (this was the condition, the difficulty, the honesty, there can be no doubt about it, of Beckett's thinking on animals, his *animal que donc je suis* [animal that therefore I am] before Derrida's).[18] Who speaks in the extraordinary line *Take into the air my quiet breath*? Connor has written admirably on breath and "breath's periodicity" in Beckett's prose ("Beckett's Atmospheres" 58). Reading *How It Is* and *Company* (works of the mid to late period) as works of breathlessness and of what is said and heard "in the bating or abatement of breath" (64), Connor traces the "secret ministry of breath" in the oeuvre (59) back to the serious psychosomatic crises Beckett suffered in the early 1930s (exactly the period of "Dante and the Lobster") featuring "spasms of breathlessness as well as paroxysms of palpitation"—in his personal correspondence Beckett would describe his "sweats and shudders and panics and rages and rigors and heart burstings" (Knowlson 181)[19]—and due to which, writes Connor, he would have seemed "to have experienced air as an alien element, and to have sought relief from the occupation of breath in fantasies of absolute expiration" ("Beckett's Atmospheres" 54–55). Is it Beckett who speaks in the line borrowed (recurrently in the 1930s writings, as critics have noted) from Keats's "Ode to a Nightingale"?—or is it the lobster?

> *and, for many a time*
> *I have been half in love with easeful Death,*
> *Call'd him soft names in many a mused rhyme,*
> *To* take into the air my quiet breath.
> *(lines 51–54; emphasis added)*

John Pilling notes that the line, addressed in Keats's ode equally to Death and to the sweet-songed bird,[20] is both savagely ironic when applied to the lobster ("Thou wast not born for death, immortal Bird! / No hungry generations tread thee down" [lines 61–62]) and unhelpful to it, "even if (for a moment or two)," he notes in passing, "it looks as though this might be the lobster's very own contribution, rather than a stray caption from Belacqua" (50–51). I favor this hypothesis, and the fleeting intuition it makes possible of a place at the heart of speaking where speakers do not add up, where voices and bodies may not line up, where a lobster may breathe without lungs. Recall what Roland Barthes wrote about literature:

> *[I]n relation to objects themselves, literature is fundamentally, constitutively unrealistic; literature is unreality itself; or more exactly, far from being an analogical copy of reality,* literature is on the contrary the very consciousness of the unreality of language*: the "truest" literature is the one which knows itself as the most unreal, to the degree that it knows itself as essentially language; is that search for an intermediary state between things and words; is that tension of a consciousness which is at once carried and limited by the words, which wields through them a power both absolute and improbable.* (Critical *160*)

Take into the air my quiet breath. This, then, the beautiful, hideous last prayer of a lobster as it prepares to go "alive into scalding water." Should one imagine it suspecting, like the voice of *The Unnamable*, later: "I never spoke, I seem to speak, that's because he says I as if he were I, I nearly believed him, do you hear him, as if he were I" (407)?

No, it is not at all clear who or what lends its voice to whom or what in that line. Rather, to quote the critic James O'Rourke on the "Ode to the Nightingale" (where the line was already, it turns out, intertextual, prosthetic and queer, its breath borrowed from Shakespeare and its logic at least partly that of a strange material passing of subjecthood to the songbird from the "I"), this is "a stylized stream of consciousness, in which involuntary events do not quite rise to the level of verbal representation" (14), but also where "the intertextual or the intrinsic materiality of Keats's language subverts [the] continuity [of perception with knowledge]" (28). An Idea, to recall Plato's term at the heart of Deleuze's and Colebrook's thinking, is not in our image. This is also to say literature's knowledge may not align straightforwardly with a subject's, nor with humans' interests,[21] nor even with a writer's affections or ethics at a given time. In the years following the war, when Beckett would visit Dublin to see his mother, Simone McKee, the wife of a close friend (Frederick McKee), remembered how "he loved lobsters" and how they would get some especially when he visited, which she would have to boil even as her "heart would sink" at the prospect: "I can still see my husband and Sam on the garden steps, cracking lobsters" (Knowlson and Knowlson 92). Yet, for whatever reason (the time it takes to realize that a lobster is alive? a gender repositioning vis-à-vis the boiling of lobsters, till then women's work? the lag between what is known through writing and what is known through living? his mother's death in 1950 from Parkinson's disease?),[22] a shift seems to have occurred some years later. For in 1953–54, James Knowlson's (earlier) biography notes, when frequenting the Paris restaurant Aux Îles Marquises ("his favorite seafood restaurant"), Beckett would sit "as far away as possible from the trout and lobster tank, because it upset [him]" (399–400).

The French for Lobster

John Pilling, who like others has located in "Dante and the Lobster" the beginnings of Beckett's leave-taking from Dublin but also from the English language, notes a higher frequency of "Irishisms" in this story than in the rest of the stories of *More Pricks Than Kicks*. Interestingly, the

main terms he cites have to do with the lobster. Thus he notes the use of
"bating" for *except*, "lepping" for *living*, "lively" or "brand spanking new"
in its freshness, and the final "it is not" that carries the trace of the Irish
way, plausibly derived from the Gaelic, of saying "no" (like "it is" instead
of "yes"). For Pilling such Irish elements work to estrange Belacqua from

his surroundings but also more generally contribute to the story's overall enigmatic multilingual texture (53). Approaching the incalculable, unrecognizable, "nervous" life that the linguistic hide-and-seek game, generalized through the story, lends to the lobster, may require, however, a more specific attention to the specter of the French language—otherwise easily overlooked by its relegation to the cartoonish subplot of Mlle Glain and her cat. For there are several ways in which the lobster, "this neuter creature," is covered up by more than a brown paper bag throughout the story: considered lepping dead when it is lepping alive, it is then passed off, remember, in the exchange with Mlle Glain, as a fish. It is highly unlikely that Beckett, who had already lived and taught for two years in France by this time, would not have known the French for *lobster*. (In the French translation of *More Pricks Than Kicks* published some years after Beckett's death, Édith Fournier would resort to the solution of having Belacqua speak to Mlle Glain in the language of Dante: "Il ne savait pas comment se dit homard en italien" [He didn't know the Italian for lobster] [*Bande* 35].)[23]

If the lobster is a "neuter creature," it is not because sex in a lobster is particularly undifferentiated or difficult to determine[24] but, I've had to conclude, quite simply because in English, unlike in French, animals are not customarily lent grammatical gender. The conditions for gender are, it would appear, the conditions for life: the effect of the neuter here is precisely that the lobster can only be referred to in what follows of the story as an *it*, with none of the effects of animate life that the French "il" might have ambiguously afforded. Thus it is the very grammar of being that the *it*'s "nervous act of life" unnerves. "Neuter"—as a designation for what is genderless—thus works as itself a kind of homonym here, a *fausse piste*, as the "it" to which the lobster is confined by this spectral return from the French names in the first instance and the last rather the objecthood of something that can unceremoniously be killed. The neuter, Barthes would note in his late seminar "The Neutral" (citing here Blanchot), is what is "constantly expelled from our languages and our truths" (*Neutral* 189). In Latin, as in certain other languages, recalled Barthes, the neuter would have named the nonsubject, the one to which subjectivity is prohibited and that is excluded from it (188). The "witless clutch" in which Belacqua carries the still-alive and yet always-already-dead lobster names language's and also the story's witless grasp on this neuter creature that nonetheless secretly upsets the count. The cruel irony of it: in *Bande et sarabande*, Fournier would herself fall prey to the homonymy of the neuter: "Soudain il vit la créature bouger, cette créature de sexe indéterminé" (Suddenly he saw the creature move, this creature of indeterminate gender) (38).

A final word on *bating* here, in this story that reads less like a story than a poem. The usual word for "lobster" in French, *homard*, is distinguished by its *h aspiré*, or its aspirated h, so that when one pronounces it, one must bate one's breath awhile to separate it silently from any word that precedes. Thus one would say not *l'homard* but *le homard*, a rule generally reserved for words of Germanic (rather than Latinate) origin but sometimes applied simply to avoid confusion with possible homonyms—so with *le héros*, "the hero," so as to avoid confusion in the plural with *les zéros* (!). In the case of "homard," it is indeed a word of Saxon or Dutch provenance, but I cannot help thinking of the fact that without the *h aspiré*, on the way to saying *l'homard* one would not be able to prevent oneself from saying *l'homme*—that is, "man." Remember James Joyce's play in *Finnegans Wake* on *l'hommelette*, or the omelette that was also a little man—taken up by Jacques Lacan (Bond 15–16). With the *h aspiré* or the bated breath of the lobster, it is prevented from carrying with it *man* and dies the death of a lobster. But we imagine Beckett, too, bating his breath here, in pretending, or in pretending to pretend, not to know the French for lobster.

In his uncommonly lucid book *Witnessness*, Robert Harvey resorts in two places to images of the hermit crab (11, 31) as a figure for "a consciousness that decided one day to call itself 'I' and dwell in my head" (46)—the shortest possible complete definition of the *I* and the best I have come across since Émile Benveniste's, even if I am left wondering whether the hermit crab here is not in fact a lobster in more radical disguise? While a chief difference between lobsters and hermit crabs is that the former grow and shed their own shells and the latter use available shells (vacated by other creatures), both periodically find themselves, when a first shell is shed (because it is too small for the growing body), exposed in soft flesh and most vulnerable, whereupon they tend to retreat awhile from view—offering a poignant analogy indeed to the *I* in the intermittences of its self-identity. Through a grammar and a scene intimately dictated by Beckett's late text *Worstward Ho*, Harvey assembles a grave model of witnessing predicated on what is most paradoxical about the event—that one is not present at it, that it is precisely what happens to one in one's absence: "When the event befalls you, your wits fail you. [. . .] But when things calm down, [. . .] you work with the martyr within you, from now on perceiving the world through those jaded, haggard eyes" (49). As plausible a description as any of one's relationship to traumatic events, but equally to one's birth or one's early childhood as events at which one was absent, the wit*less*ness at the heart of wit*ness*ness becomes the potential grounds, in Harvey's thinking, for living

Figure 3
Provincetown, MA,
July 2016

Photograph by Tina
Tryforos

and for bearing witness to the destruction or absence or silence that has affected another who may or may not have been oneself; Beckett's insight (but also Dante's and Primo Levi's), in Harvey's devastating reading, is that of "a vicariousness intrinsic to one's consciousness" (50), so that thinking is a "feel[ing] one's way around" (90) "the skull of another, occupied by me" (26). What I have been trying to get at here is that there is something like a lobster feeling its way through the skin or skull or shell of Beckett's prose and that if it emerges as a sort of irreducible other to the "I" very early in Beckett's fiction, it is because as soon as there is—and by the mere fact that there is—something other than an "I" or than *I*'s, the *I* itself is irreducibly unnerved, as if always "stuck" in the daze of learning that it may be that ever unfalsifiable sign of life, but not in fact necessary for something like life to exist.[25]

    —*Unless* these are contortions and complications of which humans alone are capable, as Beckett's unnamable narrator would write twenty years later (as if unsure of who or what was writing), in what is the only other place in the oeuvre where I have recorded a reference to the lobster: "So they build up hypotheses that collapse on top of one another, it's human, a lobster couldn't do it" (*Unnamable* 372). Rabaté points perceptively to the fact that the French original had read not "homard" but "langouste"—a "'spiny lobster [. . .],' slightly smaller than lobsters and devoid of any claw"

(*Think* 56, 215n). Is this really to say that Beckett could not bring himself to say "the French for lobster"? Certainly no lobsters appear in Beckett's near-last work, *Catastrophe*; there is only a main character with "clawlike" hands, in reference to Dupuytren's contracture, a fibrous tissue disorder ailing Beckett in the 1980s and that, in his own words, "reduces hands to claws" (qtd. in Knowlson 597; Seelig 386).

My thanks to Hannah Freed-Thall for inviting me to participate in her Queer Modernist Ecologies panel at the Modernism Studies Association Conference in 2015 (Boston), where I presented an early version of this essay. My gratitude goes also to Richard Wahle at the University of Maine's Darling Marine Center for enlightening me on gender identification in lobsters and to Douglass Morse at Brown's Department of Ecology and Evolutionary Biology for kindly mediating this communication across the disciplines. My special thanks, finally, to Elizabeth Weed for the gift of her trust and reading, and to Denise Davis for her exquisite editorship.

THANGAM RAVINDRANATHAN is an associate professor of French studies at Brown University. She is the author of *Là où je ne suis pas: Récits de dévoyage* (Presses Universitaires de Vincennes, 2012) and coauthor, with Antoine Traisnel, of *Donner le change: L'impensé animal* (Hermann, 2016). She is currently completing a book titled "Animals Passing" (or maybe "Animals Missing").

Notes

1   See also Bryden 282–84 and Casanova 52–53.

2   The line has been read in turn as forming the moral aporia at the heart of "Dante and the Lobster." For Ruby Cohn the story is about "the impossibility of reconciling divine justice and mercy in this world" (46); for Sam Slote it offers "an allegory of the horror of the realisation of the complete and utter absence of allegory in the world below" (26). Numerous other critics (see, among others, Casanova 45–53 and Rabaté, *Think* 49–58) have commented on the critical Dantean subtext in this story, where the lobster's fate is an evident reference to "the sadistic violence in the *Inferno* where damned souls are plunged in boiling blood like the violent souls of the seventh circle of Hell" (Rabaté, *Think* 50).

3   In *Think, Pig! Beckett at the Limit of the Human*, Rabaté reads "Dante and the Lobster" as a difficult meditation on moral allegory, pain, sadism, and judgment and reconsiders in the detail Beckett's processing of the lessons of Dante, Proust, and Geulincx (see ch. 4, "Burned Toasts and Boiled Lobsters," 49–58). If I take my cue, rather, from Rabaté's earlier essay, it is in partiality to a notion, presented more rawly there, of literary thinking as radically defamiliarizing, as if intercepted in the moment "before" the work of erudition (before the return of ethical or otherwise recognizable categories). Arguably, the attention to animals in the humanities today (despite Cary Wolfe's call to a view of our texts and concepts as "not our own," [*What* 88, 118–19, 123]) risks reinvesting with ethical charge a certain realist and referentialist conception of the literary (and thus ironically of reinscribing a distance between the human and the nonhuman, these rapidly becoming exhausting, dismaying words). But literature's ways

of thinking animals (of thinking its way [in]to animals and animals' way [in]to it) have—far from being evidently realist or knowing or identified with a subject or separate from its object—tended to have a rather more outlandish and creepy-crawly character; this, in any case, is my hypothesis here.

4   Provided that one considers free indirect style or discourse as implying, or at least not ruling out, following the conception of Genette and others, the possibility that it is a character's *words* (silent or spoken) that are being carried over by or merging indistinguishably with the narrator's. The perspective or focalization here is ostensibly that of the lobster; it is where the lobster stands vis-à-vis (and to what extent it supports) this "voiced" point of view lent to it that is more obscure—given, among other complicating elements, the "it" (in ontogrammatical tension with the lending to it of thoughts/speech, see further) and the surrounding point of view—Belacqua's—still governing the "his" (but also "the Frenchwoman") in the line, "It had survived the Frenchwoman's cat and *his* witless clutch."

5   I represent in the broadest brushstrokes this overlap. The place and work of literature in Derrida's thinking on the death penalty is addressed in greater depth by David Wills in a forthcoming book and also by Peggy Kamuf in lectures and interviews following the translation of *The Death Penalty* seminar.

6   "[A]t any given time," wrote Naomi Schor in 1995, "within the carefully policed precincts of the academy, some critical objects are promoted to the status of good objects (say, not so long ago, dead authors), while others are tabooed (say, in the old days, experience). I am

drawn to what I perceive rightly or wrongly as the bad objects. [. . .] To deliberately make an object choice branded as bad is risky business at worst and at best a means to go beyond certain impasses, to read at an angle, to be an intellectual bad girl" (xv).

7   Indeed, ancestors of lobsters may have lived up to 500 million years ago and were of giant dimensions, as suggested by discoveries of fossils both in Morocco and Canada last year ("The Ancient Lobster as Tall as Usain Bolt," read the *Daily Mail* headline on March 11, 2015 [Woollaston].) As for today, it is known that "[s]ince lobsters can live to be over 100, they can also get to be quite large, as in 20 pounds or more—though truly senior lobsters are rare now, because New England's waters are so heavily trapped" (Wallace 3).

8   Nerval, so goes the story, used to walk his lobster on a leash in the gardens of Palais-Royal. When asked about this, Nerval is reported to have said: "Why should a lobster be any more ridiculous than a dog? Or a cat, or a gazelle, or a lion, or any other animal that one chooses to take for a walk? I have a liking for lobsters. They are peaceful, serious creatures. They know the secrets of the sea, they don't bark, and they don't gobble up your *monadic* privacy like dogs do. And Goethe had an aversion to dogs, and *he* wasn't mad!" (qtd. in Holmes 213). Scott Horton, in a piece in *Harper's*, presents plausible evidence that Nerval had released the lobster—which he named Thibault—from a net in the Atlantic coastal town of La Rochelle, for which he had to officially apologize to the town's mayor.

9   According to David Foster Wallace, commissioned by *Gourmet* magazine to write a feature essay

on the Maine Lobster Festival in 2004, we do not. At this festival attended by 80,000 people each July and during which 25,000 pounds of fresh-caught Maine lobsters are "prepared" (a hundred at a time) and eaten, Wallace struggled with the realization that the lobsters were so heavily overlaid by gourmet culture representations, collective myths, and fun facts that their numbers, their predicament, and their still inconclusively disproven suffering at being boiled alive were rendered simply unthinkable. "[S]tanding by the bubbling tanks outside the World's Largest Lobster Cooker, watching the fresh-caught lobsters pile over one another, wave their hobbled claws impotently, huddle in the rear corners, or scrabble frantically back from the glass as you approach, it is difficult not to sense that they're unhappy, or frightened, even if it's some rudimentary version of these feelings," wrote Wallace, who, aware of the riskiness of such observations, claimed repeatedly to be merely trying "to work out and articulate some of the troubling questions that arise amid all the laughter and saltation and community pride of the Maine Lobster Festival. The truth is that if you, the Festival attendee, permit yourself to think that lobsters can suffer and would rather not, the MLF can begin to take on aspects of something like a Roman circus or medieval torture-fest."

10   John Pilling deems the line "To take into the air my quiet breath" to be "not of much help to the lobster on its way to the 'cruel pot'" (50); in more general terms, no critic I have found notes that "cruel pot" pertains literally or first to the lobster-trap.

11   "I use the words you taught me. If they don't mean anything any more, teach me others. Or let me be silent" (Beckett, *Endgame* 113).

12   In a strange reverse migration from kitchen to sea, sections of the lobster-trap may be named "kitchen," "chamber," or "parlor," depending on where the bait is placed and where the lobster is finally trapped. This information I derive from the Wikipedia "Lobster trap" entry (which is certainly reliable on the trap/pot synonymy) and do not have the heart to pursue further. Certainly, if this is true, lobster trapping appears to be the place of a curious homonymic/metaphoric creep.

13   Wallace describes the scene in the kitchen:

> However stuporous the lobster is from the trip home, for instance, it tends to come alarmingly to life when placed in boiling water. If you're tilting it from a container into the steaming kettle, the lobster will sometimes try to cling to the container's sides or even to hook its claws over the kettle's rim like a person trying to keep from going over the edge of a roof. And worse is when the lobster's fully immersed. Even if you cover the kettle and turn away, you can usually hear the cover rattling and clanking as the lobster tries to push it off. Or the creature's claws scraping the sides of the kettle as it thrashes around. The lobster, in other words, behaves very much as you or I would behave if we were plunged into boiling water (with the obvious exception of screaming).

Regarding the myth of the lobster screaming (evidence, according to Wallace, of a "low-level cultural unease about the boiling thing"), he adds in a note: "There's a relevant populist myth about the high-pitched whistling sound that sometimes issues from a pot of boiling lobster. The sound is really vented steam from the layer of seawater between the lobster's flesh and its carapace [. . .], but the pop version has it that the sound is the lobster's rabbitlike death scream" (n15).

14 Sometimes, this is a lag of time during which the lobster may still escape its fate. For instance, every year Buddhist monks release a number of lobsters into the sea. See Kelper.

15 Beckett's lobster story was apparently inspired by a real incident at his "Aunt Cissie's house in Howth" on the Irish coast (Ackerley and Gontarski 122; L. Harvey 154n), though I have not succeeded yet in following this thread to any further details.

16 Watt would presently wonder the same thing about the word *man* (*Watt* 82–85).

17 Lobsters' pincer claws are pegged or banded in tanks because otherwise, crowded in such constricted spaces, they would fight and even eat each other. Indeed, aquaculture or lobster farming has been largely unsuccessful due to lobsters' natural cannibalism in conditions of forced population density.

18 At certain points of *The Animal That Therefore I Am*, Derrida wrote about the "I" as if exactly from the other side of the question and as if commenting on Beckett's work even while never citing him. Thus, remarking on how autobiography (and, in its smallest unit, saying "I") is "[d]ischarged of every onus of proof," he would add: "As if, in speaking of oneself, I, me, my self were speaking of another, were quoting another, or as if I were speaking of an 'I' in general, naked and raw" (57). Derrida's book about the animal is perhaps his book on Beckett and his best retort to Royle: he may still not relinquish certain rituals of authorship (far from it) but is evidently fascinated by

and philosophically invested in thinking an *I* inhabited by "a little animal."

19 It is in these circumstances that Beckett would enter a two-year-long therapy with the young Wilfred Bion. The telling of this part of the story in psychoanalytic terms is most enlightening and to my mind does not preclude the possible significance of a lobster:

Wilfred Bion would write, some two decades after his experience of analyzing Beckett, of the attacks on the idea of bodily integrity and integument that characterized the thoughts and desires of psychotic patients, who would be consumed with the idea of being emptied out or vacuumed, with tears and sweat gushing through their ears, nostrils and the pores of their skins. Didier Anzieu has suggested that Beckett's sufferings took the form of a "toxic skin," in which the phantasmal epidermis that should serve as a model of containment and communication between self and world was both itself lacerated and acted as a suffocating constriction on the self. (Connor, "Beckett's Atmospheres" 55)

20 To follow Connor's helpful gloss of the Keats line: "[A]n air is a song as well as the breath from which it is shaped. If Keats is looking for blissful midnight surcease in asking that his quiet breath be taken into the air, he may also presumably be asking for his words to be taken up into the bird's song" ("Beckett's Atmospheres" 58).

21 In this sense, Rabaté's remarkable book offers conclusions more (however darkly or displacedly) humanist than I have been able to reach: "Beckett's 'human'—caught in a garden that combines dying animals and barely surviving human diggers—presents us a broader humanity, a humanity at the limit, accepting the animal in

itself, a humanity that has become stronger because of this acceptance of the stranger. It is therefore better fitted to resist oppression and humiliation" (*Think* 195).

22   This event affected Beckett deeply (his psychosomatic illness and subsequent work with Bion had very much to do with a historically difficult relationship with his mother), indeed, the characteristic symptoms of Parkinson's disease (notably the "tremulous agitations") would impress themselves upon his writing. See Culick. Were one to subscribe to a Pierre Bayard–type approach to literature as invested with a foreknowledge of future events (*Demain est écrit*; *Le "Titanic" fera naufrage*), one might see in the "faint nervous act[s]" of Belacqua's lobster—"it shuddered again," "it trembled"—weird premonitory signs of what would befall the mother's body.

23   On "fish" for "lobster," Rabaté writes: "Belacqua's exhausted indifference facing his own salvation and that of creatures as diverse as a lobster (or even Christ) seems to betray a despair about the communicability of poetry, hence of all language. Both the Dantean Belacqua and Beckett's Belacqua appear as 'bogged,' 'stuck,' caught in a dead end of history, and therefore unable to move from a passive to an active will" (*Think* 56–57).

24   Nor should it have been so in Ireland (or France) of the 1920s and 1930s, as evidenced by the "Lobster" entry in the 1911 edition of *Encyclopedia Britannica* and confirmed by my communication with Richard Wahle, marine biologist at the University of Maine. Evident features (evident at least to the scientific community and to fishermen, conceded Wahle) in external anatomy (notably the wider abdomen/"tail" in female lobsters [for carrying roe] and the distinct form of males' swimmerets specialized for copulation) easily distinguish the sexes in lobsters; besides, Wahle told me, "in commercial lobster fisheries around the world reproductive females are protected for their egg production value"; indeed "distinguishing the sexes plays a central role in fishery management" (Wahle).

25   *The auto-biographical does not have to occur to an "I," living or dead, that would come to speak of itself. The auto-bio-graphical derives from the fact that the simple instance of the "I" or of the* autos *can be posed as such only to the extent that it is a sign of life, of life in presence, the manifestation of life in presence, even if the what, or who, male or female, that thereby gives this sign of life finds itself to have passed over to the side of death, and even says "I am on the side of death or rather on the other side of life." Even if this "I"—as is always possible—is quoted, mechanically repeated by a technique of reproduction or by Descartes' animal-machine.* (Derrida, Animal *56*)

Works Cited

Ackerley, C. J., and S. E. Gontarski. *The Grove Companion to Samuel Beckett: A Reader's Guide to His Works, Life, and Thought*. New York: Grove, 2004.

Barthes, Roland. *Critical Essays*. Trans. Richard Howard. Evanston: Northwestern UP, 1972.

——————. *The Neutral: Lecture Course at the Collège de France (1977–1978)*. Trans. Rosalind E. Krauss and Denis Hollier. Ed. Thomas Clerc and Éric Marty. New York: Columbia UP, 2005.

Bayard, Pierre. *Demain est écrit*. Paris: Minuit, 2005.

——————. *Le "Titanic" fera naufrage*. Paris: Minuit, 2016.

Beckett, Samuel. *Bande et sarabande*. Trans. Édith Fournier. Paris: Minuit, 1994.

——————. "Dante and the Lobster". *More* 9–22.

——————. *Endgame. The Complete Dramatic Works of Samuel Beckett*. Boston: Faber & Faber, 1990. 89–134.

——————. *Malone Dies. Molloy* 177–289.

——————. *Molloy, Malone Dies, The Unnamable*. New York: Calder, 1997.

——————. *More Pricks Than Kicks*. New York: Grove, 1972.

——————. *The Unnamable. Molloy* 291–418.

——————. *Watt*. New York: Grove, 1959.

——————. "Yellow." *More* 158–174.

Bond, Steven. "Joyce, Beckett, and the Homelette in the *Poêle*." *Otherness: Essays and Studies* 1.1 (2010): 1–23.

Bryden, Mary. "'Stuck in a Stagger': Beckett and Cixous." *Samuel Beckett: Debts and Legacies*. Ed. Matthijs Engelberts, Matthew Feldman, Erik Tonning, and Dirk Van Hulle. New York: Rodopi, 2013. 275–87.

Casanova, Pascale. *Samuel Beckett: Anatomy of a Literary Revolution*. Trans. Gregory Elliott. New York: Verso, 2006.

Cixous, Hélène. *Zero's Neighbour: Sam Beckett*. Trans. Laurent Milesi. Cambridge: Polity, 2010.

Cohn, Ruby. *A Beckett Canon*. Ann Arbor: U of Michigan P, 2005.

Colebrook, Claire. "How Queer Can You Go? Theory, Normality, and Normativity." *Queering the Non/Human*. Ed. Noreen Giffney and Myra J. Hird. Burlington: Ashgate, 2008. 17–33.

Connor, Steven. "Beckett's Animals." *Journal of Beckett Studies* 8 (1982): 29–44.

——————. "Beckett's Atmospheres." *Beckett after Beckett*. Ed. S. E. Gontarski and Anthony Uhlmann. Gainesville: U of Florida P, 2006. 52–65.

Culick, Hugh. "Neurological Disorder and the Evolution of Beckett's Maternal Images." *Mosaic* 22.1 (1989): 41–53.

Deleuze, Gilles. "Literature and Life." Trans. Daniel W. Smith and Michael A. Greco. *Critical Inquiry* 23.2 (1997): 225–30.

Derrida, Jacques. *The Animal That Therefore I Am*. Trans. David Wills. Ed. Marie-Louise Mallet. Chicago: Fordham UP, 2008.

Foucault, Michel, and Maurice Blanchot. *Maurice Blanchot: The Thought from Outside/Michel Foucault as I Imagine Him*. New York: Zone, 1990.

Genette, Gérard. *Figures 3*. Paris: Éditions du Seuil, 1972.

——————. *Narrative Discourse: An Essay in Method*. Trans. Jane E. Lewin. Ithaca: Cornell UP, 1983.

Gibson, Andrew. *Samuel Beckett*. London: Reaktion, 2010.

Harvey, Lawrence E. *Samuel Beckett: Poet and Critic*. Princeton: Princeton UP, 1970.

Harvey, Robert. *Witnessness: Beckett, Dante, Levi, and the Foundations of Responsibility*. New York: Continuum, 2010.

Holmes, Richard. *Footsteps: Adventures of a Romantic Biographer*. New York: Elisabeth Sifton, 1985.

Horton, Scott. "Nerval: A Man and His Lobster." *Harper's* 12 Oct. 2008. http://harpers.org/blog/2008/10/nerval-a-man-and-his-lobster/.

Keats, John. "Ode to a Nightingale." *Complete Poems*. Ed. Jack Stillinger. Cambridge, MA: Harvard UP, 1991. 279–81.

Kelper, Lauren. "Lobsters Liberated by Buddhist Intervention." *Reuters* 5 Aug. 2011. http://www.reuters.com/article/us-lobsters-buddhists-odd-idUSTRE7743ZG20110805.

Knowlson, James. *Damned to Fame: The Life of Samuel Beckett*. London: Bloomsbury, 1996.

Knowlson, James, and Elizabeth Knowlson, eds. *Beckett Remembering, Remembering Beckett: A Centenary Celebration*. New York: Arcade, 2006.

O'Rourke, James. *Keats's Odes and Contemporary Criticism*. Gainesville: U of Florida P, 1998.

Pilling, John. *Samuel Beckett's "More Pricks than Kicks": In a Strait of Two Wills*. New York: Continuum, 2011.

Rabaté, Jean-Michel. "'Think, Pig!': Beckett's Animal Philosophies." *Beckett and Animals*. Ed. Mary Bryden. New York: Cambridge UP, 2013. 109–25.

——————————. *Think, Pig! Beckett at the Limit of the Human*. New York: Fordham UP, 2016.

Royle, Nicholas. *After Derrida*. New York: Manchester UP, 1995.

Schor, Naomi. *Bad Objects: Essays Popular and Unpopular*. Durham: Duke UP, 1995.

Seelig, Adam. "Beckett's Dying Remains: The Process of Playwriting in the *Ohio Impromptu* Manuscripts." *Modern Drama* 43.3 (2000): 376–92.

Slote, Sam. "Stuck in Translation: Beckett and Borges on Dante." *Journal of Beckett Studies* 19.1 (2010): 15–28.

Wahle, Richard. "A Marine Biology Question from a Colleague in the Humanities." E-mail exchange between Douglass Morse and the author. 3 Sept. 2016.

Wallace, David Foster. "Consider the Lobster." *Gourmet* Aug. 2004. http://www.gourmet.com/magazine/2000s/2004/08/consider_the_lobster.html.

Wolfe, Cary. *What Is Posthumanism?* Minneapolis: U of Minnesota P, 2010.

Woollaston, Victoria. "The Ancient Lobster as Tall as Usain Bolt: 6ft 5in Crustacean Ate Food Like a Whale and Had 'Limbs' on Its Head." *Daily Mail* 11 Mar. 2015. http://www.dailymail.co.uk/sciencetech/article-2990200/The-ancient-lobster-tall-Usain-Bolt-6ft-5in-crustacean-ate-food-like-whale-limbs-head.html.

The Decay of Sighing:
Cesare Pavese's *Lavorare stanca*

Men and Words

*I*n 1946, Cesare Pavese attempted to rewrite history. Responding to a questionnaire circulated by the newly founded, Naples-based literary magazine *Aretusa*, the poet identified his debut collection, *Lavorare stanca* (*Work's Tiring*), as his best work to date. More boldly, he also recast his own entry onto the Italian literary scene as a veritable intervention. According to Pavese, during the 1930s,

> *L'Italia era estraniata, imbarbarita, calcificata—bisognava scuoterla, decongestionarla e riesporla a tutti i venti primaverili dell'Europa e del mondo. Niente di strano se quest'opera di conquista di testi non poteva esser fatta da burocrati o braccianti letterari, ma ci vollero giovanili entusiasmi e compromissioni. Noi scoprimmo l'Italia—questo il punto—cercando gli uomini e le parole in America, in Russia, in Francia, nella Spagna."* ("L'influsso" 223)

> [*Italy was estranged, barbarized, calcified. It was necessary to shake her up, to clear her up (*decongestionarla*), and to expose*

her again to all of the spring winds of Europe and the world. It shouldn't be surprising that this work of conquering texts couldn't be done by bureaucrats or literary laborers, but had to be undertaken by youthful enthusiasms and compromises. We discovered Italy—this is the point—looking for men and words in America, in Russia, in France, in Spain.][1]

Here Pavese answers the charges of his detractors, who claimed that he had betrayed—and effectively barbarized—Italian poetry by appropriating foreign, and especially American, forms and styles. Mixing metaphors, the poet counters that the context in which he and his like-minded peers lived and worked left them with no choice but to turn outward, to borrow from new territories in order to conquer the old country. In Pavese's account, "detourism" thus becomes the cure for collective dormancy, the means by which an ailing and "estranged" Italy can be reinvigorated and restored to herself.[2] Literary, linguistic, and cultural stagnation justify both local procedures (the shaking up or awakening of the feminized national body and the administration of decongestants) and far-flung reconnaissance missions (the search for "men and words" abroad). And these missions cannot but be successful, accomplished as they are not by white- or blue-collar "literary laborers"—indeed, not by persons at all—but rather, according to the logic of a somewhat puzzling slippage, by personified forces rendered youthful, "giovanili entusiasmi e compromissioni."

It is interestingly unclear how the second of these two sets of forces relates to the first. The youths' compromises could be with national traditions or conventional forms, but they could also serve to check or channel the enthusiasms themselves. In either case, it is these enthusiasms that seem to win out, or to lead the way. Surely it is their affective potency, more than the conceptual or discursive influence of compromise, that allows for the decisive discovery of Italy. Surely it is the sublime enthusiasms, rather than the calculus of compromises, that make textual conquests and other great poetic accomplishments possible.[3]

But the poems in Pavese's *Lavorare stanca* tell another story. They stay in stagnation. They attest to a general condition of fatigue, a condition etymologically close to the one named by the titular verb *stancare*, meaning to tire or wear out and derived from the Latin *stagno*, "to form a pool of standing water, to stagnate, to be stagnant" (Lewis and Short).[4] This is a condition absent from, and indeed at odds with, the account that Pavese would give in 1946, in *Aretusa*. That later account lays stress on the cosmopolitanism of Pavese's early work and on the novelty—as well as the energy and, again, the enthusiasm—of his engagement with Anglo-American literature in particular. For this engagement, the poet was criticized by his detractors but also celebrated by his admirers, and it was no doubt this hard-won praise that underwrote Pavese's claim to have "discovered Italy" and delivered a poetic wake-up call. Yet for all their novel borrowings, the poems in question do not travel far; nor do they awaken. They are not enthused, youthfully energetic, or in any sense expansive. *Lavorare stanca*, first published in 1936 and later expanded and reprinted in 1943, programmatically restricts its geographic scope and consistently restrains its affective displays. In a series of short and famously spare lyric texts,[5] Pavese renders rural and urban worlds in which enthusiasms have been deflated and from which youthful enthusiasms in particular have been banished. These worlds are compromised in every sense—marked by "compromissioni" but also damaged, exposed to disease—and in them great accomplishments have been ruled out from the start.

Indeed, *Lavorare stanca*'s first and longest poem, "I mari del Sud" ("The South Seas"), enacts this ruling out. The poem's speaker accompanies his older cousin on a walk through the Piedmontese countryside, remembering and recounting episodes from their shared past. At first "un gigante" (a giant), a figure who is intimidating because larger than life, the speaker's cousin comes by the poem's second stanza to resemble "contadini un poco stanchi" (somewhat tired peasants) in his isolation (5).[6] His difference and distance from the speaker are then shown to be linguistic as well as generational, for the speaker's cousin uses dialect, we are told, wielding its words like so many tools, but slowly: "adopera lento il dialetto" (he slowly deploys dialect) (5). Unlike the poets whom Pavese would later champion and recast as conquerors, then, the former giant remains unaffected by other "men and words" ("L'influsso" 223)—so much so that his speech, hard "come le pietre / di questo stesso colle" (like the stones / on this very hill) (*Lavorare* 5), is left intact even after years of travel: "vent'anni di idiomi e oceani diversi / non gliel'hanno scalfito" (twenty years of different languages and oceans / have not scratched the surface of it) (6).

With his language doing double duty as both a means of working (*adoperare*) and a substance worked on ("come le pietre"), one resistant to others' work, the speaker's cousin in "I mari del Sud" cannot transform or transcend his surroundings or profit from his experience. His plan to replace the village's beasts of burden with motors fails miserably, written off in three words that seem to seal the fate of all such modernizing projects in the village of Santo Stefano Belbo: "fallí il disegno" (the scheme failed) (7). More surprisingly, despite having wrested strength from the South Seas and their silence, the sailor returns home from his voyages and from the war not rich in stories but instead, like one of Walter Benjamin's veterans in "The Storyteller," "poorer in communicable experience" (84). He remains virtually silent, able only to list the places where he has been in a "dry," paratactic style that echoes, or becomes, the speaker's own: "Mio cugino non parla dei viaggi compiuti. / Dice asciutto che è stato in quell luogo e in quell'altro" (My cousin doesn't speak of voyages taken. / He dryly says that he was in this place and in that other one) (7).[7] And "I mari del Sud" ends by demystifying even these places themselves. Far from being "tutto nuovo" (all new) (5), as they once seemed to the speaker, the islands of the South Seas were in fact, it turns out, already old for the youthful upon arrival:

> *Ma quando gli dico*
> *ch'egli è tra i fortunati che han visto l'aurora*
> *sulle isole più belle della terra,*
> *al ricordo sorride e risponde che il sole*
> *si levava che il giorno era vecchio per loro.*
>
> (Lavorare 7–8)

> *[But when I tell him*
> *that he is among the fortunate ones who saw the sunrise*
> *on the most beautiful islands in the world,*
> *at the memory he smiles and responds that the sun*
> *rose only when the day was old for them.]*

Attaching world-weariness to a specific set of gazes (those of the "fortunati" who were not, in fact, fortunate), the poem's last words—"vecchio per loro"—seem to leave open the possibility that, from other perspectives, or for other voyagers, such islands might still appear new, undiscovered.

But the poems that follow give the lie to this promise. In them, sunrises repeatedly disappoint, and youthful enthusiasms are repeatedly shown to have burnt out. Workers rise at dawn already tired ("Disciplina," *Lavorare* 48), and sons are born too late ("Ulisse," *Lavorare* 64). One wakes up only to feel "la calma stanchezza dell'alba" (the calm weariness of dawn) ("Mito," *Lavorare* 113), and the sun's birth becomes indistinguishable from its death ("Il paradiso sui tetti," *Lavorare* 114). Only drunkards talk of projects ("Lavorare stanca," *Lavorare* 54). Youth repeatedly gives way to age, and energy to exhaustion, even at would-be moments of initiation, when

ships should be launched. Losses undo efforts at accumulation and transformation before they even begin. And the sublime yields to the beautiful,
though this, too, is tempered, or tired, as is the loveliness of "le isole più
belle della terra."[8] Indeed, as these examples begin to show, the governing
affects in *Lavorare stanca* are not, to deploy Kant's distinction, "of the cou-
rageous sort," "arousing the consciousness of our powers to overcome any
resistance," but often appear, on the contrary, to be "of the yielding kind,"
making "the effort at resistance itself into an object of displeasure" (154–55).
Yet Pavese works to ensure that even these "yielding" affects are minimal;
the forms of displeasure that they entail are not allowed to eclipse the facts
that the poems report in unadorned declaratives.

Significantly, "I mari del Sud" contains *Lavorare stanca*'s only
"Oh": "Oh da quando ho giocato ai pirati malesi, / quanto tempo è trascorso"
(Oh, how much time has passed / since I played at being Malay pirates) (6).
It is as if, by means of this first and last sigh, Pavese were at once acknowledging and taking leave of the entire Italian vernacular lyric tradition,
from Dante and Petrarch to Giacomo Leopardi and the Giuseppe Ungaretti
of *Sentimento del tempo*.[9] Pavese acknowledges this tradition in that the
"Oh" in "I mari del Sud" signals his participation in the poetic enterprise
that he continues. From the first, in and then beyond the Italian context,
this enterprise is nothing if not effusive. Sighs become privileged figures
for this effusiveness, for lyric itself. We could say, therefore, of this lyric
tradition's sighs—which are as referentially empty as they are incessant, as
contentless and, indeed, as merely conventional as they are compulsively
repeated—what Jonathan Culler says of the critically "embarrassing" apostrophe foregrounded in many Romantic and post-Romantic poems: "Devoid
of semantic reference, the *O* of apostrophe refers to other apostrophes and
thus to the lineage and conventions of sublime poetry" ("Apostrophe" 143).
Registering emotion, sighs refer to other sighs and thus to the lineage and
conventions of previous poems.

But Culler's claim also begins to indicate why Pavese takes leave
of the tradition and trope that he acknowledges, sighing once in "I mari del
Sud," never overtly to sigh again in the poems that follow. As I have already
suggested, Pavese's is emphatically—or rather unemphatically—not "sublime
poetry." The poet leaves behind the vocative, the "Oh," then, because of its
association with heightened states, with the "overflow of powerful feelings"
(Wordsworth 598) with which lyric—the "sublime notion of Poetry" (607),
the expressive and emotive mode par excellence—had been synonymous at
least since Romanticism, from Wordsworth to Pavese's beloved Whitman,

from Giacomo Leopardi to Gabriele D'Annunzio and beyond. But if this is the understanding and the "lineage" of lyric from which *Lavorare stanca* departs (Culler, "Apostrophe" 143), "I mari del Sud" already makes it clear that departures, for Pavese, are not definitive. Rather, they precede returns. Perhaps this is ultimately what Pavese, writing in 1946, meant by "compromises": just as *Lavorare stanca*, eschewing "the spontaneous overflow of powerful feelings," nevertheless stays with "overflow" (another meaning of the Latin *stagno*), defined not as expression but as stagnation, an inundation that does not await modernizing, fascist improvement, so, too, does *Lavorare stanca* persist in the lyric enterprise that it redefines rather than refuses.

To be clear, I am not claiming that Pavese's "compromise" was a political one, a way of making peace with the fascist regime. On the contrary, the poet's commitment to what I am calling "staying in stagnation" would have been recognized as pointed and even polemical when read against the backdrop of the land reclamation campaigns undertaken by Mussolini and loudly publicized in official discourses of swamp drainage in the late 1920s and throughout the 1930s.[10] Likewise, Pavese's refusal of fascist bombast—his hatred of the discourse that he distills in a remarkable chiasmus in his diary: "i tumulti, l'oratoria, il sangue e i trionfi" (tumults, oratory, blood, and triumphs) (*Il mestiere* 13)—would have been patently evident to *Lavorare stanca*'s first readers, for by the mid-1930s, this discourse had reached fever pitch. The Second Italo-Ethiopian War was ongoing while Pavese completed work on, and then brought out, *Lavorare stanca*, and 1936, the year of the volume's publication, also saw the annexation of Ethiopia and the consolidation of Italian East Africa. These events were, of course, spurs to youthful enthusiasm and invitations to powerful feeling on the part of fascist-sympathizing Italians, whose ancient empire, they could feel, was at last restored.[11] To argue that Pavese remains committed to the Italian lyric tradition that he also recasts in *Lavorare stanca* is precisely not to suggest that he shares in these national sentiments.

For after the early "Oh" marking temporal distance—and associating pathos with child's play—Pavese's speakers become reticent, like the cousin in "I mari del Sud." They become reserved, that is, by lyric standards as well as fascist ones. Not only do *Lavorare stanca*'s speakers refrain from apostrophizing or personifying affective states (as the later "youthful enthusiasms" are personified ["L'influsso" 223]); they name these states only to dismiss them—"Perché vergogna?" (Why shame?)—or to render them banal through repetition: "È una gioia [. . .] / È una gioia [. . .] / È una gioia" (It's a joy [. . .] / It's a joy [. . .] / It's a joy) ("Canzone di strada," *Lavorare* 16).

At other times, such states are evoked in titles only to be pointedly absent from the poems themselves ("Mania di solitudine," *Lavorare* 28; "Donne appassionate," *Lavorare* 67).

Needless to say, however, this attenuated and indirect treatment of affect does not render the poems altogether affectless. In striving to minimize affect—to honor by *not* heightening the minimal affects of the others whom he observes—Pavese does not arrive at total apathy. After all, the feeling that one does not feel, say, mania or a longing worthy of conventional love lyric is still a feeling (Terada 13–14). I take this to be the point of Pavese's initially puzzling titles: a poem called "Donne appassionate" in which passion is otherwise absent, or one called "Mania di solitudine" whose speaker is calm, not manic, produces a disconnect, making us feel what Keats would call "the feel of not to feel it," where "it" now names the feeling, promised in the title, that the poem goes on to withhold (77). Affect thus remains not merely preferable to emotion (which implies the kind of expressive or overtly sighing subject that Pavese's poems foreswear), but a key to understanding Pavese's project in *Lavorare stanca*.

Because they have drawn attention to affect's status as economically, politically, and culturally conditioned (Berlant; Ngai), collectively transmitted (Brennan), and indeed often "transpersonal" (Altieri 54), theories of affect can offer resources for reading Pavese's move away from the "Oh" in "I mari del Sud." This move lets the poet recast lyric as an instrument for recording collective conditions, and to do so using means that differ from the more familiar Adornian "consummation of the particular" or intensification of the individual (54). At the same time, though, since *Lavorare stanca* is still a songbook—since, to repeat, Pavese continues the lyric tradition that he transforms, never pretending fully to transcend or simply to leave behind lyric's constraints—the text compels us to revise accounts of affect that dispense with lyric or address it only to set it aside (Ngai 10; Berlant 35).[12] Resisting lyric's relegation to the realm of emotion, *Lavorare stanca* at the same time makes a virtue of the very limits of lyric.

I have suggested that "I mari del Sud" is at once exceptional in *Lavorare stanca* and representative of the collection as a whole: exceptional in its recourse to the vocative "Oh" but representative in its concern with stagnation as opposed to progress, with fatigue as opposed to vitality, with burnout as opposed to sublime enthusiasm, and with limitation as opposed to expansiveness. I have also repeatedly gestured toward the derivation of the second of the two verbs in Pavese's title: *stancare*, from *stagno*. This verb brings the dynamic if unconjugated *lavorare* to a standstill. But there is another key sense in which the collocation and title, *Lavorare stanca*, motivates my reading of the reticence of Pavese's speakers, of their failure or refusal to emote. Effectively introducing Pavese's poetry to readers in the United States in 1976, William Arrowsmith translated *Lavorare stanca* as *Hard Labor*, a phrase that, the translator claimed, placed a distinct but justified "emphasis—a prison emphasis—on [Pavese's] title" (113). *Hard Labor* thus aimed to remind readers of the context of the poems' production, of their having been completed during the period of Pavese's arrest, imprisonment, and *confino* or forced exile in Brancaleone Calabro, in rural Calabria, where he had been sent by the fascist government in 1935 as punishment for "anti-Fascist activities" (Arrowsmith xi; Casapa 66–67).

In fact, the proverbial saying "lavorare stanca" has very little to do with hard labor. Or rather, it addresses hard labor only in its insistence that all labor is hard—unavoidable, but to be avoided at all costs. One dictionary of Italian proverbs offers this surprisingly vivid definition: "Work of any kind breeds weariness; it is always and in whatever form a strain; it wears down and debilitates especially if it is repetitive and long work, giving rise to boredom and discomfort" (Lapucci 576). The verbs of attrition multiply still further as the dictionary's exhaustive and, indeed, exhausting gloss continues: "Even if enthusiasm for a task makes one forget fatigue, weariness derives from it irremediably. In the long run that work bores and disheartens. In life, work slowly dulls energies and vitality."

What does it mean for a text to unfold under the sign of this saying and this *stanchezza*, this exhaustion? How and to what end does Pavese forge a poetics of fatigue? In what follows, I seek to answer these questions by closely reading several of *Lavorare stanca*'s lyrics, moving through a selection that both attests to the range of the collection's poems and retraces their shift from the personal and expressive (the opening recollections of the "I" in "I mari del Sud") to the impersonal and collective (still up against the limits of lyric), from emotion to affect. Writing against the critical tendency to recast tiring work as hard labor,[13] I show that Pavese makes the decay of sighing, already underway in "I mari del Sud," into the means by which lyric's sighs are reconstituted, exhaled otherwise.

Useless Lights

Pavese's collection shares its title with a poem that also serves as its emblem or centerpiece: "Lavorare stanca." From the first, this poem asks to be read in affective terms, given that, with their strange, self-canceling logic, its opening lines render other contextualizing or cognitive critical frameworks inoperative.[14] And "inoperative" is indeed the operative word in that last formulation, for Pavese's lines strikingly instantiate Giorgio Agamben's thesis that by definition poetry renders communicative language inoperative ("What" 70) or effects its "idling" (*Use* 208):

> *Traversare una strada per scappare di casa*
> *lo fa solo un ragazzo, ma quest'uomo che gira*
> *tutto il giorno le strade, non è più un ragazzo*
> *e non scappa di casa.* (Lavorare *34*)

> *[Crossing a street to run away from home,*
> *only a boy does that, but this man who wanders*
> *the streets all day isn't a boy anymore,*
> *and he's not running away from home.]*

Beginning with an infinitive, a grammatical echo of the subjectless *lavorare* of the poem's and the collection's title, the first part of this text's first sentence seems to deliver a decisive and impersonal verdict, to state, if not something so proverbial that it hardly needs stating, then at least something that everyone knows. But the pair of negations that follows this initial assertion doubly undermines the truism and leaves the reader doubly bereft. For it is not merely that the behavior of "quest'uomo" is boyish and thus age inappropriate ("non è più un ragazzo"); it is not even an instance of the behavior just named ("non scappa di casa"). Even if "quest'uomo" may at first appear to share the young boy's motive, he does not. Indeed, his wandering appears unmotivated as well as aimless.

As it proceeds without arriving anywhere in particular, the poem imitates the man's aimlessness:

> *Ci sono d'estate*
> *pomeriggi che fino le piazze son vuote, distese*
> *sotto il sole che sta per calare, e quest'uomo, che giunge*
> *per un viale di inutili piante, si ferma.*
> *Val la pena esser solo, per esser sempre più solo?*
> *Solamente girarle, le piazze e le strade*
> *sono vuote. Bisogna fermare una donna*
> *e parlarle e deciderla a vivere insieme.*
> *Altrimenti, uno parla da solo. È per questo che a volte*
> *c'è lo sbronzo notturno che attacca discorsi,*
> *e racconta i progetti di tutta la vita.* (Lavorare *34*)

[There are summer
afternoons when even the piazzas are empty, stretched out
under the sun that's about to fall, and this man, who arrives
on a boulevard of useless plants, stops.
Is it worth it to be alone, only to be always more alone?
Just wandering them, the piazzas and the streets
are empty. You need to stop a woman
and talk to her and decide to live together with her.
Otherwise, you talk alone. That's why sometimes
the nighttime drunkard is there, starting conversations
and talking about his plans for all of life.]

The unpredictable alternation between personal and impersonal constructions—the former first mapping the movements of "quest'uomo," then per-
taining to the drunkard's "discorsi," the latter naming what one should do
or the consequences of a failure to do it—make it difficult to keep track of a
central subject here, let alone a lyric "I." When the wandering man finally
appears to "arrive," stopping the reader as the line stops with him ("giunge /
per un viale di inutili piante, si ferma"), someone—the speaker? the man
himself? the "nighttime drunkard"?—poses a question that may be the
poem's own: "Val la pena esser solo, per essere sempre più solo?" Yet another
impersonal construction, "valere la pena," which recurs throughout Pavese's
collection and figures importantly elsewhere in his later *Dialoghi con Leucò*
(*Dialogues with Leucò*) (1947),[15] invokes an affect, or at least a sensation:
"pena," which designates at once a punishment, trouble, or travail and the
pain of undergoing it. But, significantly, in the affirmative, the phrase also
amounts to the very least that can be said in favor of an experience, perhaps
the most minimal endorsement that Italian allows.[16] The circularity of the
question here further minimizes the phrase thus colloquially minimized,
making "valere la pena" all but meaningless as an endorsement, for the
punishment of being alone is not seen to lead to anything other than the
pain of being ever more alone.

    This solitude motivates the nighttime drinker's public rants, his
one-sided conversations or "discorsi," which bear on aborted "progetti" remi-
niscent of the "disegno" declared failed in "I mari del Sud" (*Lavorare* 7). But
the explanatory "È per questo" that the speaker offers is in fact powerless to
explain anything. Presumably, the discourse of "una donna" could have cut
the drunkard's discourse short or prevented it from forming in the first place.
Yet, never offering up words of her own, the woman is only ever stopped, an

object and not a subject, and classically lyric in this sense; the wished-for decision to live together is made *for* her ("deciderla a vivere insieme"). Moreover, no encounter with any such woman is guaranteed in the first place:

> *Non è certo attendendo nella piazza deserta*
> *che s'incontra qualcuno, ma chi gira le strade*
> *si sofferma ogni tanto. Se fossero in due,*
> *anche andando per strada, la casa sarebbe*
> *dove c'è quella donna e varrebbe la pena.*
> *Nella notte la piazza ritorna deserta*
> *e quest'uomo, che passa, non vede le case*
> *tra le inutili luci, non leva più gli occhi:*
> *sente solo il selciato, che han fatto altri uomini*
> *dalle mani indurite, come sono le sue.*
> *Non è giusto restare sulla piazza deserta.*
> *Ci sarà certamente quella donna per strada*
> *che, pregata, vorrebbe dar mano alla casa. (Lavorare 34)*

> *[It's not certain waiting in the empty piazza*
> *that you'll meet someone, but whoever wanders the streets*
> *is stopped once in a while. If they were two*
> *even walking the street, the house would be*
> *the place where that woman is, and it would be worth it.*
> *In the night the piazza becomes empty again*
> *and this man, who passes, doesn't see the houses.*
> *among the useless lights, he no longer raises his eyes:*
> *he feels only the pavement that other men made*
> *with hands hardened like his are.*
> *It's not right to remain in the deserted piazza.*
> *There will certainly be that woman on the streets*
> *who, when asked, would want to give her hand to the house.]*

The strangeness of the poem's final phrase is lost in previous English translations. William Arrowsmith's "give him her hand . . . and take him home" (Pavese, *Hard* 61) and Geoffrey Brock's "lead him home by the hand" (Pavese, *Disaffections* 119) both domesticate the poem's ending by making "quest'uomo" the object of the phrase, the recipient of wifely care, which he plainly is not in the original. Even the "certain" scenario with which the poem ends, which is by no means certain (for the earlier "Non è certo" seems both to anticipate and to cancel out the "certamente" in the poem's penultimate line), paints no such picture of marital mutuality; the text offers no such return or reassurance. "There will be no gathering home," as Avital Ronell writes in another context, "even if the poet has projected a homeward turning" (31). Indeed, Pavese's unnamed woman extends her hand not toward "quest'uomo" but instead toward the house, which, in Pavese's puzzling construction, *would* be where the woman would be if "quest'uomo" were not alone, if they were two ("[s]e fossero in due"). This conditional contrary to fact whose fulfillment alone would make it—the labor of life? the work of weariness?—worth the trouble is never met in the space or time of the poem. Should the reader infer, then, that all tiring work is, like the plants and lights named in the poem, "useless"?[17] That all projects are doomed to fail? That the wanderer will not find home? To formulate these questions in this way is already to belie the poem's reserve. For even in staging "the missing of love" (François), Pavese allows for no formulation so sighingly histrionic.

"Quest'uomo" is without enumerated qualities, but he remains, importantly, singular even as he desires nothing more particular than to be one of two ("in due"). Feeling here becomes indeed "an ebbed tide, and the mind [. . .] a dry but alert shell, its life [. . .] encompassed by mechanical and formal processes" (Terada 82). The man does not dream of a particular woman (a content); he aspires only to be one of a pair (to participate in or belong to a form). Likewise, he does not see the particular houses before him but thinks only of "la casa," a placeholder rather than a place. Meanwhile, he feels only one thing, the ground that does little or nothing to ground him: "sente solo il selciato, che han fatto altri uomini / dalle mani indurite, come sono le sue." The man's isolation is thus paradoxically underscored by these lines' insistence on his sensing the surface paved by others just like him—or rather, others whose hands are just like his.

These metonymic "hardened hands" are the poem's only indication that the "uomo solo" has, in fact, been worn out by the kind of work signaled by the title, "Lavorare stanca." Work and exhaustion are not otherwise thematized in the poem, and the indirectness of their thematization suggests that fatigue in Pavese functions, or malfunctions, as a mood. A lasting rather than local, drawn-out rather than definite, state, fatigue informs gestures, inflects movements, and, as in Hegel's *Aesthetics*, aborts dialectics even, or perhaps especially, when exhaustion is not named explicitly;[18] it is ever-present, indeed, "permeant" (Wollheim qtd. in Altieri 54). Something is thus transmitted to "quest'uomo" through the pavement—"something vaguely transpersonal" (Altieri 54).[19] This something is a collective *stanchezza*, and yet the man feels it alone.

Early Risers

"Lo steddazzu," another meditation on uselessness, ends the expanded edition of *Lavorare stanca*, published in 1943. The poem's title, which Brock translates as "Morning Star over Calabria," is taken from Calabrian dialect, and its appearance at the end of a collection that begins by mentioning (without quoting) Piedmontese would seem to underscore the distance that the poet has traveled. But the "I" has, strikingly, disappeared here, as has the "we" encoded in the first word of "I mari del Sud," "Camminiamo" (*Lavorare* 5). And the tide of emotion has ebbed even further:

L'uomo solo si leva che il mare è ancor buio
e le stelle vacillano. Un tepore di fiato
sale su dalla riva, dov'è il letto del mare,
e addolcisce il respiro. Quest'è l'ora in cui nulla
può accadere. Perfino la pipa tra i denti
pende spenta. Notturno è il sommesso sciacquio.
L'uomo solo ha già acceso un gran fuoco di rami
e lo guarda arrossare il terreno. Anche il mare
tra non molto sarà come il fuoco, avvampante.
Non c'è cosa più amara che l'alba di un giorno
in cui nulla accadrà. Non c'è cosa più amara
che l'inutilità. Pende stanca nel cielo
una stella vardagnola, sorpresa dall'alba.
Vede il mare ancor buio e la macchia di fuoco
a cui l'uomo, per fare qualcosa, si scalda;
vede, e cade dal sonno tra le fosche montagne
dov'è il letto di neve. La lentezza dell'ora
è spietata, per chi non aspetta più nulla.
Val la pena che il sole si levi dal mare
e la lunga giornata cominci? Domani
tornerà l'alba tiepida con la diafana luce
e sarà come ieri e mai nulla accadrà.
L'uomo solo vorrebbe soltanto dormire.
Quando l'ultima stella si spegne nel cielo,
l'uomo adagio prepara la pipa e l'accende. (Lavorare *119*)

[The man alone gets up when the sea is still dark
and the stars are unsteady. A warmth of breath
rises up from the shore, where the sea's bed is,
and sweetens breathing. This is the hour when nothing
can happen. Even the pipe between teeth
hangs extinguished. The meek lapping is nighttime.
The man alone has already lit a big fire from branches
and he watches it redden the earth. The sea too
before too long will be like the fire, blazing.
There is nothing more bitter than the dawn of a day
when nothing will happen. There is nothing more bitter
than uselessness. In the sky a pale greenish star
hangs tired, surprised by the dawn.
It sees the sea still dark and the stain of fire
where the man, to do something, is warming himself;
it sees, and it falls with sleepiness between the dim mountains
where a bed of snow is. The slowness of the hour
is merciless for one who doesn't wait for anything anymore.
Is it worth it for the sun to get up from the sea
and begin the long day? Tomorrow
the mild dawn will return with the diaphanous light
and it will be like yesterday and nothing will happen.
The man alone would want just to sleep.
When the last star goes out in the sky,
the man slowly prepares his pipe and lights it.]

The inconsequence of the man's final gesture—his preparing the pipe and then lighting it, under extinguished stars—finds an analog in the lack of pathos with which the poet pronounces the day's uselessness. It is as if the poet, too, had written "per fare qualcosa," "to do something," to kill time while waiting for nothing to happen. The prevalence of end-stopped lines here (and throughout *Lavorare stanca*) indexes this "nulla," this nothing happening, at the level of the line. Enforcing repeated pauses or arrests, such lines undo in advance, time and again, the expectation, the slight onward rush, that enjambment would produce. But note the painstaking distribution of "nulla" in the poem: the word is used four times, twice in the middle of lines and twice at the end. Of the latter two usages, the first does, in fact, usher in an enjambment ("Quest'è l'ora in cui nulla / può accadere"). A last residue of lyric, this anomalous enjambment signals that "Lo steddazzu" and

Lavorare stanca alike remain committed to the poetic, for all their interest in the prosaic. This is not, Pavese says here, in effect, sighing otherwise, "the end of the poem" (Agamben, "End").

Pavese's speaker begins by hinting at the existence or at least the possibility of a correspondence between the man and his surroundings, as the warmth of the sea's air, likened to breath ("fiato"), meets and sweetens the man's breathing ("respiro"), a breathing that stops short of sighing even while it reminds us that sighs, too, are merely breath. This initial sweetness is then undone, however, by the bitterness that the dawn brings, ushering in as it does "un giorno / in cui nulla accadrà." This nothing and the more general "inutilità" that it bespeaks belong to a world of circularity, recursivity; days repeat themselves as do phrases ("Non c'è cosa [. . .] / Non c'è cosa"; "pende spenta [. . .] / pende stanca"; "nulla accadrà [. . .] / e mai nulla accadrà"). But this repetition does not bring comfort or even rest, as the poem's final conditional indicates: "vorrebbe soltanto dormire." The man would like to sleep (as would the speaker in "Il paradiso sui tetti," for whom heaven is endless rest [*Lavorare* 114]), but he cannot, and here the reader is not even allowed to imagine a situation, however counterfactual, in which he could (as in "[s]e fossero in due" in "Lavorare stanca").

But this is not, of course, the poem's last word. Unable to sleep though sleep is all he would like, the man alone smokes; this last gesture, at least, remains possible, if a poor substitute for rest. Suggestively, this gesture is qualified as made "adagio," slowly. The adverb invests the man's actions with a minimal musicality, as though, preparing and then lighting his pipe, he were engaging in a modestly aesthetic act. At the same time, the syntax of the line brings "adagio" closer to "l'uomo" than "prepara," so that the "uomo solo" of the poem's first line has become or has been replaced by "l'uomo adagio." That this man who moves slowly is still alone and thus still, fundamentally, the "uomo solo" after all suggests that the aesthetic (or musical or at least musically timed) gesture has not transformed either the subject or his surroundings. But it has momentarily caused being to give way to doing, the adjectival to the adverbial, matter (or number, "solo") to manner, "Lo steddazzu" says without quite sighing.

The more cryptic "La voce" ("The Voice") sounds a different and less personal kind of music:

> *Ogni giorno il silenzio della camera sola*
> *si richiude sul lieve sciacquío d'ogni gesto*
> *come l'aria. Ogni giorno la breve finestra*

s'apre immobile all'aria che tace. La voce
rauca e dolce non torna nel fresco silenzio.
S'apre come il respiro di chi sia per parlare
l'aria immobile, e tace. Ogni giorno è la stessa.
E la voce è la stessa, che non rompe il silenzio,
rauca e uguale per sempre nell'immobilità
del ricordo. La chiara finestra accompagna
col suo palpito breve la calma d'allora.
Ogni gesto percuote la calma d'allora.
Se suonasse la voce, tornerebbe il dolore.
Tornerebbero i gesti nell'aria stupita
e parole parole alla voce sommessa.
Se suonasse la voce anche il palpito breve
del silenzio che dura, si farebbe dolore.
Tornerebbero i gesti del vano dolore,
percuotendo le cose nel rombo del tempo.
Ma la voce non torna, e il sussurro remoto
non increspa il ricordo. L'immobile luce
dà il suo palpito fresco. Per sempre il silenzio
tace rauco e sommesso nel ricordo d'allora. (Lavorare *105*)

[Every day the silence of the room alone
closes in on the lapping of every gesture
like the air. Every day the small window
is opened, immobile, onto the air that is silent. The voice,
hoarse and sweet, does not return in the cool silence.
It opens itself like the breath of one who is about to speak,
the immobile air, and it's silent. Every day it's the same.
And the voice is the same, not breaking the silence,
hoarse and identical always in the immobility
of memory. The bright window accompanies
with its brief throbbing the calm of that time.
Every gesture strikes the calm of that time.
If the voice were to sound, the pain would return.
The gestures would return in the astounded air
and words and words, of a soft voice.
If the voice were to sound the brief throbbing, too,
of the silence that lasts, would give pain.
The gestures of useless pain would return,

striking things in the rumble of time.
But the voice doesn't return and the distant whisper
doesn't ripple the surface of memory. The immobile light
gives its cool throbbing. Forever the silence
falls silent, hoarse and hushed in the memory of that time.]

The poem's sibilant soundscape—its "sciacquío," "sussurro," and "sommesso"—anticipates that of "Lo steddazzu." Likewise, assertions of stasis or stagnation in "La voce" ("Ogni giorno è la stessa. / E la voce è la stessa, che non rompe il silenzio, / rauca e uguale per sempre nell'immobilità del ricordo") prepare the reader for the later poem's statements of recurrence: "Domani / tornerà l'alba tiepida con la diafana luce / e sarà come ieri e mai nulla accadrà." But in another sense, "La voce" differs markedly from "Lo steddazzu" and from most other poems in Pavese's collection; it is anomalous in multiplying disembodied voices, words, gestures, and silences. Abandoning identifiable speakers and figures observed, it offers up only traces, gathered in an empty room. A window "is opened" ("s'apre [. . .] / S'apre"), as though by itself. First the air is silent ("l'aria [. . .] / tace [. . .] / e tace"); then the voice refuses to break the silence ("non rompe il silenzio"). Then, in a series of counterfactual constructions, the reader learns that the voice, were it to return and break the silence, would bring pain. It would also bring gestures and words and hushed words ("i gesti [. . .] / e parole parole alla voce sommessa"). Returning, this voice would, moreover, make even the lasting silence hurt ("Se suonasse la voce anche il palpito breve / del silenzio che dura, si farebbe dolore"). The poem's conclusion promises perpetual silence, suggesting that the reader or listener (or the speaker himself?) need not fear the pain that the returned voice would entail. But this silence, although it at first seems permanently silent ("Per sempre il silenzio / tace"), is clearly not a true or total silence, since it is heard to be both hoarse and hushed, "rauco e sommesso."[20]

A far cry—or a far sigh—from "adagio" in "Lo steddazzu," the adjective "rauca" ("hoarse") recurs in the poem, attaching first, in the poem's first and second stanzas, to the voice, then, in its last stanza, to the silence; paired first with sweetness ("dolce"), it is then paired with sameness or indifference ("uguale"), and finally with softness ("sommesso"). The word names a physical property of the voice, not an affective quality, and still less an aesthetic charge. "La voce" would thus seem to silence what slight hope, consolation, or aesthetic compensation the other poem's "adagio" might have held out. But it does so only at the level of content, when read (reductively) for the story it tells rather than the song it sings, or the sigh it hints at without heaving. For at the level of form, with its lexical and metrical repetitions, the poem becomes in effect a protracted "palpito breve."

Work Release

Another combinatory poem, "Semplicità" ("Simplicity") reintroduces "the man alone," who replaces the "room alone" in "La voce":

L'uomo solo—che è stato in prigione—ritorna in prigione
ogni volta che morde in un pezzo di pane.
In prigione sognava le lepri che fuggono
sul terriccio invernale. Nella nebbia d'inverno
l'uomo vive tra muri di strade, bevendo
acqua fredda e mordendo in un pezzo di pane.
Uno crede che dopo rinasce la vita,
che il respiro si calmi, che ritorni l'inverno
con l'odore del vino nella calda osteria,
e il buon fuoco, la stalla, e le cene. Uno crede,
fin che è dentro uno crede. Si esce fuori una sera,
e le lepri le han prese e le mangiano al caldo
gli altri, allegri. Bisogna guardarli dai vetri.
L'uomo solo osa entrare per bere un bicchiere
quando proprio si gela, e contempla il suo vino:
il colore fumoso, il sapore pesante.
Morde il pezzo di pane, che sapeva di lepre
in prigione, ma adesso non sa più di pane
né di nulla. E anche il vino non sa che di nebbia.
L'uomo solo ripensa a quei campi, contento
di saperli già arati. Nella sala deserta
sottovoce, si prova a cantare. Rivede
lungo l'argine il ciuffo di rovi spogliati
che in agosto fu verde. Dà un fischio alla cagna.
E compare la lepre e non hanno più freddo. (Lavorare 115)

[The man alone—who has been in prison—returns to prison
every time he bites into a piece of bread.
In prison he dreamed of wild hares that flee
across winter's plowed fields. In the fog of winter
the man lives between walls of streets, drinking

cold water and biting into pieces of bread.
You believe that afterward life is reborn,
that the breath is calmed, that winter returns
with the smell of wine in the warm tavern
and the good fire, the stable, and meals. You believe that,
while you're inside you believe that. You go out one evening,
and they've caught the wild hares and they're eating them hot,
happy, the others. You have to watch them through the windows.
The man alone dares to go inside for a drink
when he's freezing, and contemplates his wine:
the smoky color, the heavy taste.
He bites into the piece of bread, which tasted like wild hares
in prison, but now doesn't taste like bread anymore
or like anything. And the wine, too, just tastes like fog.
The man alone thinks again of those fields, glad
to know that they've already been plowed. In the empty room
he tries to sing softly. Again he sees,
along the embankment, the naked blackberry bushes
that in August were green. He whistles to his dog.
And the wild hare appears and they aren't cold anymore.]

Atypically, Pavese here gives the reader a great deal of information about not only the ex-prisoner's sensory responses to his surroundings but also his thoughts, and even his dreams. The poem is also, relative to others in *Lavorare stanca*, unusually varied in that it traverses both the prison and its outside, both the tavern and its exterior. "Semplicità" is also uncommonly crowded not only with people affectively othered ("gli altri, allegri") but also with animals. The solitary male figure at the center of the poem appears to merge, at least grammatically, with one or more of these latter in the poem's last line, in which a singular verb gives way to a plural that includes, minimally, both the dog and the man. This merging follows a moment of contented, if simple, reflection ("ripensa a quei campi, contento / di saperli già arati") and, crucially, another instance of attempted, *sottovoce* singing ("sottovoce, si prova a cantare"). Perhaps this singing, preceding a more creaturely whistle, confirms the man's contentedness, announcing the thaw, the dispersal of fog, and the memory of green and August with which "Semplicità" ends. Whereas "La voce" ended by falling silent, "Semplicità" concludes with hopeful if hesitant sounds, sounds that suggest satisfaction as well as simplicity.

But as the poem's first lines make clear, reporting yet another return, what sustains the man alone is also what sends him back to the prison that he thought he had escaped: "L'uomo solo—che è stato in prigione—ritorna in prigione / ogni volta che morde in un pezzo di pane." There will be no becoming-animal, then, that does not return to the human, no hunting for hares that is not the realization of the prisoner's dream and in this sense a return to prison. Nor will there be the singing fully "reborn" that the man anticipated while still inside. Like "Lo steddazzu," "Semplicità" ends with only the most conditional of releases.

So, too, I have claimed, is Pavese's own release from the prison house of lyric a suspension rather than a break. For all his reserve and notwithstanding the spare nature of his verse, Pavese continues the poetic enterprise from which he departs or at least takes distance. That is to say, he sighs otherwise. To sigh otherwise is not to quit sighing altogether; it is instead, since sighs have long since been figures for lyric itself, to find new ways to set lyric to work—or to render it inoperative. In *Lavorare stanca*, this happens under conditions in which lyric emotiveness has not simply been played out by being continued for centuries; such emotiveness has also been politically compromised, claimed by protofascists like D'Annunzio and later repurposed (and rendered "epic") in scenes of national sentiment staged by the regime itself. This is one reason why another poet, Eugenio Montale, writes of the necessity of *attraversare D'Annunzio* (crossing D'Annunzio) ("Gozzano" 1279). For Montale, there can be no bypassing D'Annunzio, no real way of avoiding a reckoning with his effusive lyrics. In Montale's own work, as in Ungaretti's, this reckoning takes the form of a poetic enclosure, often called hermeticism, still compatible with apostrophe, with the vocative, the "oh," that, sigh-like, signals emotion's overflow.

Indeed, sighing marks the time in one of Montale's poems, "Casa sul mare" ("House by the Sea"):

> *Tu chiedi se così tutto vanisce*
> *in questa poca nebbia di memorie;*
> *se nell'ora che torpe o nel sospiro*
> *del frangente si compie ogni destino. (Ossi 128–29)*

> *[You ask if everything vanishes this way,*
> *in this bit of fog made of memories;*
> *if every destiny is fulfilled in the hour that*
> *grows torpid or in or the breaker's sigh.]*

Montale's speaker is "tired" (*stanco*), he will later say, and yet this state does not prevent him from projecting emotion outward, onto the sea whose sublime breakers sigh. The hour does not become so torpid, then, as to rule out this movement at least. Animation persists in the world said to be slowing down, going numb, growing torpid, for the breakers produce the sounds made by animate beings, beings that are also emotional and expressive. It is as if the sea were speaking in apostrophes, answering the speaker and his companion in vocatives, in poetry's own figures and sounds. Thus although at first these lines from Montale may seem to come close to rendering the feeling of *not* feeling that I have located in Pavese's *Lavorare stanca*, there is a plenitude—an overflowing that is not that of *stagno*, of stagnation—in Montale's poem absent from Pavese's project. This project, I have claimed, proceeds from an ebbing or emptying out of the lyric "I" that is not for all that a simple abandonment of lyric's generative limitations.

Torpor takes over in *Lavorare stanca*: not total apathy, that is, but a fatigue that inhibits expression, dampens emotion. This is why "nemmeno un sospiro" (not even a sigh) is heard in the silence of a poem significantly called "Poetica" ("Poetics"), written, like much of Pavese's collection, from within the confines of the *confino* but not published during his lifetime (*Poesie* 125). Sighing has gone the way of the "Oh" in "I mari del Sud" (*Lavorare* 6), and the emotion that still saturates the world of Montale's "Casa sul mare" has given way to affect, gathered in Pavese's poems from a collective weighed down by *stanchezza*, as in these arresting lines from late in *Lavorare stanca*: "Ora pesa / la stanchezza su tutte le membra dell'uomo / senza pena" (113). (Now weariness weighs on all the man's limbs, without suffering.) Note that the phrase "senza pena" minimizes suffering, even while the condition named in these lines is grave indeed, for exhaustion weighs on more than the body and on more than this man alone. It weighs on the words of the lyricist who thus participates in the condition that he describes.

In what sense, then, is he still a lyricist? Montale's poetry anticipates and instantiates the Adornian account of lyric in modernity, according to which poetry's very "self-absorption," its distance from the social world, becomes dialectically its most social feature and its most critical (Adorno 43). I have argued that *Lavorare stanca* lets us see another lyric possibility, one in which the lyricist is no longer "opposed to the collective" (41), but instead forms part of it. Pavese writes from within—again, he stays in—the collective stagnation that another poet, and not only a Montale, might flee from or resist through reanimation. Yet even the most conventional lyricists were not unacquainted with stagnant states. In fact, the verb *torpere*, used by Montale in one of the untranslatable lines quoted above from "Casa sul mare"—"se nell'ora che torpe o nel sospiro"—sounds a Petrarchan echo, recalling a line from Petrarch's sonnet 335: "di che pensando ancor m'aghiaccio et torpo" (thinking of it I still freeze and grow torpid) (532–33; translation Durling's). Or rather, it sounds the first of two Petrarchan echoes in the single line, since "sospiro" also inevitably calls the repeatedly, even ceaselessly sighing author of the *Canzoniere* to memory.[21] Already in that founding lyric sequence, moreover, we read: "Il sempre sospirar nulla releva" (Always sighing relieves nothing) (Petrarch 209, canzone 105; my translation). The poet thus sighs that sighs are good for nothing, just as he claims in a *canzone*, a song, to be giving up the singing that he will continue in hundreds of songs to come: "Mai non vo' più cantar com'io soleva, / ch'altri non m'intendeva" (I never want to sing the way I used to / for no one understood me) (209; my translation). Wastes of breath that know themselves to be wasted and that understand that they are not understood: such are Petrarch's poems, which persist in the singing and sighing that they relinquish.

If Pavese turns away from the effusiveness of this lyric tradition, his poems nevertheless pursue the engagement with futility that we can see compellingly begun in poems like canzone 105—and continued in Montale's much later "Casa sul mare." I am thinking of the number of times that things—plants, lights, days—are called "useless" in *Lavorare stanca*, a collection that keeps bringing the "nulla," the nothing, into relief even while its poems repeatedly withhold the lasting relief, the rest, that its subjects seek. This rest is withheld most explicitly in "Lavorare stanca" and "Lo steddazzu," but recall the voice that does not return in "La voce" or the release that is shown to be short-lived, a work release, in "Semplicità." In this sense, despite their reticence, all of the poems that I have read are indeed sighs that relieve nothing, as Petrarch's singer might complain. Giving voice to this complaint—hoarse and hushed, to be sure, unemphatic but repeated, repetitive—Pavese's poems remain lyrics.

The poems are not therefore, to be clear, examples of affect unbound. They do not open onto oceanic feelings, as some theories of affect might claim.[22] Instead, time and again, they let us see the limits in which they, and the anonymous figures that they treat, remain. These are also the limits of the "estranged," "calcified" Italy—the dormant and stagnant nation—that Pavese would later claim to have overcome ("L'influsso" 223). Writing in 1946, a decade after *Lavorare stanca* was first published, Pavese sounds like Gilles Deleuze, another firm believer in "the superiority of Anglo-American literature."[23] I have worked to show, however, that unlike the manic Deleuzian heroes who manage to become free men—"to flee the plague, organize encounters, increase the power to act, to be moved by joy, to multiply the affects which express or encompass a maximum of affirmation" (Deleuze and Parnet 62)—Pavese's speakers, workers, prisoners, prostitutes, and vagrants are all infected without hope of cure. Or rather, for them, any partial remedy must emerge from within their exhaustion, which they cannot deny. They experience "the plague" not as a catastrophe, then, but rather as a fact of life, a part of their environment, breathed in like atmosphere.[24] The events and upheavals, crashes and crises of the first decades of the twentieth century are nowhere named in *Lavorare stanca*'s poems, which instead bear witness to—by becoming—nonevents, minor recurrences, or brief reprieves. To read these poems is thus to stay in stagnation, like Pavese, his speakers, and those they observe. But since such staying turns out to require attunement, to stay is also to produce the minimal possibility of doing something else.

I thank Charles Altieri, Alessia Ricciardi, and Shaul Setter, this essay's first readers, as well as those who have read and responded to more recent versions of the text: Natalie Adler, Paco Brito, Joan Copjec, Lorenzo Fabbri, Katie Kadue, D. A. Miller, Julia Nelson, Ellen Rooney, Jocelyn Saidenberg, Suzanne Stewart-Steinberg, and Elizabeth Weed.

RAMSEY MCGLAZER is a postdoctoral scholar at the University of California, Berkeley, where he works in both the Department of Comparative Literature and the International Consortium of Critical Theory Programs.

Notes

1   Unless otherwise noted, all translations from the Italian are my own.

2   On "detourism" defined as a process by which "home is constructed retroactively as a result of the 'detour' that is travel," see Spackman 39.

3   In the *Critique of the Power of Judgment*, Kant classifies enthusiasm as sublime: "The idea of the good with affect is called enthusiasm. This state of mind seems to be sublime, so much so that it is commonly maintained that without it nothing great can be accomplished. [. . .] [E]nthusiasm is aesthetically sublime, because it is a stretching of the powers through ideas, which give the mind a momentum that acts far more powerfully and persistently than the impetus given by sensory representations" (154).

4   *Stagno* itself derives from *stare*, which gives both Italian and English "stasis," on the one hand, and "resistance," on the other. For recent and moving reflections on the implications of this "primal word," see Comay (esp. 238–41). My reading proceeds from and hinges on the observation that such states are not strictly, or not always, opposed. Registering stillness, stagnation, or "stuckness," impasse or arrest, can thus become a precondition for acting otherwise (Comay 266).

5   For now I bracket recent critical debates about "lyric" and "lyricization," debates most visibly associated with the work of Virginia Jackson and Yopie Prins (*Lyric Theory Reader*), on the one hand, and Jonathan Culler (*Theory*), on the other. In what follows, I use "lyric" and "poetry" interchangeably to name Pavese's early literary production, not least because I want to draw attention to his engagement with an Italian tradition—a lyric tradition—that precedes his work and makes it possible, even when he takes distance from this tradition (Culler, *Theory* 3–4, 6–7). Attending more closely to the history of "lyric" in the Italian context might, then, complicate the historicist account that defines "lyricization" as a recent invention and legacy of the New Criticism. That is, it might lead to an account closer to Culler's than Jackson's and Prins's.

6   In translating Pavese's poems, I have consulted both Brock's and Weaver's translations, but I have made my own renderings as literal as possible, maintaining Pavese's word order and lineation whenever English allowed.

7   Jacques Rancière reads parataxis in Pavese's fiction as a form of "faithful[ness] to the ways of mediocre and commonplace characters, working-class or middle-class characters without depth" (59). In an earlier essay, Susan Sontag, too, underscores the "flat, dry" style of Pavese's novels (39), and she notes that these take a diminution or dampening of feeling, related to what I am calling the "decay of sighing," as given: "A certain atrophy of the emotions, an enervation of sentiment and bodily vitality, is presupposed" (40).

8   To be sure, Kant maintains that "even affectlessness [. . .] is sublime," but he qualifies this by attributing such sublimity only to apathy "in a mind that emphatically pursues its own inalterable principles" (154). Thus, whereas the speaker's cousin in "I mari del Sud" may approach the sublime in his "noble" affectlessness, the speaker himself falls short of sublimity in his unemphatic pursuit of principles that are not his own but rather those of others, those called "fortunati." If, then, in the economy of the Kantian sublime, the subject's advances outpace declines (as the encounter with "insufficiency" gives way to a recognition of reason's difference from and superiority over nature [145]), Pavese's texts envision no comparable gain or consolation.

9   See Erich Auerbach's discussion of the role of apostrophe in Dante's lyrics, and especially his reading of the concluding command in "Tanto gentile e tanto onesta pare": "Sospira!" (Sigh!) (29–30, 36–38). Whereas Auerbach hears an "abrupt" "shift from sterile old age to youth" in this imperative (35), I am arguing that Pavese stages an inverse process, whereby youth recedes and old age must be taken as a given, even for the young. In this sense, *Lavorare stanca* can be seen to belong to a modern, male, Italian narrative tradition that extends from the "stanchissima virilità" (exhausted manhood) of Ippolito Nievo's 1867 novel *Le confessioni di un italiano* (5) to Paolo Sorrentino's film *Youth* (2015), in which "youth" names second childhood or senescence. But as I have already indicated, it is *Lavorare stanca*'s relation to the Italian lyric tradition that most interests me. Petrarch's *Canzoniere* begins by recasting its verses as youthful sighs: "Voi ch'ascoltate in rime sparse il suono / di quei sospiri ond'io nudriva 'l core / in sul mio primo giovenile errore" (You who hear in scattered rhymes

the sound / of those sighs with which I nourished the heart / in my first youthful error) (37). Sighs continue to function as figures for lyric, as well as indices of suffering, throughout Petrarch's songbook, and they likewise recur in Leopardi's much later collection of *Canti*. First published in 1933, Ungaretti's relatively spare but obsessively apostrophizing *Sentimento del tempo* gathers poems written just before *Lavorare stanca* made its first appearance in 1936. Compared to earlier lyricists, Ungaretti sighs sparingly; there are four explicit references to sighs or sighing in *Sentimento del tempo*. But frequent apostrophes continue the work or play of sighs, and in this respect the contrast between the two poets' approaches is instructive. Ungaretti's collection opens with the poem "O notte," which "I mari del Sud" seems, in some ways, to answer: "O gioventù, / Passata è appena l'ora del distacco. / [. . .] Oceanici silenzi, / Astrali nidi d'illusione, / O notte" (O youth, / the hour of separation has just passed. / [. . .] Oceanic silences, / astral nests of illusion, / O night) (103; see also Coletti).

10 Simonetta Falasca-Zamponi describes the work of these campaigns as follows: "Transformed marshes exemplified the regime's victory over nature and the elements, papers and newsreels indefatigably claimed. The reclamation of the Pontine Ager [in Lazio, southeast of Rome], one of the most publicized symbols of the fascist era's achievements, epitomized the regime's ability to build life from death" (153). Pavese thus opposes the regime's discourse of "indefatigable" effort and limitless improvement with a poetics of fatigue. On fascist land reclamation, see also Stewart-Steinberg, and for a more general account of

the fascist regime as modernizing rather than strictly regressive, see De Bernardi.

11 In 1935, Pavese wrote in his diary that he could only summon superficial enthusiasm for revolutions: "[I]o non mi entusiasmo per loro se non a fior di pelle" (*Il mestiere* 13). This was at a time when the discourse of revolution had long since been co-opted by the fascist regime. Ruth Ben-Ghiat briefly but illuminatingly reads this entry in Pavese's diary against the backdrop of the fascist invasion of Ethiopia (122).

12 On *Lavorare stanca* as *canzoniere*, see Mutterle 1–47.

13 For an influential instance of this recasting—which heightens, amplifies, and energizes there where Pavese's poems do the opposite—see Italo Calvino's account of Pavese as "a man of careful industriousness in his studies, in his creative work, in his work for the publishing house, a man for whom every gesture and every hour had its function and its fruit, a man whose terseness and unsociability were the defense of his doing and his being, whose nervousness was that of one who is entirely seized by feverish activity, whose moments of idleness and whose amusements, parsimonious but savored with wisdom, were those of one who knows how to work hard" (60). Whatever truth this may have at the level of biography, it falls short as an engagement with Pavese's work. Nevertheless, Calvino's Pavese has arguably become the canonical Pavese, and this version of the poet lives on, informing recent critical discussions, for instance, of the poet's refusal of "literary idleness" in favor of "a total commitment to 'making'" (Casapa 109).

14 On affective as opposed to cognitive critical approaches, see Altieri 1–6. In another context, Alejandro Zambra attests to Pavese's tendency to frustrate critical and even commemorative energies: "Algo va mal en este artículo" (Something's wrong with this article), Zambra writes, beautifully, just a few paragraphs before his article ends (205). I thank Paco Brito for bringing Zambra's text to my attention.

15 See, for instance, in *Lavorare stanca*, "Mediterranea": "Val la pena incontrarlo un mattino di vento?" (57); "Paesaggio": "Val la pena tornare, magari diverso" (73); and "Lo steddazzu," discussed below (118). See also Pavese's astonishing rewriting of the myth of Orpheus in the *Dialoghi*'s "L'inconsolabile" ("The Unconsolable"). Here Orpheus remembers asking himself, on his way back from the underworld, "Valeva la pena di rivivere ancora?" (Was it worth the pain of living again?) (99). He answers—for Eurydice—in the negative and therefore turns around to face her not out of weakness, but because he has come to understand that life's not worth the effort—or what the *Dialoghi*'s English translator renders initially (a bit too loudly, to my mind) as "the anguish" (71): "[C]redi a chi è stato tra i morti," Orpheus concludes, "non vale la pena" (Believe one who's been among the dead[, . . .] it's not worth it) (101). (This repetition of the phrase is missing from the English translation [73].) Pavese thus radicalizes—even while his Orpheus refuses—the Virgilian definition of poetic production as *effusus labor*, work that is wasted or, literally, poured out (*Georgics* 4: 492). This is Orpheus exhausted: a new figure for the lyricist as belated and beleaguered.

16 I am grateful to Alessia Ricciardi for this formulation.

17 Niva Lorenzini notes that elsewhere in *Lavorare stanca* Pavese's repetition of the word *work* ("lavoro") itself indexes a sense of futility, of stalled development and negated collectivity (102).

18 "The poorest mode of apprehension, the least adequate to the spirit, is purely sensuous apprehension," says Hegel. "It consists, in the first place, of merely looking on, hearing, feeling, etc., just as in hours of spiritual fatigue (indeed for many people at any time) it may be an amusement to wander about without thinking, just to listen here and look round there, and so on" (36).

19 I should note that I depart slightly from Altieri's discussion of moods in that my reading of *Lavorare stanca* limits the "immense psychological expansiveness" that Altieri locates in moods (55) as well as "the need to submit [the] absoluteness of mood to some kind of judgment" (267). As I have already indicated, Pavese's poems tend not to foster sublime feelings of expansiveness (again, "giovanili entusiasmi" and "conquest[e] di testi" notwithstanding ["L'influsso" 223]). Nor do these texts seem to me to foreground the evaluative or reflective processes that attend being in moods, according to Altieri.

20 On silence in Pavese, see Gioanola, which, though intertextually sensitive, exemplifies a preference for such timeless categories as myth and symbol, shared by many of Pavese's critics. My turn to affect is meant to counter this critical tendency, even while it resists the kind of historicist account that would reduce the poems to their context, ignoring what Culler calls

the reversibility of poetic forms (*Theory* 4).

21   On sighing in Petrarch's *Canzoniere*, see note 9, above.

22   For critiques of theories that celebrate affect unbound, see Ball; and Brinkema.

23   For recent attempts to reimagine Deleuze as a thinker of negativity, see Culp; and Schuster. For a compelling account of Pavese's relationship to the literature of the United States, see Catalfamo. My aim has not been to deny Pavese's abiding engagements with this literature or the importance of his work as a literary and cultural translator. On the contrary, I borrow Deleuze's phrase here in order to call attention to these engagements and this work precisely, and it would be absurd to argue that the poet's influences were strictly national. I hope to have shown, however, what is missed when readers of *Lavorare stanca* follow the poet's lead in his account of the cosmopolitan rediscovery and poetic reawakening of Italy. What is missed is, in a word, *stanchezza*.

24   On affect and atmosphere, see Altieri 54–55; Berlant 100; and esp. Brennan 1.

Works Cited

Adorno, Theodor W. "On Lyric Poetry and Society." *Notes to Literature.* Vol. 1. Ed. Rolf Tiedemann. Trans. Shierry Weber Nicholsen. New York: Columbia UP, 1991. 37–54.

Agamben, Giorgio. "The End of the Poem." *The End of the Poem.* Trans. Daniel Heller-Roazen. Stanford: Stanford UP, 1999. 109–16.

——————. *The Use of Bodies.* Trans. Adam Kotsko. Stanford: Stanford UP, 2016.

——————. "What Is a Destituent Power?" Trans. Stephanie Wakefield. *Environment and Planning D: Society and Space* 32.1 (2014): 65–74.

Altieri, Charles. *The Particulars of Rapture: An Aesthetics of the Affects.* Ithaca: Cornell UP, 2003.

Arrowsmith, William. Introduction and Translator's Notes. *Hard Labor.* By Cesare Pavese. Trans. William Arrowsmith. New York: Viking, 1976. xi–xlii; 113–23.

Auerbach, Erich. *Dante: Poet of the Secular World.* Trans. Ralph Manheim. New York: New York Review of Books, 2001.

Ball, Karyn. "Losing Steam after Marx and Freud: On Entropy as the Horizon of the Community to Come." *Angelaki* 20.3 (2015): 55–78.

Ben-Ghiat, Ruth. *Fascist Modernities: Italy, 1922–1945.* Berkeley: U of California P, 2001.

Benjamin, Walter. "The Storyteller: Reflections on the Works of Nikolai Leskov." *Illuminations.* Trans. Harry Zohn. Ed. Hannah Arendt. New York: Schocken, 1968. 83–109.

Berlant, Lauren. *Cruel Optimism.* Durham: Duke UP, 2011.

Brennan, Teresa. *The Transmission of Affect.* Ithaca: Cornell UP, 2004.

Brinkema, Eugenie. *The Forms of the Affects.* Durham: Duke University Press, 2014.

Calvino, Italo. "Pavese: essere e fare." [Pavese: Being and doing.] *Una pietra sopra: Discorsi di letteratura e società.* [A stone above: Speeches on literature and society.] Turin: Einaudi, 1980. 58–65.

Casapa, Valerio. *Un'esigenza permanente: Un'idea di Cesare Pavese.* [A permanent need: An idea of Cesare Pavese.] Bari: Pagina, 2008.

Catalfamo, Antonio. "La tesi di laurea di Cesare Pavese su Walt Whitman e i suoi studi successivi sulla letteratura americana." [Cesare Pavese's thesis on Walt Whitman and his later studies on American literature.] *Forum Italicum* 47.1 (2013): 80–95.

Coletti, Vittorio. "La diversità di *Lavorare stanca.*" [The difference of *Lavorare stanca.*] Introduction. *Lavorare Stanca.* By Cesare Pavese. Turin: Einaudi, 1998. v–xxiv.

Comay, Rebecca. "Resistance and Repetition: Freud and Hegel." *Research in Phenomenology* 45.2 (2015): 237–66.

Culler, Jonathan. "Apostrophe." *The Pursuit of Signs: Semiotics, Literature, Deconstruction.* Ithaca: Cornell UP, 2001. 135–54.

—————————. *Theory of the Lyric.* Cambridge, MA: Harvard UP, 2015.

Culp, Andrew. *Dark Deleuze.* Minneapolis: U of Minnesota P, 2016.

De Bernardi, Alberto. *Una dittatura moderna: Il fascismo come problema storico.* [A modern dictatorship: Fascism as a historical problem.] Milan: Mondadori, 2001.

Deleuze, Gilles, and Claire Parnet. "On the Superiority of Anglo-American Literature." *Dialogues 2.* Trans. Hugh Tomlinson and Barbara Habberjam. New York: Columbia UP, 2007. 36–76.

Falasca-Zamponi, Simonetta. *Fascist Spectacle: The Aesthetics of Power in Mussolini's Italy.* Berkeley: U of California P, 1997.

François, Anne-Lise. "'Not Thinking of You as Left Behind': Virgil and the Missing of Love in Hardy's *Poems of 1912–13.*" *ELH* 75.1 (2008): 63–88.

Gioanola, Elio. "Pavese e il silenzio." [Pavese and silence.] *Cuadernos de Filología Italiana* 9 (2002): 121–38.

Hegel, G. W. F. *Aesthetics: Lectures on Fine Art.* Trans. T. M. Knox. Oxford: Oxford UP, 1975.

Jackson, Virginia, and Yopie Prins, eds. *The Lyric Theory Reader: A Critical Anthology.* Baltimore: Johns Hopkins UP, 2014.

Kant, Immanuel. *Critique of the Power of Judgment.* Trans. Paul Guyer and Eric Matthews. Ed. Paul Guyer. New York: Cambridge UP, 2000.

Keats, John. "In drear nighted December." *Selected Poems.* Ed. Elizabeth Cook. New York: Oxford UP, 1994. 77.

Lapucci, Carlo, ed. *Dizionario dei proverbi italiani.* [Dictionary of Italian proverbs.] Florence: Le Monnier, 2006.

Lewis, Charlton T., and Charles Short. "Stagno." *A Latin Dictionary.* Oxford: Clarendon, 1879.

Lorenzini, Niva. "Lavoro, città, spaesamento: Sul set di *Lavorare stanca.*" [Work, city, disorientation: On the set of *Work's Tiring.*] *Letteraria* 2 (2009): 101–4.

Montale, Eugenio. "Gozzano, dopo trent'anni." [Gozzano, thirty years later.] *Il secondo mestiere: Prose, 1920–1979.* [The second occupation: Prose, 1920–1979.] Vol. 1. Ed. Giorgio Zampa. Milan: Mondadori, 1996. 1270–80.

——————. *Ossi di seppia.* Milan: Mondadori, 1976.

Mutterle, Anco Marzio. *I fioretti del diavolo: Nuovi studi su Cesare Pavese.* [The little flowers of the devil: New studies on Cesare Pavese.] Alessandria: Edizioni dell'Orso, 2003.

Ngai, Sianne. *Ugly Feelings.* Cambridge, MA: Harvard UP, 2005.

Nievo, Ippolito. *Le confessioni d'un italiano.* [The confessions of an Italian.] Ed. Simone Casini. 2 vols. Milan: Fondazione Pietro Bembo, 1999.

Pavese, Cesare. *Dialoghi con Leucò.* Turin: Einaudi, 1960.

——————. *Dialogues with Leucò.* Trans. William Arrowsmith and D. S. Carne-Ross. Ann Arbor: U of Michigan P, 1965.

——————. *Disaffections: Complete Poems, 1930–1950.* Trans. Geoffrey Brock. Port Townsend: Copper Canyon, 2002.

——————. *Hard Labor.* Trans. William Arrowsmith. New York: Viking, 1976.

——————. *Il mestiere di vivere.* [The business of living.] Ed. Marziano Guglielminetti and Laura Nay. Turin: Einaudi, 1990.

——————. *Lavorare stanca.* Turin: Einaudi, 1998.

——————. "L'influsso degli eventi." *Opere.* Vol. 12. *Saggi letterari.* Turin: Einaudi, 1968. 221–24.

——————. *Poesie edite e inedite.* [Published and unpublished poems.] Ed. Italo Calvino. Turin: Einaudi, 1962.

Petrarch, Francesco. *Petrarch's Lyric Poems: The* Rime sparse *and Other Lyrics.* Trans. and ed. Robert M. Durling. Cambridge, MA: Harvard UP, 1976.

Rancière, Jacques. *The Politics of Aesthetics.* Trans. Gabriel Rockhill. London: Continuum, 2004.

Ronell, Avital. "On the Misery of Theory without Poetry: Heidegger's Reading of Hölderlin's 'Andenken.'" *PMLA* 120.1 (2005): 16–32.

Schuster, Aaron. *The Trouble with Pleasure: Deleuze and Psychoanalysis.* Cambridge, MA: MIT P, 2016.

Sontag, Susan. "The Artist as Exemplary Sufferer." *Against Interpretation and Other Essays.* New York: Farrar, Straus, and Giroux, 1966. 39–48.

Spackman, Barbara. "Detourism: Orienting Italy in Amalia Nizzoli's *Memorie sull'Egitto.*" *Italianist* 25.1 (2005): 35–54.

Stewart-Steinberg, Suzanne. "Grounds for Reclamation: Fascism and Postfascism in the Pontine Marshes." *differences* 27.1 (2016): 94–142.

Terada, Rei. *Feeling in Theory: Emotion after the "Death of the Subject."* Cambridge, MA: Harvard UP, 2003.

Ungaretti, Giuseppe. *Sentimento del tempo: Tutte le poesie.* [Sentiment of time: The complete poems.] Milan: Mondadori, 2005.

Virgil. *Georgics. Eclogues, Georgics, Aeneid.* Books 1–6. Trans. H. Rushton Fairclough. Rev. G. P. Goold. Cambridge, MA: Loeb Classical Library, 1999.

Wordsworth, William. "Preface to *Lyrical Ballads* (1802)." *William Wordsworth: The Major Works.* Ed. Stephen Gill. New York: Oxford UP, 2000. 595–615.

Zambra, Alejandro. "Buscando a Pavese." [Looking for Pavese.] *No leer: Crónicas y ensayos sobre literatura.* [Not to read: Chronicles and essays on literature.] Ed. Andrés Braithwaite. Barcelona: Alpha Decay, 2012. 193–207.

Learning Nothing:
Bad Education

No Future argued that social relations that imagine an end to their structural antagonism in a tomorrow perpetually deferred invoke the future as guarantee of meaning's realization (Edelman). Such a future, in its status as supplement, as the empty placeholder of totalization, works at once to preclude and assure the social system's closure, denying its totalization in the present while filling the gap that denial opens with the pledge of the yet-to-come. The Child, as the privileged figure of that pledge—one with no markers of identity in advance, such that any child, in the proper context, can instantiate its logic—compels us take our social value from our various relations to *it* and to make ourselves, in whatever way, the guardians of *its* future.[1] A class of persons must therefore emerge to materialize the *danger* to that future, a class of persons whose failure to invest the Child with the privilege of value pits them not only against the Child but also against the future's assurance of social viability. I called those persons *sinthomosexuals* to propose a link between the Lacanian *sinthome*, the symptomatic knot that binds each subject to a meaningless jouissance, and the emergence in the

Volume 28, Number 1   DOI 10.1215/10407391-3821724

"West" of homosexuality as a figure for the stigmatized relation of "sexuality" to a death-driven jouissance.

Though homosexuality, in certain Western democracies, may be shedding (in part) its connection to queerness, continuing the process of normalization by which it mirrors and so reinforces dominant ideologies of social relation, sinthomosexuality, as a signifier, affirms the anxiogenic intimacy of "sexuality" and the sinthome, of jouissance and what, as Jacques Lacan expresses it in "L'Étourdit," "ab-sens designates as sex" (452).[2] In the sinthomosexual, the social order posits and localizes the enemy of the Child as the paradoxical object form of jouissance itself: a violently disruptive enjoyment that threatens the integrity of the object insofar as that object is nothing but a catachrestic positing intended to foreclose the primal negativity of *ab-sens* as the subtraction from being and meaning without which neither can arise. Such an "antisocial" jouissance may be disavowed by the social order and read into whomever it sinthomosexualizes (those, that is, whom it queers as figures of ontological negation, and so of a socially destructive violence charged with libidinal enjoyment), but it pulses within as the motor force of social organization, repeatedly erupting in violence against those assigned to that stigmatized class. Thus, reproductive futurism's investment in the Child as the icon and promise of meaning doesn't alter the fact that futurism, too, embodies sinthomosexuality, enacting in its aggression against those it queers the enjoyment it disavows. We are all sinthomosexuals, as I put it in *No Future*, but those who are queered by a given social order are figures, historically contingent, for the ab-sens that threatens its sustaining logic by materializing the void that ruptures the imagined consistency of its world.

It follows that queerness, as the figure of such a radical unbecoming, maintains a persistently negative link to the logic of education. Queerness, wherever it shows itself (in the form of a catachresis), effects a counterpedagogy, refuting, by its mere appearance, the reality that offers it no place—or that grants it the place of what nullifies as well as the nonplace of the null. Like poetry in W. H. Auden's well-known phrase, queerness makes *nothing* happen; it *incises* that nothing in reality with an acid's caustic bite. Like a flame that affords the hapless moth an unsentimental education, so queerness dissolves the coherence to which our reality pretends, belying the comprehension, the unifying framework of the world, that the Child as meaning's cynosure ostensibly preserves.[3] Futurism compels us to indoctrinate children in what *ought to be*, not what is, shrouding them in the blinder of the putative innocence associated with the Child and imposed on children the better to enable the social control of adults. In the eyes of this all-pervasive regime, "the queer," like a counterfactual assertion produced in the land of the Houyhnhnms, represents, wherever the Child is concerned, the Swiftian *thing which is not*: it represents, that is, the being who intends the negation of being as such—the negation of being as defined, at least, by reproductive futurism. Thus queerness, from the normative perspective, promotes what I'm calling here *bad education*, the education that teaches us nothing but the nothing of the *thing which is not*. Like the Child, the queer is a fantasy figure catachrestically produced to fill in the void that precludes the world's totalization. The Child, however, signals the attainment of that totality in the future while the queer stands in for the obstacle impeding its realization in the present. Fleshing out the cut of division in terms of contingent historical identities constructed to ontologize ontological exclusion, those who are queered are libidinally stained with the negativity of the *thing which is not*. They threaten the Child, and therefore the future, by desublimating its "innocence," reducing it from privileged object of desire to the void at the core of the drive.[4]

But what exactly does *innocence* mean and how does it manage to sublimate the negativity of that void? Jean-Jacques Rousseau, who helped to enshrine it as the privilege of the Child, reminds us that it frequently coincides with a passion for wholesale destruction: "A child wants to upset everything he sees. He smashes, breaks everything he can reach. He grabs a bird as he would grab a stone, and he strangles it without knowing what he does" (Rousseau 37). Seen from this angle, the Child can preserve its "natural" state of innocence only to the extent that it preserves as well its "natural" state of ignorance. While hardly a comfort to the strangled bird, the thoughtless Child, knowing nothing of death, bears no guilt for its murderous act. It kills with an innocent exuberance, unconscious of what it does. But the Child confronts a worse threat in the bush than the slaughtered birds in its hand. Heaven help it the day it takes pleasure in "strangling" a bird of a different feather, which is to say, in "choking the chicken." At that point, the drives of the Child must be made to submit to parental law. In the words of the French psychoanalyst Lucien Israël, "From this period interdictions from outside intervene to deter the child from masturbating, from sucking his thumb, from pissing all over the place whenever he wants to do so" (86; my translation). One must, in effect, limit innocence in defense of innocence itself.

Rousseau understood this necessity well, whether or not he recognized it as inherently self-deconstructing. Regardless of the author's intentions, *Émile* unfolds the contradictions of an educational program that claims to find its model in "nothing but the march of nature" (34). Specifying the fractured logic on which that assertion must rest, Jacques Derrida produced his widely influential reading of the supplement. As he writes in *Of Grammatology*: "According to Rousseau, the negativity of evil will always have the form of supplementarity. Evil is exterior to nature, to what is by nature innocent and good. It supervenes upon nature. But always by way of supplementing what *ought* to lack nothing at all in itself." Does nature, and with it "innocence," *require* the "negativity of evil"? Derrida suggests just that: "Yet all education, the keystone of Rousseauist thought, will be described or presented as a system of substitution [. . .] destined to reconstitute Nature's edifice in the most natural way possible" (158).

The prime example afforded by Rousseau of this perverse or contradictory logic centers on the Child whose innocence, perversely, occasions its own perversion. Derrida, who carefully traces this logic, situates the Child in the place of negativity associated with the cut or the gap that constitutes an originary "deficiency" for Rousseau: "Childhood is the first manifestation of the deficiency which, in nature, calls for supplementation [*suppléance*]. [. . .] Without childhood, no supplement would ever appear in Nature. Now the supplement is here both humanity's good fortune and the origin of its perversion" (159–60). In its lack of self-sufficiency, in its need for acculturation, the Child exposes an absence internal to the fullness of nature itself. The natural, of course, in a perfect world, would need no supplementation since the supplement evinces a "negativity of evil" *un*natural by definition. The Child, however, as the "first manifestation of the deficiency [. . .] in nature," introduces, in its very innocence, supplementarity as original sin. It opens, that is, the dimension of futurity imagined as *redeeming* the lack to which such futurity attests.

Consider how Eve's punishment in the book of Genesis, that she must bring forth children in pain, reenacts the transgression that occasioned it: the pursuit of a supplement (the fruit of knowledge) to make up for loss or lack. But by positivizing the lack whose excessive presence made Eden incomplete, a lack figured by the serpent as the world's first "queer" and first agent of bad education, the supplement costs us paradise by dividing paradise from itself. (Could Eden have ever been paradise if it seemed to need supplementation?) Like the fruit of the tree, the fruit of Eve's loins makes supplementarity infinite as the fatal fall into time opens up the void in the form of futurity. No wonder we protect the Child from the knowledge of and at its origin; by reading as "innocence" the Child's luxurious immersion in nonknowing, we deny our own knowledge that the Child confirms the *deficiency* in Nature, the impossibility of Eden. "Perfection [. . .] cannot have children," as Sylvia Plath declares (262). Produced in response to, and in order to deny, the "evil" of knowledge as supplement, the Child embodies "innocence" as the negation of knowledge's negativity. Because "knowledge" of that negativity involves the unconscious, the Thing, and the drive, the negation of that negative knowledge effectively positivizes the Child, which then, by virtue of its sublimation, can reinforce the law's intertwining of prohibition and desire. Framed as the Child's antithesis, though, the queer, like that negativity, deconstructs the law in the very process of desublimating the Child and exposing its implication in the pulsion of the drive.

In order to obviate such a reduction, the Child, Rousseau argues, ought to be given a *minimal* amount of knowledge to protect it from the greater knowledge its innocence couldn't survive. *Émile* proposes that the Child receive, where "the organs of the secret pleasures and those of the disgusting needs" are concerned, an education that explicitly "turns [it] away from a dangerous curiosity" (217). Rousseau's text urges parents to make sure that "the first fire of imagination is smothered" by associating the sexual organs with excrement, dirt, disease, and death, inducing, thereby, a connection between "coarse words" and "displeasing ideas." The Child "is not forbidden to pronounce these words and to have these ideas," in the Rousseauian program, "but without his being aware of it, he is made to have a repugnance against recalling them" (217). Thus the armor most likely to protect the Child's innocence is a sort of aversive knowledge, one that effects a disinclination to "dangerous curiosity" and that does so surreptitiously, without the Child's even knowing that an aversion is being instilled.

Given the major role he plays in the history of the Child's sublimation, we should hardly be surprised that Rousseau idealizes the innocence he deconstructs. But Israël sees the Child's education from a starkly different perspective, reading the Child's relation to excrement and to its various "disgusting needs" without supposing, like *Émile*, some innate and "innocent" repugnance before such filth. It's rather, as Israël points out, "[g]ood housewives and housekeepers, [who] don't like the child's smearing itself with its shit." "Education," he continues, "is education against the drive. To lead out of [. . .], that's what educate means, to lead out of the universe of the drive" (87).[5] Education, in other words, instills and enacts the imperative to sublimate insofar as "the operations of sublimation are always ethically, culturally, and socially valorized" (Lacan, *Ethics* 144).

Good education thus always intends and assures the *social* good by negating whatever refuses that good and so endangers the Child, even if that danger inheres in the very nature *of* the Child. Education becomes, like sexuality, compulsory reproduction, procuring the Child for an order of truth that denies the foundational negativity, deficiency, perversion on which it rests. In the aftermath of such an education, as Israël concludes, "one no longer knows anything about the universe of the drive, because the only small way to safeguard something of it is by knowing nothing about it" (87).[6] This is the context in which he defines "education as antidrive [l'éducation comme antipulsion]" (87). Education, that is, as understanding, seals off and displaces the incomprehensible element, the *ab-sens*, that always drives its systematizations, while maintaining that element, dialectically, as the destabilizing other of education and knowledge. Not the negation of knowledge, then, this internal element bespeaks, instead, the negativity inherent in knowledge as such.

Adorned with its innocence as privileged *non*knowledge, the Child perpetuates through sublimation the *enforced* nonknowledge as and in which the "universe of the drive" insists, allegorically instantiating the Thing's sublimation as the creation of something out of nothing, as the dialectical negation of negativity that generates presence through reference to futurity. Allegory, sublimation, and dialectic, then, share a logic with one another, each naming a mode of production that displaces into systematic knowledge a negativity impossible to comprehend and at odds with all totalized forms.[7] It follows that a fourth term, education, belongs beside these three: the education that perfectly complements the Child as the promise of coherent totality—the education that is always, as Friedrich Schiller would have it, an aesthetic education.

For Schiller the attainment of humanity to its proper moral state depends on this assumption of unity as an ideal: "Every individual man, it may be said, carries in disposition and determination a pure ideal man within himself, with whose unalterable unity it is the great task of his existence, throughout all his vicissitudes, to harmonize" (31). The process of this harmonization, for Schiller, as effected by the "cultivation of Beauty," constitutes "the education of humanity" (55) and depends on the coordination of life in time, the life of the human as animal, with the development of moral possibility through and as the State. Schiller notes:

> *The great consideration is, therefore, that physical society in* time
> *may not cease for an instant while moral society is being formed*

> *in* idea, *that for the sake of human dignity its very existence may not be endangered. When the mechanic has the works of a clock to repair, he lets the wheels run down; but the living clockwork of the State must be repaired while it is still in motion [. . .]. We must therefore search for some support for the continuation of society. (29–30)*

As Paul de Man points out, the Schillerian aesthetic aims at the unification of sensory content and abstract form, linking the "sensuous world to a world of ideas" (Schiller 115) for reasons that have everything to do with the future that the Child is meant to secure. "[T]he necessity of this synthesis," de Man remarks, "is made in the name of an empirical concept, which is that of humanity, of the human, which is used then as a principle of closure. The human, the needs of the human, the necessities of the human are absolute and are not open to critical attack" (*Aesthetic* 150).

Needless to say, the "human," whose continued survival the Child guarantees, constitutes a recurrent site of ideological contestation. But insofar as "We are all Schillerians" (de Man qtd. in Warminski 7) according to de Man—which is to say, adherents, consciously or not, of an aesthetic ideology bound up with reproductive futurism—such contestation concerns the definition, not the *value*, of the "human."[8] Though the regime of aesthetic ideology protects that value from "critical attack," queerness refers to whatever conveys the *threat* of such attack by opening a critical gap within the logic of the aesthetic itself, exposing thereby the negativity from which Schiller and the Schillerian tradition retreat.[9] To confront such negativity would require a loss of the only ground on which the "empirical concept" of "humanity" could sustain the fantasy of its sovereignty; as Schiller puts it, "The person must therefore be its own ground, for the enduring cannot issue from alteration; and so we have in the first place the idea of absolute being grounded in itself, that is to say of *freedom*" (61).

To clarify the stake in this aesthetic ideology—and so, in the sublimation of the Child—I want to touch on de Man's account of an even more rigorous effort to produce a self-grounding philosophical system. In "Pascal's Allegory of Persuasion," de Man focuses on what happens when Blaise Pascal, observing geometry's refusal to define its principal objects (movement, number, and space), asserts that this "lack of definition is rather a perfection than a fault" and then claims that these principal objects have a "reciprocal and necessary relation" in which he implicates time as well (Pascal 151–52).[10] To exemplify this reciprocity, he asserts the homology among these "principal objects" with reference to the "two infinities [ces deux infinis]" of enlargement and contraction. Just as a movement can always be made faster or slower, and numbers can always be made larger or smaller, so space can always be increased or diminished and a temporal duration extended or reduced. Movement, number, space, and time thus are always infinitely distant from their radical extremes: nothingness and infinity ("le néant et l'infini" [Pascal 154]).

The demand that these realms remain perfectly homologous, though, runs into a certain difficulty when Pascal confronts the status of the "one" (which, as described by Euclid, is and is not a number at once) and tries to locate it in relation to what is not included in the realm of space because "indivisible" and lacking spatial extension. Pascal declares, "[T]he only reason that the one is not included in the ranks of the numbers is that Euclid and the first authors who dealt with arithmetic, having several properties to give it that were common to all the numbers other than one, excluded the one from the meaning of the word *number*, so as not to have to say all the time *we find such and such a condition in all numbers other than one*" (160).[11] Euclid recognizes, however, as Pascal observes, that the one, insofar as it is not a nothing ("un néant"), belongs to the same "genre" as number. As soon as they are added together, after all, two ones will produce a number, but two indivisible spatial entities, two elements lacking spatial extension, could never yield a spatial expanse by being joined together. If no homology exists between the one in the realm of number and an indivisible entity in the realm of space, then Pascal, according to de Man, had to "suspend this separation while maintaining it—because the underlying homology of space and number, the ground of the system, should never be fundamentally in question" (*Aesthetic* 59). So Pascal finds a corollary for the indivisible entity by adducing the zero in the order of number, which, while not a number itself, is presupposed by number and has clear equivalents in terms of motion, space, and time: "If you want to find a comparison in the realm of numbers that accurately represents what we are considering in the realm of extension, it would have to be that of zero to numbers. Because zero is not of the same genre as numbers, [. . .] it's a veritable indivisible of numbers just as the indivisible is a veritable zero of extension" (163–64).[12] As Ernesto Laclau describes it, "the zero is radically heterogeneous with the order of number" but "crucial if there is going to be an order of number at all" ("Identity" 68). It allows, moreover, "the homology between number, time and motion [. . .] to be maintained" insofar as it provides "the equivalent of 'instant' or 'stasis' [. . .] in the order of number" (67). Much as the aesthetic, for Schiller, restores, in de Man's words, "equilibrium, harmony, on the level of principles" (*Aesthetic* 151), so for Pascal, as de Man maintains, "the homogeneity of the universe is recovered" (59) by way of the zero.

For de Man, however, its true importance lies in its allegorical relation to what Pascal understands as the arbitrariness of linguistic definition—the arbitrariness that lets Euclid exclude the one from definition as a number while still offering a definition of magnitudes by which it belongs to the "genre" of number. The zero, as de Man expands upon its brief appearance in Pascal's text, correlates with geometry's nondefinition of its own initial principles and the lack of any demonstrable ground to undergird its logic: "All these truths," Pascal writes, "are incapable of demonstration, and yet they are the foundation and the principles of geometry" (154). This leads de Man to characterize Pascal's project in the following terms:

> *The continuous universe [. . .] is interrupted, disrupted* at all points *by a principle of radical heterogeneity without which it cannot come into being. Moreover, this rupture [. . .] does not occur on the transcendental level, but on the level of language, in the inability of a theory of language as sign or as name [. . .] to ground this homogeneity without having recourse to the signifying function [. . .] that makes the zero of signification the necessary condition for grounded knowledge. The notion of language as sign is dependent on, and derived from, a different notion in which language functions as rudderless signification and transforms what it denominates into the linguistic equivalent of the arithmetical zero. It is as sign that language is capable of engendering the principles of infinity, of genus, species, and homogeneity, which allow for [. . .] totalizations, but none of these tropes could come about without the systematic effacement of the zero and its reconversion into a name. There can be no* one *without the zero, but the zero always appears in the guise of a* one, *of a some(thing). The name is the trope of the zero. The zero is always* called *a one, when the zero is actually nameless, "innommable." (Aesthetic 59)*

The importance of this account for my argument lies in its evocation of the zero's "effacement" and its concomitant "reconversion" into, its tropological representation as, a positivized and enumerable entity, which is to say, a "one."[13]

The "systematic" effacement of the zero as the disruptive and heterogeneous principle on which the "continuous universe," as a totalized system, nonetheless depends, enacts a logic that underlies the aesthetic for Schiller, the supplement for Derrida, education for Rousseau, and sublimation for Lacan. Not that these terms are interchangeable or designate the same thing, but each reinforces the social imperative toward the "marriage" of "mind and world" (Warminski 8), toward a unified system, a comprehension, that strives to efface its internal rupture or structural impossibility, its predication on *ab-sens*, through repetitive tropological substitutions that continuously turn zero into one by making the ontological exclusions articulated as queerness or blackness, for example, assume the substantial status of the "queer" or the "black" as identity.[14] Consonant with such a logic, though, the negativity of this repetition, the drive that underlies it, undergoes "reconversion" into the "truth" of reproduction, refiguring the stasis of its iterations as movement toward futurity.[15] This, of course, is the function of the Child, and so of the Child's education. Could teachings at odds with this logic add up to anything at all, having nothing at all to add but the persistence of nothing in the "guise" of the one—nothing to add but the negative sign that signals a primal subtraction, the negativity added to the sign as such in order to show, as de Man writes above, that "language as sign is dependent on, and derived from, a different notion"?

If sublimation, aesthetics, and logic turn the zero into one, this "different notion" reverses the process and so makes the one, the referential entity, into something unintelligible, the "linguistic equivalent" of zero. This "different notion" recalls what Brian Rotman has in mind when he discusses the insistence of the sixteenth-century Flemish mathematician, Simon Stevin, "on a semiotic account of number, on an account which transferred zero's lack of referentiality, its lack of 'positive content,' to *all* numbers" (29). Such a "notion," like queerness as ontological negation, leads to nothing in the social order of meaning: which is to say, to the nothing of the "zero of signification" that always subtends that order. Andrzej Warminski views this zero as the "stutter of sheerly mechanical enumeration" (31), a phrase that echoes de Man's own words in "Hegel on the Sublime," words to which we might turn in order to gloss the zero as well: "Like a stutter, or a broken record, it makes what it keeps repeating worthless and meaningless. [. . .] Completely devoid of aura or *éclat*, it offers nothing to please anyone" (*Aesthetic* 116).

How could the nothing of the zero, then, with its mechanistic repetitions, ever generate something of value and make a contribution to life? Simply put, it can't. The very value of "value" enshrines sublimation as a good insofar as it privileges positive production and the dialectical

logic that undertakes to make something out of nothing, to turn a profit on
negativity. A teaching that profits no one and that "offers nothing to please":
to what could that teaching amount if not a radical threat to the one, to the
Child, to the good, and so to the future? In an aesthetic order based on the
harmonization of sign and meaning, that teaching could serve as nothing
more than the sign of a bad education.

So let's turn to the sign of a bad education to frame this another
way—or turn, at least, to the sign used to advertise Pedro Almodóvar's *Bad
Education* (*La mala educación*, 2004) (see fig. 1). At the center of the graphic
stands Ignacio Rodríguez, the boy whose love for his classmate, Enrique,
enrages Father Manolo, the school's director and Ignacio's literature professor, who passionately desires Ignacio, though his advances have been
rebuffed. To shield his friend from the wrath of the priest when the boys
are discovered together, Ignacio gives in to Father Manolo in exchange for
the latter's implicit agreement not to expel Enrique. *Bad Education* unfolds
this narrative in a film within the film: a film by the grown-up Enrique
based on an autobiographical story, *La visita*, written by the grown-up
Ignacio. Enrique acquires the tale from Ignacio's younger brother, Juan,
a would-be actor who, with the assistance of his former lover, the same
Father Manolo (no longer a priest but now a publisher who goes by his family name, Berenguer), murdered Ignacio four years earlier. When he brings
Enrique the story, Juan has assumed Ignacio's identity, hoping to gain the
director's affection, a part in one of his films, and perhaps the starring

role in the version of *La visita* that, as he rightly anticipates, Enrique will decide to make.

Depicted as a Spanish auteur who has moved from underground movies to wider fame for his films in the spirit of *la movida*, Enrique is linked to Almodóvar from the outset; the latter's title-sequence credit as writer and director of *Bad Education* fades into a similar, diegetic card that refers to Enrique Goded. The poster for Almodóvar's film, moreover, extending this identification, bears an image that refers to a sequence that takes place, narratively, in Enrique's film. That image, a full-length black-and-white shot of Ignacio confronting the camera head-on, shows the boy in the t-shirt, sneakers, and shorts that he wears in a scene from *La visita*—the scene in which he realizes his betrayal by the priest, as Enrique, despite Father Manolo's promise, is forced to leave the school. In the film, Ignacio chokes back a sob; in the poster he glowers instead, suggesting that the camera, and by extension the viewer, is aligned with Father Manolo.

But Ignacio, with his sullen, reproachful gaze, forms only one part of the poster's logo for Almodóvar's film. His image appears in a bright red circle that it bisects like a diameter. The difference between this vivid sphere and the black-and-white picture of the Child contrasts the naturalism of the photographic image with the abstract, nonrepresentational space on which it is superimposed. It produces, in the process, a correlative contrast between two geometric elements: the circle and the upright line of the boy, which function, in relation to each other here, as versions of the zero and the one: the noncognizable cipher and the Child whose human pathos displaces it; the gaping void and its sublimation in the *einziger Zug*, the single stroke, the Lacanian "first signifier" (*Fundamental* 256). Precisely as signifier of the singleness or unity of an entity, which alone permits the concept of an "entity" to emerge, this stroke or notch, this one, asserts the coherence of the signifying system in which the "zero of signification," like the Thing as primal loss or division, always appears "in the guise of a *one*," always appears through the sublimation that denies it a place *as zero*.

The field of the poster's red circle, by evoking the zero that threatens the human—while also alluding to the presence of the camera (both Almodóvar's and Enrique's)—might seem, on the one hand, to engulf the boy, reducing him to a mere geometric form by inscribing him as nothing but the single stroke, the material mark of the signifier at risk of sinking into the void. But that circle, on the other hand, might also be seen as receding before Ignacio's incarnation of the Child: as dissolving, that is, before the figure of meaning that positivizes and displaces it. The aesthetic education explored by the film (but from which it never can break), the normative imperative of education as such toward the concord of the good, compels us to approach the relation between these opposing hands dialectically, to resolve it into an allegory and so to sublate its persistent antagonism. In doing so, education repudiates the "stutter" of the zero whose insistence makes "what it keeps repeating worthless and meaningless," according to de Man. Such education denies, in other words, what J. Hillis Miller asserts: that the zero, which remains "unknowable," "does not 'generate' the one. The one, however, any one, 'generates' a glimpse of the zero that is at the same time its hiding or covering over by a false or fictional name" (241). Such a name, a catachresis misrecognized as a substantive identity, affirms the aesthetic unity whose ultimate signifier is the "human."[16] Returning to the work of the philosopher most closely associated with aesthetic education, de Man ventriloquizes the reasoning behind Schiller's insistence on effecting a reconciliation of the sensory and the formal drives: "Because the category of the human is absolute, and because the human would be divided, or would be reduced to nothing if this encounter between the two drives that make it up is [*sic*] not allowed to take place, for that reason a synthesis must be found. It is dictated, it is forced upon us, by the concept of the human itself" (*Aesthetic* 150). Almodóvar's *Bad Education*, too, engages this division of the human, its reduction to the "nothing" of the zero, which threatens, like queerness, the *regime* of the human by destroying the Child as its supplement and guarantee of meaning. This confluence of queerness as ontological negation with the zero or void of ab-sens approaches the end of the Child, as I'll argue, by approaching the Child through its end, performing the sort of bad rearing that seizes the Child itself from the rear, overturning thereby its human face and teaching us to construe it as nothing more than the nothing we *posit* as more. Such is the bad education whose lesson, from the standpoint of aesthetic ideology at least, invariably lessens us all.

We can see this better by approaching the poster's reading of *Bad Education*. The picture of Ignacio, as I mention above, alludes to the moment in Enrique's film when he learns that he's been betrayed. The import of the poster depends, however, on the formal and visual connection it makes between that scene and what precedes it. Earlier in *La visita*, Enrique, no more able than Ignacio to fall asleep after an afternoon at the movies that included their first sexual contact with each other (mutual masturbation while watching Sara Montiel in *Esa mujer*), follows Ignacio to the washroom in order to talk about what they did. Their conversation breaks off, however, when Father Manolo enters the dorm, intending to enlist Ignacio as his acolyte at daylight mass. Anticipating their teacher's wrath were he to find them in the washroom together, the boys attempt to avoid his gaze by hiding in a stall. But the priest, now livid with jealousy at the sight of their empty cots, discovers their place of concealment and orders them to come out. When they open the door, Enrique makes an effort to shield Ignacio, but Father Manolo, furious, throws Enrique to the floor and sends him back to the dorm after leveling a threat to deal with him later.

In the chapel, Ignacio assists at Father Manolo's mass absent-mindedly, disdainful of the priest but worried about what lies in store for Enrique. As Father Manolo intones the words that consecrate the wine, "Hic est enim calix sanguinis mei," Ignacio shoots him a withering glance and begins to speak in voiceover: "I think I've just lost my faith at this moment and, lacking faith, I no longer believe in God or in hell. And as I don't believe in hell, I'm now without fear. And without fear, I'm capable of anything" (Almodóvar 130).[17] Once the mass ends, the priest, unable to stay angry with his favorite for long, absolves Ignacio of responsibility for what happened in the washroom. He reiterates, however, his intention to expel Enrique from the school. Ignacio, making a bold calculation, offers the priest a deal: "If you don't expel him, I'll do what you want" (132). As he speaks these words, the camera captures his upward gaze at the priest, whose shoulder obtrudes on the screen as a block of darkness on the left (see fig. 2). A reverse shot shows us the teacher's response. Urging Ignacio to silence, he starts to move forward to embrace him, and the film, cutting back to the previous shot, shows Ignacio's face in eclipse as the priest's black cassock blocks the lens and the entire screen goes dark (see figs. 3–5).

Given the Hitchcockian texture of the film, established in the opening credits with their musical and visual citations of *Psycho* and maintained through the film's revision of *Vertigo*'s take on identity and loss, this shot should recall the hallmark of *Rope*, where the camera's cuts are masked four times by a man's back blocking its view. In his indispensable account of that film, D. A. Miller, connecting this strategy with "the very operation of the closet," observes that these blackouts conceal two things, the anus and the cut, and he adds that by doing so imperfectly these blackouts *call attention* to them as well (133). By quoting this signature gesture of *Rope*, Almodóvar, though free to show gay male sex, adduces the *form* of the closet without its indicative social function. Or rather, he *alerts* us to the form of that closeting, which he thereby brings out of the closet, so as to closet something else: not gay male sex, nor pedophilia, nor even Ignacio's sodomization (about which the film leaves the viewer no doubt), but rather

Figures 2–5
Ignacio offers him-
self to Father Manolo
to protect Enrique
from expulsion.

Bad Education,
Pedro Almodóvar,
2004

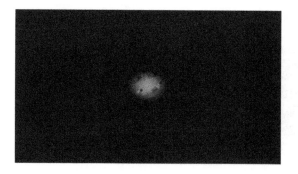

the jouissance of Ignacio in this moment of erotic education, the voiding of his subjectivity through his reduction to the anal opening, the hole, that renders him unintelligible, a zero instead of a one, a site of ab-sens at odds with the Child as the promise of social meaning.[18]

    Though the opening of and onto that hole is concealed by Father Manolo's back (which covers the *camera's* opening and thus completely blacks out the screen), that hole, as the trace of jouissance, asserts itself nonetheless. The screenplay for *Bad Education* suggests that the blackout gives way to a fade-in—"The screen remains black for two or three seconds. Slowly, from within the darkness of the frame, a group of students begins to define itself (twenty or thirty of Ignacio's schoolmates) doing Swedish gymnastics in the soccer field" (Almodóvar 132)—but Almodóvar (or, alternatively, Enrique, whose film, *La visita*, we are watching) makes the transition by way of an iris shot, tattooing on Father Manolo's back the hole that the film brings out of the closet through its displacement to the level of form (see fig. 6). As a reference to the camera's mechanical eye, the characteristic dilation of the iris-in shot evokes the compulsion of the ocular drive and with it the automatism of the drive as such. The annular form of the shot, in this context, links the contraction and expansion of the ocular iris with the sphinctral tightening and relaxation associated with the anus. The expansion of the camera's eye thus evokes what the darkness of the screen concealed: Ignacio's opening to Father Manolo, which situates Father Manolo inside Ignacio in more ways than one.

    I'll explain that more fully in what follows, but for now let me linger on the iris shot, which inscribes a relation between the anus and the eye that returns us to the zero and the one. Images that the eye desires to take in (like Ignacio's picture on the poster) reaffirm the integrity of the object as such, an integrity or coherence that the anus (like the poster's red circle) threatens to void. If *Bad Education* (or *La visita*) associates the Child's penetration by the priest with the blacked-out screen, with seeing nothing, then

Figures 7–8
The expansion of the
iris reveals an over-
head shot of young
boys in rows doing
push-ups.

Bad Education,
Pedro Almodóvar,
2004

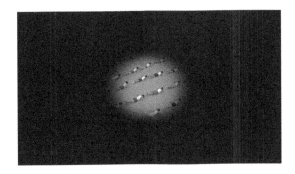

this eclipse of Ignacio as image, this desublimation of the Child, conflates the negation of the object with the opening of the anus. As the sphinctral trace of *nothing*, which is also, in this case, *nothing to see*, the hole of the iris attempts the visualization of zero *as zero* without its reconversion into the meaningfulness of an entity, of a one. That the effort fails, that representation substantializes the zero, putting *something* in *nothing*'s place, can be seen precisely by the *seeing* that the iris-shot invites in its shuttle between ocular and anal figurations. Almodóvar's shot takes the form of a hole, but that hole, while troping on the anus as an opening onto nothingness, opens a hole in the *nothing to see* through which the desired image returns. Reaffirming the objects that the eye desires and, by extension, the reality of the object world *as* object of desire, these images fill up the iris's hole, negating the negative force of the drive, which it reconstructs as desire.

What widens the camera's eye, however, as the iris expands on the screen is an overhead shot of boys in rows, like multiples of Ignacio, all offering the camera, which takes in the scene from its vantage point far above, the sight of their asses rising and falling in the course of their morning gymnastics (see figs. 7 and 8). Though framed as a Hitchcockian "god's-eye view" that dissociates its angle of vision from that of any particular character, the Olympian perspective cannot efface the shot's pederastic import or its conversion of the anus as *nothing to see* into the positivized form of the image, itself the guarantee of form. *Bad Education* (like *La visita*) realizes this positivization cinematically when the sphinctral inscription of *nothing to see* gives way to the iris's expanding image of row after row of Ignacios facing down with their bottoms up.

Perversely, the movement from nothing to number, from zero to multiples of one, conceals the hole of the anus, which endangers the integrity of the Child, by offering the viewer, instead, an image filled with young boys' asses seen through a pederastic lens; but that lens, in its function as the lens of desire, *redeems* the *nothing to see* that broaches the void of jouissance, and it does so by reasserting desire for the image as desire for the image of the human.[19] This returns us to de Man's account of Schiller as compelled to affirm the synthesis of sensual reality and pure form; as de Man writes in a passage I cited above, "Because the category of the human is absolute, and because the human would be divided, or would be reduced to nothing if this encounter between the two drives that make it up [the formal and the sensory drives—*Formtrieb* and *sinnlicher Trieb*] is not allowed to take place, for that reason a synthesis has to be found. It is dictated, it is forced upon us, by the concept of the human itself" (*Aesthetic* 150).

In this context, whatever effects the division that reduces the human to "nothing" brings the force of a "radical evil" to bear on the logic of "reality." It performs an inherently violent act against which the whole of the social order, like the ego as the organized portion of the id, mobilizes itself to defend. Alenka Zupančič describes with precision what follows in its wake: "The gap opened by an act (i.e., the unfamiliar, 'out-of-place' effect of an act) is immediately linked in this ideological gesture to an *image*. As a rule this is an image of suffering, which is then displayed to the public alongside this question: *Is this what you want?* And this question already implies the answer: *It would be impossible, inhuman, for you to want this!*" (95). The question, however, in another sense, implies the opposite answer: whether or not we want what it shows, we desire the image *as such*. To negate the image (which signifies, if only dialectically, the image of reality) would be "impossible, inhuman," the work of the death drive as embodied in whomever a given culture sinthomosexualizes.

As a synecdoche for the object-world, the image is charged with mirroring back our coherence as objects/subjects brought into "being" within that world's frame (though the toggle between object and subject already dismantles that putative coherence). If pederastic vision (not only here, but throughout Almodóvar's film) becomes paradigmatic of vision as such, if it instantiates the object-fixation of the law (understood as the law of desire) by taking the Child as the object that has to be raised to the dignity of the Thing, then the object-wasting drive through which desire acquires its motion takes the form, instead, of the flaming hole that the poster's red circle evokes, the hole by which, as de Man observes, the human is "divided, or [. . .] reduced to nothing."[20] That division expresses the persistence of the zero we never can know as such, the ubiquitous access to jouissance we never can endure as such, and the ceaseless pulse of the death drive we never can master as such.

Tearing open what "is" in response to the constant pressure of what "is not," such division, in its primal negativity, preoccupies Almodóvar's *Bad Education*. From the outset, when the credits show collages of images (mostly focused on sex, religion, and film) being ripped and peeled back to disclose something else (encapsulating thereby the logic of montage, which paradigmatically cuts to "something else" to fill what it also opens: the atopia of the cut), the film reads division as inherent in the psychic insistence of a "queer" negativity inseparable from the Symbolic's correlation of reading as such with making sense. That order has no need to teach its subjects what its every institution hammers home: "that interpretation only works by way of meaning," to quote Lacan ("Dissolution"). It's precisely that belief that makes us subjects in the first place, pursuing Imaginary meaning through the circuits of the signifying chain. But Lacan, by aligning the psychoanalytic act with the Real as external to meaning or sense, and thereby leading interpretation back to the signifier as *ab-sens* or pure division, asserts the difference between education and the act while broaching, as Almodóvar does, the valences of "bad" education.

In the narrative of Almodóvar's film, that badness finds its referent first and foremost in Father Manolo, the educator whose fixation on Ignacio leads, in the moment simultaneously announced and elided by the blacking out of the screen, to the Child's undoing as meaning. Expressed in the visual eclipse of Ignacio (both as image and as Child), that undoing inflects the voiceover accompanying the transition to the iris shot, too. As embedded in the multiple layers of *Bad Education*'s textuality, the voice belongs to the Ignacio who narrates parts of *La visita*, his autobiographical story recounting his childhood and what came after. Almodóvar's *Bad Education* unfolds the contents of that story by incorporating scenes from Enrique's cinematic treatment of it—scenes we witness, for the most part, proleptically within the diegesis of *Bad Education* while Enrique, reading *La visita*, imagines the film it will become. In a sort of structural reversal, though, where Almodóvar's film uses prolepsis, Enrique's shows a preference for hindsight instead, offering up Ignacio's childhood in flash-back while thirteen years later Father Manolo, under the adult Ignacio's gaze, reads, like the Enrique of *Bad Education*, the text of *La visita*.[21] Now presenting as Zahara, who lies to the priest by announcing Ignacio's death and pretending to be his sister (Zahara herself is played in Enrique's film by Juan, Ignacio's real-life brother in *Bad Education*), the former Ignacio pays the visit to which his story's title refers: Zahara's visit with Father Manolo in which she threatens to publish *La visita* unless he pays her enough money to give her "a better life and a better body."[22] As the author of the story that recalls her childhood experiences as Ignacio, a story that includes in its narrative Zahara's visit with Father Manolo, Zahara herself ought properly to supply the voiceovers in *La visita*. But it's the boy Ignacio, not Zahara, who delivers them in Enrique's film, reflecting the fact that Father Manolo, understanding the story as Ignacio's recollections, "hears" its words as emerging from the Child that Ignacio was for him. So when our view of the screen is blocked by the priest and we're given nothing to see, it's the young Ignacio's voice that declares: "I sold myself for the first time in that sacristy to prevent Enrique's expulsion."

The tension between this, the voice of the Child, and the words that Ignacio speaks—calling the nonvisualized scene of sodomy his *first* act of prostitution—opens a gap in "Ignacio" like the hole that the iris-shot opens on-screen. The boy whom the screenplay describes as possessing a voice of the greatest purity ("la voz blanquísima de Ignacio-niño" [Almodóvar 96]) here lifts his voice to depict this moment as a beginning instead of an end. He looks back on what happened less as a rape or a *sexual* violation than as the violation of a legitimate contract on whose terms the priest reneged: "I sold myself for the first time in that sacristy to prevent Enrique's expulsion, but Father Manolo conned me." In the aftermath, Ignacio/Zahara reenacts that fraudulent transaction in reverse, symptomatically robbing her clients as if to make good on Ignacio's loss. She avenges herself by cheating the men who have purchased her body for sex just as Father Manolo, Ignacio's first client, brazenly cheated him. This invests her sexual exchanges with a supplementary jouissance while funding her access to the jouissance she enjoys through the use of drugs.

Having sold himself "for the first time" in the transition between the blacked-out screen and the iris shot (a transition that, rather than keep-ing something out of sight, attempts to visualize *nothing*), Ignacio's coher-ence as a Child disappears. As a result, in the scene that follows, the one to which the photo on the poster refers, we catch our last glimpse of Ignacio as

Figures 9–13
Ignacio, on discov-
ering that Enrique
has been expelled,
is thrust out of *La
visita* as he meta-
morphoses into Juan.

Bad Education,
Pedro Almodóvar,
2004

the Child we've been prompted to desire (in all the many ways such desire creates and destroys the Child). On the sports field introduced by the iris shot, as he watches Enrique being led from the school, Ignacio is wracked by a force from within that morphs the Child of Enrique's film into the Juan of Almodóvar's, the Juan who has murdered the real-life Ignacio and later performs as Zahara, the woman Ignacio becomes in Enrique's film, *La visita* (see figs. 9–13). Split open by Father Manolo, and so by the experience of jouissance (the priest's, of course, but also his own, which attaches to the sexual power he deploys in attempting to rescue Enrique); divided both from his faith in God and from his trust in the word of the priest; crossing the ontological barrier that separates the fiction of *La visita* from the "reality" of *Bad Education*, Ignacio translates the Child in all its innocence as a blank screen ("blanquísima," like Ignacio's voice), into nothing but nothing's substantialization, the positivization of the internal void that ceaselessly drives the subject toward its expression in jouissance.

An earlier sequence in Enrique's film anticipates the effects of this negativity, permitting what J. Hillis Miller calls "a glimpse of the zero" in the one. When Zahara hands Father Manolo her story, indicating a particular passage with which his reading should begin, we see the typewritten leaves of the text and hear Ignacio in voiceover speaking the words to which she points. He recalls that those students who earned the best grades were rewarded with outings in the country, always escorted by Father Manolo, whom the camera shows us in profile as he reads the words we hear. With the voice of the Child as a bridge to the past, the film cuts from Father Manolo's face to the scene the text evokes. A group of young boys in bathing attire runs toward the river for a swim while the camera, countering their forward movement, tracks in the other direction, drawn toward something hidden from view by the overgrowth of a canebrake. On the other side of its sheltering barrier, we discover Father Manolo, in his clerical robes, sitting beside Ignacio, whose uneasiness is palpable. The priest begins to strum a guitar as Ignacio, lending his choirboy tones to a popular song from the sixties, starts singing "Moon River" in a Spanish version rewritten by Almodóvar.[23] The purity of Ignacio's voice imbues the song with a deep ambiguity; in the screenplay's words: "There is something hypnotic and perverse about the fact that a child is singing it" (Almodóvar 96). With the hungry eyes of Father Manolo fixed upon him yearningly, Ignacio squirms to avoid his teacher's startlingly naked gaze; but he finds himself, almost against his will, meeting and holding it anyway. As he sings how he'll neither forget Moon River nor permit the flow of its turbid waters to carry him away, he expresses his own unsettling contradictions, bringing out the play of attraction and repulsion, desire and resistance in the scene.

Eager, like Ignacio, to look somewhere else, to escape the sexual tension revealed by his exchange of glances with the priest, the film cuts away to a series of slow-motion shots while Ignacio continues to sing—shots that observe his classmates playfully cavorting in the stream. This cut provides, on the one hand, a respite from Ignacio's encounter with the priest by immersing the audience in the sights and sounds of what seems like an ethical alternative: the openness, exuberance, and joy of the schoolboys enjoying themselves in the river tacitly rebuking the furtiveness, constraint, and uneasiness of the priest and his favorite in the canebrake. In that sense, the film implicitly captions these shots with a tag that reads "innocence," weighing them against the events in the reeds, soon to literalize the fall. On the other hand, the camera's luxuriance in the lithe young bodies of the boys, its idealization of their comradeship and its loving attention to their natural athleticism, on which the lingering of the spectatorial gaze is mimed by the slow-motion of the shots, stains this same sequence with the pederastic import of the scene from which it turns. In this logic that associates vision with the compulsion imposed by the law of desire (as desire for the Imaginary object capable of securing the "oneness" of meaning by halting the signifier's slide), compulsion also attaches to the desire that determines our relation to the Child. That desire itself takes on the negativity of the drive; the image of the Child raised up to fill the void of the scopic imperative is divided from the meaning it promises by the very void whose place it takes. It proves, that is, to be nothing more than the division of that void from itself, the positivization of the zero to which jouissance leads us back.

That recognition, perhaps, brings the camera back to the scene from which it had turned. Over the image of two boys bobbing in the water, Ignacio's voice, through the lyrics of "Moon River," inquires where God and Good and Evil are found; but when he confesses his desire to know what it is that hides itself in the darkness ("Yo quiero saber / qué se esconde en la oscuridad"), the film cuts away from the river (on the word *saber*, "to know") and returns to the canebrake behind which Ignacio, hidden by its foliage, sings. The camera stays with that shot of the reed-bed over the words "qué se esconde" ("what hides itself") and then slowly tracks in toward the greenery as Father Manolo's guitar goes silent and Ignacio continues a capella: "en la oscuridad / y tú lo encontrerás" ("in the darkness, and you will find it"). With the vegetation still filling the screen, Ignacio goes silent for a moment too, and then we hear him call out, "No!" The camera pans

Figures 14–16
Fleeing from Father
Manolo's sexual
advances, Ignacio
encounters his divi-
sion as a subject.

Bad Education,
Pedro Almodóvar,
2004

left, following the movement of Ignacio as he dashes out from behind the reeds then trips and falls flat on his face. Father Manolo cries out after him and follows anxiously (buttoning his cassock as he does so), until he reaches the boy's prone body, over which he pauses, looking down. The film then cuts to a close-up of Ignacio, as seen from the priest's point of view, turning toward Father Manolo, whom he fixes with his gaze. His expression conveys neither fear nor anger. Only in his impassivity, only in the steadiness of his knowing and unblinking eyes, could one read, or project, reproach (see fig. 14). A stream of blood slides down his forehead, tracing a line along which his image splits open, exposing the darkness of a void that anticipates the emptiness of the blacked-out screen we will see when he first "sells himself" (see fig. 15). Out of that darkness emerges his teacher's face, as if from within the boy (see fig. 16), as Father Manolo, in the "real time" of Enrique's film, reads the words Ignacio speaks: "A trickle of blood divided my forehead in two. I had a feeling that it would be the same with my life: I would always be divided and I could do nothing to avoid it" (Almodóvar 100).

Most accounts of the film, responding to the legal and ethical consensus on sexual relations between children and adults, interpret this episode as Ignacio's harassment, abuse, or victimization. The screenplay lends weight to this view, describing Ignacio's look as "defiant" (98) and the boy himself as the priest's "adored victim" (100). But the film, in exploring the libidinal investments to which its characters respond, poses a challenge to the binarism of victim and abuser, innocence and guilt. Ignacio's inability, while singing, to keep his eyes from meeting his teacher's; his confession, by way of the lyrics, that he wants to know what the darkness hides; his literal opening onto that darkness when his face is torn in two: all of these signal his drive toward a knowledge of something within him that the film and the culture around it dismiss as nothing. What divides Ignacio as he lies on the ground foreseeing a life of division is not, then, the aftermath of Father Manolo's traumatizing advances, but rather Ignacio's recognition of his own internal Father Manolo, his recognition, that is, of his own susceptibility to what Father Manolo signifies: the submission to a power beyond one's control that undoes one's coherence as a subject by reducing "one" to the zero it approaches in the moment of jouissance.

Like the "masques à transformation" used to metaphorize plasticity by Catherine Malabou, Ignacio's image gives way to Father Manolo's as its own self-difference, which is to say, as "a line of division between two ways of representing the same face."[24] But that face possesses no authentic or positive presence of its own. It gives, instead, the illusion of substance to the void that the subject "is": the void in the signifying chain that we compulsively try to fill with sense (by constantly adding more links to that chain, thus enchaining us to reproductive futurism). In this way the one, if not "generated" by the zero, according to J. Hillis Miller, can be viewed as its symptom instead. The one sublimates or positivizes—in the form of "presence" or "being"—the negativity of primal division, which in consequence becomes unthinkable, just like the zero *as* zero. The one grounds our faith in reality's consistency by construing it as replete with meaning and not as a network of mobile signifiers with nothing to hold them in their place. Insofar as education, according to Israël, "lead[s] out of the universe of the drive," it rests on escaping the negativity of the signifier's movement by equating reading or interpretation with the process of making sense, of positivizing meaning, even with regard to reading practices identified as nonhermeneutic.

The shot that literalizes Ignacio's division thus highlights the nested-doll logic of reading that structures *Bad Education*. More specifically, its literalization of fracture tropes upon the fracture introduced in the film by letters of various sorts; it collocates the division of Ignacio with the division of the subject by the drive and with that of the manuscript or text by the signifier. Not for nothing (though precisely to *conceptualize* "nothing") does the filmic splintering of Ignacio's face, which makes Father Manolo's visible, show us the priest, some thirteen years later, reading Ignacio's text. As framed within Enrique's film, this displacement crosses barriers understood as temporal and ontological both: the flashback shows Ignacio's narrative as Father Manolo, in the act of reading it, sees it in his mind's eye, while the shot that returns us to this act of reading returns to the "reality" from which he conjured those images of Ignacio as he read. That conjuring is what the shot's traversal of these barriers asserts: that the flashback suffuses the manuscript with meaning by investing its differential signifiers with Imaginary plenitude. Fleshing them out in images, it accords them the "presence" that Ignacio's voiceover gives the typewritten words on the page—words it raises from testamentary inscriptions of the "dead" Ignacio to the living speech in which the Child that he was survives forever, unchanged.

If the return to Father Manolo in the cinematic present of Enrique's film deconstructs the Imaginary status of Ignacio's voice as the *token* of "presence," then it reads the Child, the figure of meaning, as Imaginary too, as a fantasy designed to seduce us into cathecting a reality that can open at any moment, like Ignacio's divided face, onto the zero of the Real. Reinforcing that point by challenging the tenability of any interpretative ground, the transition from Ignacio to Father Manolo links up with the next two shots, the first of which cuts to the page that the priest is reading in Enrique's film (the text of *La visita* he received from Zahara's hands), the second of which cuts to Enrique reading that page in Almodóvar's (the text of *La visita* Enrique was given by Juan). The wipe that fractures Ignacio's face coincides with the reduction of his image to the mere effect of a linguistic signifier (the words we see on the page); the cut from those signifiers to Enrique's face so reduces the priest as well. The Imaginary status of Child-Ignacio for Father Manolo in Enrique's film attaches to the boy and the priest alike in the diegesis of Almodóvar's (see figs. 17–19).

Figures 17–19
The image of Father
Manolo reading
Ignacio's story gives
way to an image of
Enrique reading that
story's description of
Father Manolo read-
ing it while being
watched by Zahara.

Bad Education,
Pedro Almodóvar,
2004

But I must slightly reframe my reading of these shots to account
for another aspect of the film that bears on their signification: the aspect ratio
that determines the proportions of the image we see on the screen. Usually
no more than a technological given, the meaningless frame that divides the
film's space of inscription from what it excludes, the aspect ratio, for obvious
reasons, rarely signifies diegetically.[25] For the most part, it simply shapes
the area in which the image is allowed to appear by serving as the window
through which we construct its Imaginary space. But Almodóvar treats the
aspect ratio as a signifying element by changing *Bad Education*'s format (in
general, 2.35:1) to an earlier norm of aspect ratios (1.85:1) whenever he wants
to designate scenes that take place in Enrique's film.[26] The first instance of
this transition, which occurs as Enrique starts reading *La visita*, coincides

with Enrique's voice (not Ignacio's) pronouncing its words in voiceover. A long shot of Enrique absorbed in the text fades into an establishing shot of a cinema, the one in which, as we subsequently learn, Enrique and Ignacio experienced their first sexual contact with each other. As the cinema comes into focus, the change in the aspect ratio narrows the image before our eyes. This marks a shift in the temporality and the ontological status of what we see, though only in retrospect do we understand that it defines these sequences as proleptic glimpses of Enrique's version of *La visita*. The image of the Cine Olympo, as carefully framed onscreen, thus serves as a switchpoint to foreground the very framing of the cinematic image—its framing both *within* the dimensions of the visual field and *by* them.[27] Though the content of the image directs our attention to the place for viewing films, its reformatting asks us to consider what has no place in the films we view: the framework wherein the Imaginary topology of cinema unfolds (see figs. 20–24).

As evinced by the trimming of the image and the insertion around it of an "empty" border, this reformatting signals the signifying function of the "nothing" that meaning relies on and at once forecloses. It introduces a diegetic frame that differentiates, in the context of *Bad Education*, the representation of filmic representation (the scenes from Enrique's movie) from the representational practices that are naturalized in Almodóvar's. Such a naturalization, however, soon overtakes the diegetic frame produced by the change in aspect ratio too; the identificatory lure of the image effaces the signifying function of its border, which becomes no more than the space of nonmeaning, or the nonspace of *nothing to see*. The more we find ourselves caught up in the image-world of Enrique's film, the more its literal margin gets marginalized as nonbeing, as ontological exclusion. But our investment in the narrative reality of visual images in *Bad Education* suffers disturbance, in turn, by repeated transitions from one representational level to another. When the splintering of Ignacio's face reveals Father Manolo's, some thirteen years later, as he reads Ignacio's text, the scenes of Ignacio's schooldays, with their animation of pederastic desire, melt back, like our image of Ignacio as a Child, into mere linguistic signifiers given Imaginary substance by the priest; but Father Manolo himself dissolves into a linguistic signifier too once we realize that the text he seems to be reading (see figs. 17–18) is actually the text in which his experience of reading the story is being read by another. Though it consists of the same page with the very same words from the very same story by Ignacio, the text we see in the reverse shot is read by Enrique, not the priest, as the change in aspect ratio

Figures 20–24
Almodóvar's manip-
ulation of aspect
ratio can be seen in
the movement from
the image of Enrique
reading *La visita*
to the final image
of the Cine Olympo
as envisioned in
Enrique's film of that
story.

Bad Education,
Pedro Almodóvar,
2004

makes clear *before* the film cuts to Enrique's face (see fig. 19).[28] The image of Father Manolo (in fig. 17) takes shape retrospectively as a mere effect of the signifiers Enrique encounters in Ignacio's text (see fig. 18). Thus: while Enrique reads Ignacio's story, Almodóvar envisions that reading through scenes from the movie Enrique will make of it; and Father Manolo, as portrayed in those scenes, reads Ignacio's story too, similarly envisioning the events it describes like a movie that plays in his mind. From the perspective of Almodóvar's film, these envisionings—Enrique's and Father Manolo's—find their common provenance "in a fiction, in a dream of passion," making them as insubstantial as the "nothing" that Hecuba is to Hamlet, while producing, like Hamlet's meditation on the players, a *mise-en-abyme* that calls its own ontological ground into question (Shakespeare, *Hamlet* 2.2.536, 541).

The "airy nothing[s]" of poetry and fiction, as Shakespeare's Theseus describes them (*A Midsummer Night's Dream* 5.1.16), express the world that is given to be thought, but Almodóvar invokes them, on the contrary, to broach what thought itself excludes. If he seems to substantialize those nothings at first by fleshing them out in images, then by fracturing those images or by blacking them out he makes them "nothing" as well, suggesting that the world as given attains its Imaginary positivization by occluding the negativity that ruptures its ontological consistency. He does so specifically with reference to the specter of child-adult sexual relations, the proscription of which reinforces our fantasy of knowing what sex "is" insofar as that proscription construes the Child as the locus where sex "is not."[29] Bringing sex together with the question of the zero, Almodóvar proposes that we can no more "know" the former than the latter—that both, because they pertain to *ab-sens*, are absented by attempts to comprehend them.

Sex in *Bad Education*, that is, as figured through children's sexuality, gender fluidity, pederastic desire, and the compulsions of the drive, denotes a constitutive gap in knowledge around and against which the world takes shape in all its social meanings. As the pressure of an unintelligibility that arouses a libidinized will to master it, generating ideology in order to suture, in the words of Slavoj Žižek, an "ontological 'crack'" in "every notion of the universe qua totality," sex eludes representation except by virtue of disrupting or undoing it (*Tarrying* 26). Like the filmic apparatus or the linguistic text, on both of which *Bad Education* insists, sex is the machinery of difference, inherently meaningless in itself, on the basis of which an Imaginary meaning is posited nonetheless; like the zero *as* zero, it denotes a negativity whose every conceptualization, appearance, or image works to efface it. *Bad Education* approaches the void of this unintelligibility, the originary cut of primal division, through the ontological flicker that implicates the image, and in particular the cinematic image, in the negativity that sunders what "is." As the cynosure of meaning, moreover, and the instantiation of the "one," the Child in Almodóvar's film looms large in its thinking of queerness as the ontological exclusion to which sex, *ab-sens*, and the zero all refer.

 The image of Ignacio as a Child, for example, though conjured as a spur to the spectatorial desire it also intends to sublimate, remains, diegetically, a *cinematic* image, only seen in Enrique's film. Though *Bad Education* provokes a longing in the audience for the lost Ignacio, a longing that parallels Enrique's and Father Manolo's in the narrative, it brings out, in its image of a *fictional* Ignacio as portrayed in *La visita*, not only the illusionary aspect of the Child but also the presence of something that disfigures and destroys that Child from within: a death drive evinced through the instability, the self-difference, of its very image. When the face of Ignacio splits in two, making visible his internal division, its disclosure of Father Manolo's face (as seen in Enrique's film) anticipates a subsequent visual effect that attends the shift shortly thereafter between Enrique's film and Almodóvar's: the effect by which Ignacio morphs into Juan while the aspect ratio of the image changes from 1.85:1 to 2.35:1 (see figs. 9–13). In both instances the passage from one level of narrative "reality" to another distorts the Child by revealing the inner presence of its own antagonist, whether Father Manolo (an accomplice to the murder of Ignacio in Enrique's *La visita*) or Juan (who devises the plan for Ignacio's murder in *Bad Education*). The plasticity of the image, bespeaking its openness to the negativity that undoes it, thus registers the fatality of the drive to which the Child as fantasy succumbs.

 When Ignacio morphs into Juan, however, *Bad Education* has not yet exposed the latter's imposture of his brother. Despite Enrique's incipient suspicions (from the outset he fails to recognize in Juan any signs of his former schoolmate), the audience continues to take Juan at his word when he claims to be Ignacio (all the more so since Juan has been seen as Zahara, the woman Ignacio becomes in the visualized scenes of Ignacio's narrative, which have not as yet been identified as prolepses of Enrique's film). Only in retrospect do we fully grasp the otherness that erupts in Ignacio—an otherness that marks the continuous tension between the Imaginary fixation of the image and the Symbolic movement of the signifier, the very tension that gives rise to the drive as the negativity of their relation, as the insistence of the chasm between them that constitutes the Real. The morphing itself, like the bifurcation that tears open Ignacio's face, evinces the nothing of the zero as the desublimation of the image. As violent as the exposure of the death drive is on the occasions when Ignacio's image turns into that of one of his murderers, a more shocking transformation takes place when we see the "real" Ignacio at last. If the Child to whom *Bad Education* binds us appears diegetically only as embodied by an actor in Enrique's *La visita*, Almodóvar shows us the "real" Ignacio only in the flashback that accompanies the confession to Enrique by Father Manolo (now a publisher, Sr. Berenguer, who looks nothing like the actor in Enrique's film whom we "know" as Father Manolo) of how he and Juan killed Ignacio.

To the extent that the Child of Enrique's film both excites and instantiates desire (the desire whose form is the image itself in its status "as materialized Nothingness," to quote Žižek's characterization of the sublimated object), the "realization" of that desire, which also effects the unveiling of the image itself as a veil (covering, but also embodying, the negativity of the Real), enacts its desublimation by the pressure of the drive (*Looking* 83). In the case of the grown-up Ignacio, the compulsion of that drive gets figured in the addiction that leaves him gaunt and sickly. Unlike the charming Zahara portrayed by Juan in Enrique's film, the adult Ignacio in "reality" is shrill, unattractive, and deceitful—far removed from the Child (portrayed diegetically in *La visita*—and in *Bad Education*—by the actor playing Ignacio) whose beauty is meant to seduce us. Indeed, when Manolo/Berenguer recalls his first glimpse of Ignacio as an adult, he says to Enrique in voiceover before we see Ignacio himself, "This was not the Ignacio that you and I loved." When the film then cuts to Ignacio as seen from the publisher's point of view, we must share his disappointment. Shot in a crimson light that bathes his angular face with a tint that might suggest the poster's red circle (see fig. 25), he lacks the appeal of the young Ignacio as depicted in Enrique's film or the prettiness of Zahara as brought to life by Juan (see fig. 26).

Figures 25–26
The "real" adult
Ignacio as evoked by
Señor Berenguer dif-
fers markedly from
the adult Ignacio
portrayed by Juan in
Enrique's film.

Bad Education,
Pedro Almodóvar,
2004

Like *Vertigo*'s Judy in relation to Madeleine, the "real" Ignacio,
when he appears on-screen, effects a desublimation that disturbs our attachment to the Child of *La visita*. The screenplay, which calls him "Ignacio
Adulto" and describes him as "el travesti," paints him in the following terms:
"In person he is much deteriorated. He is tall, extremely thin, with long,
disordered hair, teeth in an awful state, and more feminine than masculine"
(Almodóvar 208).[30] Blackmailing Father Manolo for money to complete his
gender confirmation surgery, this Ignacio might seem to embody the condition of division he expressed in *La visita*, yet the corporeal transformation
he anticipates aims to resolve, not affirm, such division; it aims, that is, to
realize Ignacio's idealization as desired object. The division that matters in
Bad Education, and that nothing can ever resolve, lies less in the object of
desire, however, than in the tension between desire and the drive, between
the futurity elaborated in the former and the latter's insistence on the Real.
Hence Ignacio's oscillation between saving his money for the surgery he
dreams of and his compulsion to squander it, notwithstanding those dreams,
on the drugs to which he is driven. The one impulse pushes him forward and
holds out the promise of future becoming; the other affords the immediacy
of an *un*becoming instead. In the grip of the drive that takes him beyond the
object-form of desire, and so, in effect, beyond his very survival as himself,
Ignacio confronts the intractable Real of his attachment to jouissance.

That, we might say, is the zero degree of queerness in the film—the queerness of the zero as negativity, and therefore, as *ab-sens*; the queerness that designates sex as nothing but the cut, the division, that forever divides it from being as being "one." Prerequisite for being countable, and so for representation, such a oneness affirms not only the fictive coherence of an entity but also the fantasmatic totalization of a world. And what props that world up is precisely the legibility of the image as such, its legibility as a representation of the world's *availability* to representation. Queerness, by contrast, though always fleshed out in catachrestic figures, refers to what never accedes to representation in itself. Instead, it denotes what eludes the stabilization of the "in itself," referring to what is not itself and so to what is not, *tout court*, in a given regime of meaning. Like the zero, it enacts the negation of what is—opening onto the space of the imageless, the impossible, the unthinkable—while occasioning phobic embodiments in particular types of beings (those a given culture queers) made to stand in for the death drive in its stubborn ineducability.

The *nothing to see* that emerges differentially with the opening of the iris onscreen, or with the vivid red circle of the poster that frames the image of the boy, reinforces the ontological negations subtending both Ignacio's divided face and his morphing into Juan; it bespeaks the pressure of the zero in and against the logic interimplicating meaning, sociality, and the Child. Perhaps that explains why the obscuring of the camera by the body of Father Manolo gets repeated during Manolo/Berenguer's account of the "real" Ignacio's death. Besotted with Ignacio's younger brother and fearful of being exposed as a sexual predator by the student he loved, Manolo/Berenguer, as the latter tells Enrique, conspired with Juan to get rid of Ignacio by giving him a dose of pure heroin. In the flashback that accompanies this recollection, Ignacio is seen writing a letter to Enrique—we watch the typewriter print the words, "Dear Enrique, I think I have succeeded" ("Querido Enrique: Creo que lo conseguí")—when the sound of the buzzer interrupts him and he discovers Manolo/Berenguer at his door. The latter hands Ignacio the packet of drugs (as fatally "pure" as the image of the Child, though Ignacio doesn't know it) and follows him back to the study. While Ignacio returns to his typewriter, Manolo/Berenguer remains on the threshold, promising Ignacio the money he demands in exchange for keeping silent. The framing here echoes the scene of Ignacio's selling himself in the sacristy (see fig. 27), though the former priest's back now impinges on the right-hand side of the screen (see fig. 28).

Figures 27–28
The framing of the
shot in the sacristy
is mirrored in the
scene of Ignacio's
death.

Bad Education,
Pedro Almodóvar,
2004

Unlike its counterpart in that previous sequence, this shot is not followed by a total blackout, or at any rate, not immediately. Although Manolo/Berenguer, as he did before, moves closer to Ignacio, he does so now with murderous rather than sexual intent. In fact, when Ignacio, getting ready to inject himself, misinterprets the former priest's interest as admiration for his silicon breasts, Manolo/Berenguer can barely conceal his erotic distaste for the troublesome person the boy he loved has become. Uncomfortable being watched as he prepares the heroin, Ignacio sends Manolo/Berenguer away ("Váyase. No me gusta ponerme delante de Vd." [Almodóvar 242]), suggesting, by substituting the formal "Vd." for the "tu" he uses elsewhere, his embarrassment at the prospect of his former teacher witnessing his jouissance. His interlocutor, who knows better than Ignacio the dissolution this enjoyment will entail, nervously turns to leave the room and, in exiting, repeats the blackout of the image so noticeable in the earlier sequence. But he does so, as in the shot above where he blocks the screen's right side, with a directional reversal, frontally obscuring the camera's lens while turning his back on Ignacio, as if to literalize as nothing to see, as a negated negativity, this unbearable remainder and reminder of the Child's desublimation (see figs. 29–32).

These two homologous blackouts, each construing the zero of the *nothing to see* as a purely differential relation, not as an ontological given,

Figures 29–32
Señor Berenguer's
frontal blockage of
the camera repeats
in reverse the dor-
sal blockage by
Father Manolo in the
sacristy.

Bad Education,
Pedro Almodóvar,
2004

read jouissance as the cut of division that can never appear in itself to the extent that it desublimates the fantasy on which the "in itself" depends. Desublimation, as this suggests, is less the encounter with an entity unaltered by the gloss of idealization than the *undoing* of the entity as already idealized, already sublimated, in its framing *as* an entity. Desublimation, like jouissance, thus functions in a purely negative register (as its prefix already indicates), performing an act of subtraction from the givenness of what is. In doing so it opposes itself to the work of education, which reinforces the "one" of the entity in the form of knowledge, meaning, and legibility. Education, especially in the mode of critique, may look like desublimation, but it works to shore up the idealization of reading as making sense that allows us, if only negatively, to comprehend a world. As the iris shot, in the earlier sequence, oscillates between figural associations with the anus and the eye, with the void that wastes the value of the Child and the Child as object of desire, so the shots that follow the blackout here also approach the zero of the Real, the zero of jouissance, by evoking the persistent division between the Imaginary and the Symbolic.

When the blackout, for example, gives way to an image, the camera, as it did in the iris shot, looks down at the scene from on high, its perspective apparently dispassionate and detached from what it observes. Floating in air, its ambient attention scans the objects that litter the floor while it pivots to focus on Ignacio's head as seen from above and behind (see fig. 33). A cut to the side of Ignacio's face makes clear that he has taken the fatal dose in the time lapse of the blackout; his eyelids slide shut, and he starts to fall forward as the heroin reaches his heart ("cuando la heroína roza su corazón" [Almodóvar 244]), finally collapsing onto the typewriter and hitting the keys with his face (see fig. 34). The film then cuts to a startling shot from the perspective of Ignacio's letter, still unfinished on the platen, as the jangle of typebars strikes it by striking at the camera and at the screen (see fig. 35). No reverse shot shows us the text itself; instead, what the screenplay identifies as Ignacio's final message ("su último mesaje" [242]) is imprinted, at any rate figuratively, on the surface of the screen: a "message" providing an Imaginary rendering of the Symbolic's signifying machinery at the moment when Ignacio succumbs to the Real of the death drive as jouissance.[31]

Though unseen at the moment of Ignacio's death, this "message," imprinted on his letter to Enrique, appears at the end of the film. Having discovered exactly how Ignacio died (a discovery he makes on the day that principal photography on *La visita* wraps), Enrique, who shared both his home

Figures 33–35
Ignacio's death is
visualized as a jam-
ming of the Sym-
bolic's machinery of
signification.

Bad Education,
Pedro Almodóvar,
2004

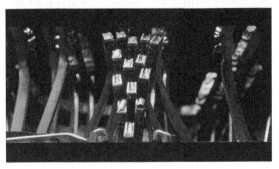

and his bed with Juan throughout the shoot, sends him packing, appalled to have been involved with the murderer of his lost first love, Ignacio. But Juan has a parting gift for Enrique. He hands him, just before he leaves, a folded piece of paper, which he identifies, without further explanation, as coming from Ignacio. After literally closing the door on Juan, Enrique opens the paper and reads the last words Ignacio wrote. A cut from Enrique's face to the text lets us see how its words gain an added "meaning" from their seemingly meaningless surplus: the randomly clustered characters struck by the fall of Ignacio's head (see fig. 36). Indicators of a death they cannot "mean" and of an enjoyment they could never convey, these marks attest to the division inherent in the structure of signification that turns arbitrary signifiers into messages and meaningless letters into the substrate of sense.

Figure 36
The meaningless
inscription of the
Real.

Bad Education,
Pedro Almodóvar,
2004

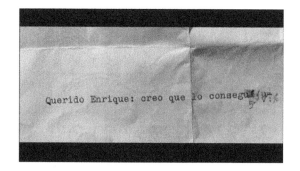

Lacan makes this point concisely in "The Signification of the Phallus": "[T] he signifier plays an active role in determining the effects by which the signifiable appears to succumb to its mark, becoming, through that passion, the signified. This passion of the signifier thus becomes a new dimension of the human condition in that it is not only man who speaks, but in man and through man that it (*ça*) speaks; in that his nature becomes woven by effects in which the structure of the language of which he becomes the material can be refound; and in that the relation of speech thus resonates in him, beyond anything that could have been conceived of by the psychology of ideas" (578). The unreadable surplus of the signifier to which the "signifiable" must succumb denotes, like the frame of the aspect ratio, the mark of articulation routinely cut off from the meanings its cut alone permits us to articulate. This surplus is the energy of difference or division incapable of appearing as such: the zero degree of (il)legibility that constitutes the drive.

This image of a text with its textualized image of what threatens the logic of imaging—the "nothing" of the Real, jouissance, and death—brings the film to its conclusion. Though not the final image we see (we're granted one last shot of Enrique refolding the letter while deep in thought and staring into space), it puts a term to Enrique's "education." While reflecting on Ignacio's "message" he too will be textualized as an inscription, as a mechanical product or effect, when his image is captured in freeze frame as a series of textboxes open onscreen. Each sketches the fate that befalls the film's characters, until, with the last one's account of Enrique—"Enrique Goded continues to make films with the same passion" ("Enrique Goded continúa hacienda cine con la misma pasión")—the textbox expands beyond the screen, leaving nothing visible but "pasión" (see fig. 37).[32] But what does that image invite us to see? The word *pasión*? The letters that shape it? The digital generation of those letters? While its enlargement intensifies its semantic allusion to emotional intensification, this onscreen image of the signifier, or of the letters that spell it out, effaces Enrique, its putative subject,

Figure 37
The passion of the
signifier.

Bad Education,
Pedro Almodóvar,
2004

as if literalizing what Lacan refers to as "the passion of the signifier." Like the marks on Ignacio's letter that get imprinted by his fall, such a literalization puts into question the signifier as such by emphasizing the materiality of the letters that compose it, those characters, here literally heightened, that displace the character they describe while unleashing what Parveen Adams calls "the access to jouissance that the reduction of the signifier to the letter yields" (131). But to whose jouissance could this refer? Is there ever a subject of jouissance? Or is jouissance the undoing, the zeroing out, of the (constitutively divided) subject as the subject succumbs to the negativity, the contentless energy of pure division?

    Bad Education suggests the latter through its efforts to show us the *nothing to see* as which queerness, like the zero, "appears": the *nothing to see* of the signifying energy never signifiable "in itself," but without which signification, like sense or the subject or the world, is impossible. That excess of signifying energy, though, as experienced in momentary eruptions of jouissance, makes those entities impossible too, exposing the subject, in the words of Jonathan Lear, to "the deepest form of human helplessness: helplessness in the face of too much energy. As Freud points out, we are vulnerable to repetitions of this helplessness from the beginning to the end of our lives. But this is a peculiar kind of 'repetition'—because it is the repetition of something that is in itself without content" (109). But only the repetition of this energy's too muchness in the compulsions of the drive can bind the ideational energy we register as "content," as the reality we know. Lear expands on this as follows:

> *For Freud, the fundamental mental molecule was an idea-plus-quota of energy (which he called affect). It was the transfer of this energy along varying paths of ideas that allowed Freud to explain the formation of neurotic symptoms and dreams. In this use, psychic energy seems to be the "matter" of a form-and-matter*

> *unity. But, then, how could there be a case of pure, formless mat-*
> *ter? How could there be* mental *energy without an idea? I think the*
> *answer is to take this as a limiting case of the mental—somewhat*
> *analogous to treating zero as a number. The reason for doing*
> *this is to capture the phenomena of trauma and of momentary*
> *breakthroughs: these are vicissitudes of the mental. (111–12)*

More than *vicissitudes* of the mental, though, these breaks or breakthroughs
are foundational or even, as Lear's usage suggests, "fundamental." Energy
itself is the trauma that demands, by way of homeopathic defense, the energy
of ideational binding. But that binding depends on an excess never contained
by ideational bonds, an excess that every attempt to bind it reproduces yet
again. In calling this a *formal* excess, then, I refer to the surplus of forming
energy over any totalized form and thus to the surplus informing form that
threatens to deform it. Comparing mental energy uncoupled from ideational
binding to "treating zero as a number," Lear implicitly evokes the place of
the Real in thought itself, where the Real names the constitutive excess of
negativity in Symbolic structuration. The imbalance created by that excess
and the necessity of finding a way to manage it give rise at once to jouissance
and to the law that defends against it. If the zero stands in for jouissance
as the opening onto the Real, then the one into which the *innommable*, the
zero, is reconverted identifies the compulsion to identity that inheres in the
logic of desire. As the void included but never counted or represented in a
situation, the zero maintains the place of queerness as ceaseless negativity.

This means that Almodóvar's film concerns itself less with something like sexual abuse or the passion for making films than with the drive's
ineducability, with the aspect of the drive that resists sublimation and that
Žižek illuminates thus: "This minimal distance between the death drive
and sublimation, between the negative gesture of suspension-withdrawal-
contraction and the positive gesture of filling its void, is not just a theoretical
distinction between the two aspects, which are inseparable in our actual
experience: [. . .] the whole of Lacan's effort is precisely focused on those
limit-experiences in which the subject finds himself confronted with the
death drive at its purest, prior to its reversal into sublimation" (*Ticklish* 160).
As a name for this limit-experience, this impossible encounter with the zero's
negativity before its reconversion into a one, queerness inhabits the place of
jouissance as inextricable excess, as antagonistic nonidentity, that animates
the Symbolic with its traumatizing energy. It stands, that is, beside other

terms (including Woman, Black, Brown, Trans, Subaltern, and Terrorist) as the aporia of ontological exclusion on which a given ontology depends.

Eric Santner comments tellingly on the passage from Lear that I cite above: "Fantasy is the name for the process that 'binds' this remainder, converts it into a support of social adaptation, a way of being in the world. I am suggesting that the task of truly inhabiting the 'midst of life' involves the risk of an unbinding or loosening of this fantasy as well as the social bond effectuated in it" (33). Santner, however, invested as he is in a messianic temporality, retreats from this negative moment, from its ontological threat, and from the risk, from the queerness, that inheres in such a prospect of social unbinding, affirming some thirty pages later that "'[u]nplugging' [...] need not signify a radical break with social reality, with the rule of a community's law, or even from historical agency" (64). This retreat, of course, is exactly what good education always effects: a retreat from the drive at its purest in favor of its reversal into sublimation, a retreat that recuperates "social reality" on behalf of "a community's law."

Almodóvar hews more closely, though, to Santner's first formulation, treating the Child as the fantasy object by which we bind the unbound remainder (the traumatic energy of jouissance), thus serving precisely as an instrument of "social adaptation." The Child, that is, like the photographic image of Ignacio on the poster, enforces the law of desire's disavowal of the excess that cannot be bound—the excess that presses for a "radical break" from every ideational content, from anything we could know. The object of desire, as Imaginary entity conceptualized as a one, makes desire itself the ultimate object of reproductive futurism: the desire that propels us forward by fantasizing our survival in an object imagined as able to fill the void around which the drive forever circles. The temporality thus established, the temporality of the law, constitutes the very movement of turning zero into one.

In the process it enacts the logic de Man associates with allegory, which aspires to a "stance of wisdom" by tracing a passage from a then to a now—a now that corresponds to the attainment of insight by virtue of having surmounted what de Man calls "radical discontinuity" (*Blindness* 224). Like the permanent parabasis as which Schlegel famously characterized irony, however, anticipating the violence of language by which, according to de Man, the "continuous universe" is "interrupted, disrupted *at all points*," the insistence of the zero refutes the claims of allegorical historicization, enacting instead the structuring force of division, contradiction, negativity. Irony, like the drive, like the letter, like the Real, inheres in every moment, destroying the coherence of the one that we cling to in moving *from* moment to moment and undoing, therefore, the meanings procured by allegory and the logic of desire. But the very sketch that I've offered here of the irony at work in the film and the poster as they offer a glimpse of the zero getting allegorized as a one has itself been condemned to perform that very same act of allegorization. To read is always to allegorize, even if only by allegorizing a reading resistant to the allegorical compulsion. Even an education in irony must turn irony into allegory, its queerness into familiarity, its meaninglessness into sense, the "radical discontinuity" of the illegible marks that conclude Ignacio's letter into a figure for the Real of the zero and, therefore, into a one.

Education thus opposes irony as it also opposes the drive, constraining us always to allegorize the overcoming of irony, even as "always" exposes the irony of allegory's repetition compulsion, its internalization of the very drive it undertakes to negate. Bad education can never escape the status of an oxymoron, gesturing only by way of allegory toward the zero that refuses allegorical reconversion into a one. That void is the nonplace of queerness, and it functions as the irony, the negativity, that is allegory's sinthome, and the sinthome, as well, of the aesthetic as our model of education. But the aesthetic remains the horizon within which we construe the human itself, the horizon within which "social adaptation" gains its status as the good. Faced with the "needs" of the human that find their face in the figure of the Child, queerness has nothing but nothing to teach, the nothing of the zero that's never raised to the status of a concept or a one.[33] We can never *know* the zero *as* zero or approach its void directly; but its queer persistence seizes us, like Ignacio, from behind, in moments of traumatic jouissance from which there is nothing to learn. That's the queer lesson that merits Almodóvar's title, *Bad Education*, the lesson that no one can ever learn and that no "one" could ever survive.

LEE EDELMAN is the Fletcher Professor of English Literature at Tufts University. He is the author of *No Future: Queer Theory and the Death Drive* (Duke University Press, 2004), *Homographesis: Essays in Gay Literary and Cultural Theory* (Routledge, 1994), and *Transmemberment of Song: Hart Crane's Anatomies of Rhetoric and Desire* (Stanford University Press, 1987), and coauther, with Lauren Berlant, of *Sex, or the Unbearable* (Duke University Press, 2014). A collection of new and previously published essays, *L'impossible homosexuel*, appeared in French in 2014 and the French translation of *No Future*, titled *Merde au futur*, was published in 2016, both titles with Epel Éditions.

Notes   1   Since the publication of *No Future*, many critics have written about   the presumed "whiteness" of the Child in Western culture. While the figure of meaning and cultural promise in a racist and antiblack order will disproportionately find representation in images of the dominant racial class, the Child itself does not have any intrinsic relation to whiteness and can, where useful, be embodied, even by that dominant order, in (the image of) children of color as well. Antiabortion activists, for example, have used representations of black and Hispanic children to demonize abortion as a form of genocide and thereby to mobilize antiliberal agendas in communities of color. Many of these same activists, of course, also promulgate the myth of the "welfare queen," the excessively reproductive woman whose class and color coincide with excessive reproductivity and so threaten the future defined by the Child of the white, middle-class social order. The Child, therefore, has no qualities in itself, but will assume those qualities as needed in the context of a dominant social order. At the same time, racial and ethnic communities within that social order may hold out their own hopes for the future in the form of a Child of their own.

2   "Freud nous met sur la voie de ce que l'ab-sens désigne le sexe: c'est à la gonfle de ce sens-absexe qu'une topologie se déploie où c'est le mot qui tranche" (Freud puts us on the path of that which ab-sens designates as sex; it's by the swelling up of this sens-absexe that a topology spreads out where the word is determining).

3   Lauren Berlant has cogently observed that "subjects are not usually shocked to discover their incoherence or the incoherence of the world" (Berlant and Edelman 6). But such experiences of the world's "inconstancy and contingency" (6) do not preclude such subjects from having an

ideological investment in meaning or from clinging to a faith in the coherence of reality, even if it seems incoherent *to them*. See Berlant and Edelman.

4   See Ohi for a brilliant reading of our ideological construction of childhood sexuality in relation to questions of "purity, guilt, and predation" (6).

5   "L'éducation, c'est l'éducation contre la pulsion. Faire sortir hors de [. . .], c'est que veut dire éduquer, faire sortir hors de l'univers pulsionnel."

6   "On ne sait plus rien de l'univers pulsionnel parce que le seul petit moyen d'en sauvegarder quelque chose est de n'en rien savoir."

7   The Child, as an allegory of this dialectic, as an allegory of sublimation, would thus be an allegorization of allegory. And the piling up of these synonyms wherever the Child is at issue would point to a repetitive insistence on the production of knowledge as social positivity, as social reproduction—an insistence that marks, as *repetition*, the structurally determining negativity internal to reproduction itself.

8   Andrzej Warminski quotes this phrase in "Allegories of Reference," his introduction to de Man's *Aesthetic Ideology*. A very similar assertion appears in de Man's "Kant and Schiller": "Whatever writing we do, whatever way we have of talking about art, whatever way we have of teaching, whatever justification we give ourselves for teaching, whatever the standards are and the values by means of which we teach, they are more than ever and profoundly Schillerian" (*Aesthetic* 142).

9   For de Man, of course, Schiller's aesthetic ideology retreats from,

by misreading, Kant, who, as de Man declares in "Kant and Schiller," "disarticulated the project of [. . .] the aesthetic [. . .] he had undertaken and which he found [. . .] by the rigor of his own discourse, to break down under the power of his own critical epistemological discourse" (*Aesthetic* 134).

10   All translations of Pascal's "Réflexions sur la géométrie en general" are mine.

11   "[L]a seule raison pour laquelle l'unité n'est pas au rang des nombres, est qu'Euclide et les premiers auteurs qui ont traité de'arithmétique, ayant plusiers propriétés à donner, qui convenaient à tous les nombres hormis à l'unité, pour éviter de dire souvent qu'en *tout nombre hors l'unité, telle condition se rencontre*, ils ont exclu l'unité de la signification du mot *nombre*."

12   "Mais si l'on veut prendre dans les nombres une comparaison qui représente avec justesse ce que nous considérons dans l'étendue, il faut que ce soit le rapport du zéro aux nombres. Car le zero n'est pas du même genre que les nombres, [. . .] c'est un véritable indivisible de nombre, comme l'indivisible est un véritable zéro de'étendue."

13   This reading of Pascal can be understood better in relation to Brian Rotman's excellent account of zero as "the meta-sign which both initiates the linguistic system and participates within it as a constituent sign" (27). Rotman goes on to describe the consequences of this in terms that correlate closely with de Man's account of "rudderless" signification: "To make the zero the origin of number is to claim for all numbers, including the unit, the status of free, unreferenced signs. Not signs *of something*, not *arithmoi*, certainly not

real collections, and not abstractions of 'units' considered somehow as external and prior to numbers, but signs produced by and within arithmetical notation" (29). These discussions would allow us roughly to map the order of units, number, and the zero onto the three orders of the Lacanian system, collocating the substantiality of the unit with the Imaginary, the abstraction of number with the Symbolic, and the negativity of the zero with the Real.

14   The metaphor of the "marriage" of "mind and world" is quoted from Terry Eagleton's *Ideology* by Warminski in his introduction to de Man's *Aesthetic Ideology*.

15   Ernesto Laclau, in his reading of de Man, arrives at a similar understanding, though by means of a different path: "[I]f the zero as moment of closure is impossible as an object but also necessary, it will have to have access to the field of representation. But the means of representation will be constitutively inadequate. It will give to the 'innommable' a body, a name, but this can be done only at the price of betraying its true 'nonbeing'; thus the tropological movement that prolongs sine die the non-resolvable dialectics between the zero and the one" ("Politics" 234).

16   Of course, the allegory that installs the human as value necessarily reduces the human to an instance of allegory itself insofar as allegorization introduces a distance or division within the unity of the signifier's referential function. In this sense, the very allegory that attempts to rise beyond the permanent disruption of irony merely refigures that disruption, recalling what de Man affirms in "Pascal's Allegory of Persuasion": "[A]llegory (as sequential narration) is the trope of irony (as the

one is the trope of zero)" (*Aesthetic* 61).

17 Translations of Almodóvar's scenario from Spanish into English are mine. Page references are to the original (French/Spanish bilingual) screenplay.

18 This is not to say that Ignacio takes any pleasure in the encounter; the film, quite literally, leaves us in the dark about his affective response, offering, in its place, his pained reaction to Enrique's expulsion.

19 Almodóvar repeats this trope of pederastic enticement later in the film when he shows us, through Father Manolo's eyes—or rather (since by then he has left the priesthood) through the eyes of the publisher, Berenguer—the seductively undulating body of Juan as he performs, wearing only a pair of shorts and a look of studied indifference, a series of pushups that awaken the excitement (and perhaps the memory) of the former priest.

20 As Carlo Freccero's presentation on animal subjectivity at the MLA convention in 2016 suggests, this reduction of the human allows us to begin to think queerness in relation to animality as well—or, at any rate, in relation to the figural logics by which the categories of *human* and *animal* have been variously constructed and reinforced at different moments and in different places.

21 See my discussion of (be)hindsight in *Homographesis: Essays in Gay Literary and Cultural Theory.*

22 Although this is the primary referent of the story as written by Ignacio, its resonances expand throughout the text of *Bad Education* to include Juan's visit with Enrique, during which he gives

him the text of *La visita*, and Enrique's visit with Ignacio's mother, during which she gives him a last letter from Ignacio, which similarly contains the text of *La visita*. The visit of Sara Montiel to her former convent in the film watched by Ignacio and Enrique, *Esa mujer*, and the visit of Sr. Berenguer to the film set when Enrique completes the filming of *La visita* also figure in the significations of the title.

23 The Spanish version of the lyrics, written by Almodóvar, change the sense of the song dramatically, describing the river itself as muddy and touching on matters involving memory, God, good and evil, and concealment.

24 See Malabou 13–16.

25 Tad Leckman gives a useful overview of some films that have made changes in aspect ratio play a role in their narrative construction, citing, among others, Abel Gance's *Napoléon*, Frank Tashlin's *The Girl Can't Help It*, and Doug Trumbull's *Brainstorm.*

26 Almodóvar uses yet another aspect ratio in the film to indicate shots taken by the video camera Sr. Berenguer gives Juan.

27 The insistence on framing is heightened by the camera's glimpse of Enrique through the visible frames of a window as the film fades into the shot of the cinema.

28 To be as precise as possible: the text that Father Manolo reads is the one given him, in the diegesis of Enrique's *La visita*, by Zahara, while the text Enrique is reading is the one given him by Juan. Enrique will later receive, from the hands of Ignacio's mother, an envelope containing another typescript of Ignacio's story. Insofar as

the scene of Father Manolo reading *La visita* in Enrique's film of
La visita is shot after Enrique has
received this second manuscript,
it is quite possible that either one
could *literally* be the prop that
the actor playing Father Manolo
is reading from in Enrique's film.
But the change in aspect ratio
from Father Manolo's face to the
manuscript makes clear that
Father Manolo has now melted,
like the Child Ignacio, back into
the signifier of which he is only the
imaginary effect.

29   Before "selling" himself to Father
      Manolo, Ignacio is with Enrique in
      the movie theater, where they jerk
      each other off; this sexualization
      of the Child may anticipate his fall
      into adult "perversion" (especially
      insofar as it expresses his love for
      another boy), but the film ideal-
      izes, even sublimates, the encoun-
      ter in the theater by showing us
      scenes of Sara Montiel, whom the
      boys, even while masturbating,
      are gazing at on the screen.

30   Unlike Zahara, who is given a
      female pronoun, Ignacio Adulto is
      depicted in the screenplay as male
      (for example, he is called "el inqui-
      lino" [Almodóvar 210] instead of
      "la inquilina"). I take my cue from
      the screenplay, therefore, in refer-
      ring to Ignacio Adulto with the
      male pronoun.

31   That shot of the typewriter's
      mechanism as figure for cinematic
      inscription recalls an equally
      surprising shot from earlier in the
      film when the camera observes
      the interior workings of the cin-
      ematic camera itself just after we
      see Enrique fuck Juan (who still
      is pretending to be Ignacio) and
      just before Enrique discusses the
      revisions he has made to the final
      script of *La visita*. This should
      remind us that the only "sex"
      scenes we see in the course of
      Bad Education recurrently play

out in relation to film. The scene
in which Zahara has sex with an
intoxicated Enrique takes place
only in the film of *La visita* and
represents a fantasy Ignacio never
realizes. His only other "encounter" with Enrique also takes place
in *La visita*, when they jerk each
other off in the theater; later Juan
and Manolo/Berenguer will begin
a sexual encounter while Juan
excitedly records it on a video
camera he receives as a gift. "Sex"
takes place as the division between
the body, its signification, and the
signifying mechanism itself.

32   The freezing of the image should
      be considered in relation to the
      beginning of the film where
      Enrique, seeking inspiration for
      a screenplay, clips a newspaper
      article about a motorcyclist found
      frozen to death while his motorcy-
      cle drives on. This anticipates the
      questions of mechanicity, desire,
      and the death drive engaged by the
      film.

33   Perhaps that explains an unre-
      marked feature of the opening
      credits. Along with scabrous sex-
      ual graffiti, religious images, and
      cinematic signifiers, this sequence
      three times depicts a passage from
      Marcel Duchamp's "The Green
      Box," the notes in which he com-
      ments on one of his masterworks,
      Large Glass (*Grande verre*), also
      known as *The Bride Stripped Bare
      by Her Bachelors, Even*. Specifi-
      cally depicting the notes that dis-
      cuss *The Illuminating Gas*, these
      citations from Duchamp bring to
      the fore the questions of sublima-
      tion, desire, and the image as they
      figure in his investigation of sex-
      ual division and the alternatives
      to "retinal" art. In this context the
      following remarks by Jacques-
      Alain Miller may be relevant to
      its relation to the film as I have
      approached it:
         *Can the subject align him-
         self with the drive and with its*

*surefootedness? The problematic
of removing fantasy, of travers-
ing the screen it represents, aims
at a laying bare of jouissance. It
is, as Duchamp says, "The Bride
Stripped Bare by Her Bachelors,
Even."*

   *The bride is jouissance. Can
one marry her? [. . .]*

   *The bride is stripped bare
by her bachelors, even. Who wants
her to be laid bare? Who wants to
lay bare jouissance? Who wants*

*to discover it underneath the
[fundamental] fantasy?*

   *There are two bachelors: the
analysand and the analyst. Lacan
completes his "On Freud's 'Trieb'"
with "and the Psychoanalyst's
Desire" by saying that the one who
wants to lay bare jouissance is the
analyst bachelor: his desire is to
lay bare the subject's jouissance,
whereas the subject's desire is sustained only by the misrecognition
of the drive known as fantasy. (426)*

Works Cited

Adams, Parveen. *The Emptiness of the Image: Psychoanalysis and Sexual Difference.* New York: Routledge, 1966.

Almodóvar, Pedro. *La mauvaise éducation: Scénario bilingue.* Trans. Véronique Foz. Paris: Cahiers du cinema, 2004.

Bad Education. Dir. Pedro Almodóvar. Warner Sogefilms, 2004.

Berlant, Lauren, and Lee Edelman. *Sex, or the Unbearable.* Durham: Duke UP, 2014.

de Man, Paul. *Aesthetic Ideology.* Ed. Andrzej Warminski. Minneapolis: U of Minnesota P, 1996.

—————. *Blindness and Insight: Essays in the Rhetoric of Contemporary Criticism.* 2nd ed. Minneapolis: U of Minnesota P, 1983.

Derrida, Jacques. *Of Grammatology.* Trans. Gayatri Chakravorty Spivak. Baltimore: Johns Hopkins UP, 2016.

Edelman, Lee. *Homographesis: Essays in Gay Literary and Cultural Theory.* New York: Routledge, 1994.

—————. *No Future: Queer Theory and the Death Drive.* Durham: Duke UP, 2004.

Freccero, Carla. "Animal Subjectivity." MLA *Convention,* Austin, TX, 9 Jan. 2016. Unpubl. Conference Paper.

Israël, Lucien. *Pulsions de mort: Séminaire, 1977–1978.* Strasbourg: Arcanes, 1998.

Lacan, Jacques. "Dissolution." *Espaces Lacan* 18 Mar. 1980. http://espace.freud.pagesperso -orange.fr/topos/psycha/psysem/dissolu9.htm.

—————. *The Ethics of Psychoanalysis, 1959–1960.* Trans. Dennis Porter. Ed. Jacques-Alain Miller. New York: Norton, 1992.

—————. *The Four Fundamental Concepts of Psychoanalysis.* Trans. Alan Sheridan. Ed. Jacques-Alain Miller. New York: Norton, 1981.

—————. "L'Étourdit." *Autres écrits.* Paris: Éditions du Seuil, 2001. 449–95.

—————. "The Signification of the Phallus." *Écrits: The First Complete Edition in English.* Trans. Bruce Fink. New York: Norton, 2006. 575–84.

Laclau, Ernesto. "Identity and Hegemony: The Role of Universality in the Constitution of Political Logics." *Contingency, Hegemony, Universality: Contemporary Dialogues on the Left.* Ed. Judith Butler, Ernesto Laclau, and Slavoj Žižek. New York: Verso, 2000. 44–89.

———. "The Politics of Rhetoric." *Material Events: Paul de Man and the Afterlife of Theory.* Ed. Tom Cohen, Barbara Cohen, J. Hillis Miller, Andrzej Warminski. Minneapolis: U of Minnesota P, 2001. 229–53.

Lear, Jonathan. *Happiness, Death, and the Remainder of Life.* Cambridge, MA: Harvard UP, 2000.

Leckman, Tad. "Shapeshifting Films." *Los Angeles: 2019* 29 Oct. 2012. https://tadleckman.wordpress.com/2012/10/29/shapeshifiting-films/.

Malabou, Catherine. *La plasticité au soir de l'écriture: Dialectique, destruction, deconstruction.* Clamecy: Éditions Léo Scheer, 2005.

Miller, D. A. "Anal *Rope.*" *Inside/Out: Lesbian Theories, Gay Theories.* Ed. Diana Fuss. New York: Routledge, 1991. 119–41.

Miller, J. Hillis. "Three Literary Theorists in Search of o." *Provocations to Reading: J. Hillis Miller and the Democracy to Come.* Ed. Barbara Cohen and Dragan Kujundžić. New York: Fordham UP, 2005. 210–27.

Miller, Jacques-Alain. "Commenting on Lacan's Text." *Reading Seminars 1 and 2: Lacan's Return to Freud.* Ed. Richard Feldstein, Bruce Fink, and Maire Jaanus. Albany: SUNY P, 1996. 422–28.

Ohi, Kevin. *Innocence and Rapture: The Erotic Child in Pater, Wilde, James, and Nabokov.* New York: Palgrave MacMillan, 2005.

Pascal, Blaise. "Réflexions sur la géométrie en general." *Oeuvres complètes.* Paris: Gallimard. 2000. 154–70.

Plath, Sylvia. "The Munich Mannequins." *The Collected Poems.* Ed. Ted Hughes. New York: Harper and Row, 1981. 262–63.

Rotman, Brian. *Signifying Nothing: The Semiotics of Zero.* Stanford: Stanford UP, 1987.

Rousseau, Jean-Jacques. *Émile, or On Education.* Trans. Allan Bloom. New York: Basic, 1979.

Santner, Eric L. *On the Psychotheology of Everyday Life: Reflections on Freud and Rosenzweig.* Chicago: U of Chicago P, 2001.

Schiller, Friedrich. *On the Aesthetic Education of Man.* Trans. Reginald Snell. Mineola: Dover, 2004.

Shakespeare, William. *William Shakespeare: The Complete Works.* Rev. ed. Ed. Alfred Harbage. Baltimore: Penguin, 1974.

Warminski, Andrzej. "Allegories of Reference." Introduction. *Aesthetic Ideology.* By Paul de Man. Ed. Andrzej Warminski. Minneapolis: U of Minnesota P, 1996. 1–33.

Žižek, Slavoj. *Looking Awry: An Introduction to Jacques Lacan through Popular Culture.* Cambridge: MIT P, 1991.

———. *Tarrying with the Negative: Kant, Hegel, and the Critique of Ideology.* Durham: Duke UP, 1993.

——————. *The Ticklish Subject: The Absent Centre of Political Ontology.* New York: Verso, 2000.

Zupančič, Alenka. *Ethics of the Real: Kant, Lacan.* New York: Verso, 2000.

TULSA STUDIES IN WOMEN'S LITERATURE

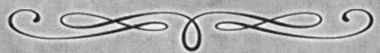

Subscribe now for
Spring 2017, Vol. 36, No. 1

@TSWLjournal
Utulsa.edu/tswl
Like us on Facebook!

Printed and bound by CPI Group (UK) Ltd, Croydon, CR0 4YY

13/04/2025

14656486-0001

ISBN   9780822368786

9 780822 368786

ISBN 978-0-8223-6878-6